THE WISDOM OF
Leone Levi

One of the Last to Know Almost
Everything About Almost Everything

George S. Sacerdote

Translations of his two books of maxims
with a biographical introduction

Massime, Volume A © 1872 Leone Levi
Massime, Volume B © 1874 Leone Levi

Translations and Translator's Introduction © 2023
George S. Sacerdote

ISBN: 978-1-7333541-2-7 (Print Edition)

Library of Congress Control Number: 2023920700

Dedicated to Leone Levi's many
North American descendants,
that they might be
inspired and educated by
his wit and writings.

TABLE OF CONTENTS

Translator's Introduction 1

Maxims Volume A 17
    Preamble 21
    Maxims 27
    Illustrations 85
    Index 135

Maxims Volume B 141
    Preamble 149
    Maxims 159
    Illustrations 227
    Appendix 303
    Index 315

Translator's Appendices 321
    The Bodonian Epigrams 323
    Partial Bibliography of Leone Levi's Writings 335

TRANSLATOR'S INTRODUCTION

Who Was Leone Levi, and Why Should We Care About Him?

Leone Levi (1824-1876) lived in tumultuous times in 1800s Europe. He was a keen observer of his time's political, economic, scientific, technological, and social upheavals[1]. During his lifetime he experienced firsthand:

- The post-Napoleonic period with its reactionary return to despotic government, aristocratic monopoly of government and academic posts, and the re-segregation of Hebrews[2] into ghettos that were walled off city districts whose gates were locked from dusk to dawn.

---

1 [Levi included a number of footnotes in his books; these are translated directly. Footnotes added by the translator to explain elements of his books are formatted in brackets.]

2 [Italian Jews always refer to themselves as *Ebrei, Hebrews*, following the Biblical usage, *Ivrit*. I will follow this usage.]

- An education in segregated ghetto schools that nonetheless qualified him to enter the university to study law.

- The shift in 1848 to a constitutional monarchy that included the restoration of full citizenship rights to Hebrews and Protestants and the reopening of government offices and the professions to educated middle-class people.

- Major scientific and technological changes including steam-powered transportation, the spread of the telegraph, the promulgation of Darwinian evolution, and great advances in the understanding of basic physics and chemistry.

- Italian Unification through a series of wars that ran in the periods 1848-1849 and 1860-1870.

- The battles between the Catholic Church and the Italian state that resulted in the king being excommunicated three times.

Levi was a remarkable polymath and one of the last people to know nearly everything there was to know, just as the great scientific discoveries of the 19th century were causing the modern explosion of knowledge with which we all continue to grapple to this day. He was deeply learned in classics, Hebrew and Christian religion, philosophy, the arts, history, jurisprudence, government, literature, economics, the social sciences, and several scientific disciplines. He read and probably spoke many languages, ranging from classical Greek, Latin, and Hebrew to an assortment of modern languages including Italian, Piedmontese, French, German and English. He had read broadly and deeply the writings of the great authors of ancient Greece and Rome, the

Italian Renaissance, and virtually all of the important Enlightenment figures from Italy, France, Germany, and Great Britain, including the works of Kant, Voltaire, Leibniz, Newton, Mill, Hume, Locke, Hobbes, Adam Smith, Montaigne, Montesquieu, and more minor writers than I can list. He was a great admirer of Benjamin Franklin. He had studied the American experiment in republican government and was well aware of the issues of racial injustice in that country that continued after the South's defeat in the American Civil War.

In 1851, shortly after the Piedmontese universities were opened to Hebrews, Levi enrolled in the Faculty of Law at the University of Turin. The bulk of his career was devoted to his legal practice,[3] and later in life he became a prolific author producing five books, numerous articles in the popular press and a number of public lectures over a ten-year period. He was elected to the *Società Filotecnica di Torino* in 1867, one year after it was founded. This society grew to include among its members many of the leading intellectuals in Turin. At the time Turin was perhaps the leading intellectual center in Italy. Notwithstanding the society's technical-sounding name, it included writers, artists, scientists, engineers, doctors, and legal and medical scholars; among them were Leone's younger brother and law partner, Samuele, and his brother-in-law, Cesare Lombroso, the celebrated professor of medicine and penology. In addition to this intellectual group, Levi was also a corresponding member of a similar organization in Milan, the *Accademia Fisico-Medico-Statistica di Milano.*

Philosophically, he advanced many leading-edge ideas that came to be accepted over the century following his death. His youthful

---

3 [In various documents and newspaper accounts Levi is listed as a *causidico* or a *procuratore capo*. These are legal occupations that correspond to British *solicitors*, i.e., what are usually termed in the US *transactional lawyers* as opposed to *litigators* who appear in court.]

4 | THE WISDOM OF LEONE LEVI

experience of growing up in the ghetto led to his advocacy of religious and racial tolerance[4] and equality before the law regardless of religion, race, or social class.[5] His observations of political repression in the various Italian pre-unification principalities and the power of demagogues during revolutions led straight to his views on good democratic government and how to achieve it. He advocated legalizing divorce,[6] permitting limited liability companies to foster economic development,[7] labor unions,[8] freedom of the responsible press,[9] freedom of religion, compulsory free public education,[10] laws against domestic violence between spouses and against children and the elderly, uplifting the poor by giving them the tools, education, and encouragement to improve their lot, and many other ideas that we now take for granted. Such ideas were quite advanced for his time.

He felt that society was on a straight trajectory of progressive improvement based on broadly disseminated education and new scientific discoveries. On the other hand, he was greatly concerned that as nation states became ever more populous and socially complex,

---

4 [See the Frontispiece to Volume B of his *Massime.*]
5 [While he advocated equality before the law, he also recognized the natural tendency of societies to organize themselves into different social classes.]
6 [Italy did not legalize divorce until the 1970s largely because of the doctrinal opposition of the Catholic Church.]
7 [The laws permitting such companies were enacted in 1882, six years after his death.]
8 [His younger brother and law partner, Samuele Levi, served for many years as general counsel to the railroad workers union and won for them the right to strike for better wages and working conditions.]
9 [Levi abhorred the scandal sheet newspapers. While he argued strongly for a free press, he also thought that there should be a requirement that editors be well-educated and responsible to the public for the quality what they publish.
10 [Pope Pius IX issued a Syllabus of Errors in 1859 listing 80 doctrinal dictates, among which was Church opposition to democracy, public education and liberal politics]

the number of leaders with the intellectual strength and leadership skills to manage them was becoming ever smaller.

Levi was deeply committed to the proper administration of justice and how to arrive at true and correct judgments and allocate guilt among the multiple contributors to a given legal case. He also sought to distinguish between true and pretended virtue; he despised fakers.

He argued forcefully in favor of careful study before major legal, public policy, and scientific decisions were made, so that these would be based on facts and logical arguments. He thought that arguments based only on opinions (e.g., most political and theological arguments) led only to intolerance and bloodshed. He also noted that most people preferred to be told what to think and do rather than thinking things through on their own; for such people religious education was the only path to public morality.

Religiously, he was deeply learned in both the Hebrew and Catholic religions and fully conversant in their main holy texts; his own beliefs bordered on Deism in which God set the universe in motion and defined its basic laws but left it to man to discover and apply those laws. He was a great admirer of Sir Isaac Newton's discoveries in science and mathematics. On the other hand, he criticized Newton's attempts to draw theological inferences from physics, but nonetheless ended up going down the rathole of trying to prove the existence of God using only his somewhat flawed understanding of Newtonian mechanics.

Levi also had a clear understanding of mankind's follies. He was concerned about people who falsely pretended to great wisdom, riches, and/or power and how to protect the public from them. He railed against those who were physically or intellectually lazy. He made many astute observations about corrupt players in both the public and private domains and their adverse impact on society. He urged everyone to judge people based on their deeds rather than their words.

Levi was acutely sensitive to the major scientific and technological discoveries that occurred during his lifetime, such as Darwin's theory of evolution and Faraday's and Gauss' discoveries in electromagnetism. He saw science as the best vehicle for driving the use of fact-based reasoning to displace arguments based merely on ungrounded opinions. He came within inches of discovering the random mutation process by which evolution works, but rejected the idea on the grounds that God does not play dice;[11] with that conclusion he rejected Darwin. He also detailed many of the impacts of new technologies such as the telegraph and steam power on society and on bringing the disparate parts of the world closer together.

One area in which the vast majority of contemporary readers would strongly disagree with Levi was his ideas about the education of women and their role in society. He felt strongly that they belonged in the home, seeing to the efficient running of the household and the proper upbringing of their children. As such, he saw no point in their receiving higher educations. He took this position even as he admired such luminaries as Novella d'Andrea, (c.1270–c.1349), the first female judge and professor of law in Italy, Vittoria Colonna (1492-1547), a great poet and mother figure to Michelangelo, and Gaetana Agnesi 1719-1799) the first Italian woman to hold a university chair in mathematics. Notwithstanding his biases, all his daughters went to university after his death[12] as did virtually all his granddaughters and most of them made important contributions to society. One of

---

11 [Two generations later, Einstein used the same argument to reject quantum mechanics.]

12 [Levi died in 1876, when his oldest child was only 15 years old.]

his granddaughters, Rita Levi-Montalcini, earned a Nobel Prize in medicine.

Levi captured the best elements of his ideas in his two volumes of maxims, which he published in 1872 and 1874 as a legacy to his nine surviving children. Each volume listed three hundred maxims together with twenty essays expanding on the most important of his ideas. Some of those maxims are traditional truisms that are much in the spirit of Aesop and Poor Richard. For example, Maxim 1 in Volume A advises:

Early risers live longer.

Other maxims combine delightful wit with wisdom such as such as Maxim 59 in Volume A:

Excellent doctors are rare, and great politicians are yet rarer, but they all claim to be so, be they doctors or politicians. One who diagnoses you with an illness without recommending an effective treatment or who carries on about a public problem without suggesting how a king, minister, or governor should address it in this or that way shows you only that he does not understand the issue.

But the most interesting of his maxims are those that expose deep insights, such as Maxim 119 in Volume B:

Conscience is built largely upon what a person has been taught: his knowledge and his experience. To believe that the consciences of two different people are the same is like confusing the universal natural human feelings with the knowledge of one's duty, or the wild ignorant passions with morals illuminated by knowledge.

When we yoke together equality before the law, and the necessary training, we replace ignorance with serious analysis in dealing with the issue of injustice; conversely, if one transgresses in favor of ignorance in dealing with this issue, he succeeds in making injustice the norm. Thus, education is a necessary and canonical part of justice.

Biographical sketch of Leone Levi

Leone Levi was descended from a Renaissance banking family that had moved to Piedmont from the Duchy of Milan[13] in the mid-1500s in response to Spain gaining control of the latter principality and threatening to institute its anti-Semitic policies. According to family tradition, the family had originated in Central Europe and moved to the much more prosperous Italy in the 1400s.

Levi's early life is tightly bound up with the battle between Europe's reactionary despotic governments, reimposed by the Council of Vienna after the overthrow of Napoleon in 1814, and liberal ideas unleashed by the French Revolution and propagated across Europe during Napoleon's conquest of most of the continent. Levi's father, Israele was born in 1795 in Nizza Monferrato, a small regional city. He grew up during the period in which Napoleon had conquered most of Italy, opened the ghettos and restored civil rights to the Hebrews and Protestants.[14] Leone Levi, the oldest of Israele's

---

13 [More or less the modern region of Lombardy]

14 The Hebrews and Protestants lost their civil rights in Piedmont in two steps. In the late 1670s, Louis XIV of France waged war against the French Protestants and induced his

five children was born in 1824 in the same city, shortly after the ghetto had been reimposed after the defeat of Napoleon.

Leone grew up in the ghetto, and at the tender age of eleven was sent to the *Collegio Israelitico Elia Emanuele Foa* in the somewhat larger city of Vercelli. That school was part of the segregated educational system that the Hebrews had set up since they were banned from the public schools and universities. The school was in part the religious school for the children in the ghetto of Vercelli, and in part a boarding school for more academically oriented Hebrew students from several regional cities. For these latter students it provided not only religious instruction but also most of the classical education[15] provided by the state-run and Church-controlled public schools. A number of its graduates went on to hold academic posts at major universities after the end of the ghettos, while several others became noted rabbis.

In 1848 King Carlo Alberto (1798-1849) was faced with one of the popular uprisings that occurred all over Europe in which the people were demanding that the despotic royal systems that had been

---

niece, the Dowager Duchess of Piedmont and regent during the minority of her son, Duke Vittorio Amedeo II, to force the Hebrews in the Piedmontese capital, Turin into a ghetto, a walled-off district in the city locked from dusk to dawn; the Waldensian Protestants were isolated in certain Alpine valleys after a failed attempt to annihilate them. Both communities lost most of their civil rights. In 1723, Vittorio Amedeo II, now also king of Sardinia, decreed that all of the remaining Hebrews had to move into ghettos in various regional cities. The second confinement was probably the result of a corrupt bargain with the Pope, in which the Church ceded the right of sanctuary on Church property and control of the public school system to the state in exchange for the state's changed policy toward the Hebrews. After the death of Victor Amadeus II, the Church rescinded the first two concessions, but the Hebrews' remained locked in the ghetto.

15 [The Hebrews were prohibited from studying Latin as that was considered a sacred language for Catholics only. Thus, they read the Latin classics only as Italian translations. Nonetheless, Levi managed to learn that language and also Greek on his own.]

Timeline

Ghettoes established in provincial Piedmontese cities	1730	
	1745	
	1795	Birth of Israele Levi, Leone's father
French Occupation and Opening of the ghettoes; King exiled to Sardinia.	1798	
Napoleon defeated, King returns, ghettoes re-imposed.	1814	
	1824	Leone Levi born.
Collegio Foa opened	1828	
	1835	Leone Levi enters Collegio Foa; Samuele Levi (his brother) born
	1840	Benedetta Debendetti (Leone's wife) born.
King Carlo Alberto grants Hebrews full civil rights	1848	
First War of Italian Unification fails; Carlo Alberto abdicates.	1849	
	1851	Leone enrolls in Law Faculty at U. of Turin
	1855	Samuele enrolls in Law Faculty at U. of Turin

Timeline

Vittorio Emanuele II begins Seocnd War of Unification	1859
	1860 Leone marries Benedetta Debenedetti
Victory unites much of of Italy outside regions around Rome and Venice	1862
Capital moved from Turin to Florence	1865
Venetia ceded to Italy	
	1866 Levi publishes first book, *Piemonte e Italia*
	1867 Leone elected to *Società Filotecnica*
	1868 Leone's first article in popular press
	1869 Levi's Second book published, *Lampi sulla Società Comtemporanea*
Italy conquers Rome makes it the national capital	1870
	1872 Levi's third book published, *Massime*.
	1874 Levi's fourth book published *Massime, Seconda Seria*
	1876 Levi died. his fifth book published posthumously, *Il Tempio Israelitico*
	1908 Samuele Levi died
	1920 Benedetta Debendetti died

reimposed after the defeat of Napoleon be replaced with democratic governments. Carlo Alberto was advised that he could either fight to retain the old system and probably be deposed, or he could assume a leadership role in bringing democratic reform, first to his own domain, the Kingdom of Sardinia and Piedmont, and perhaps elsewhere in the Italian peninsula. He granted a constitution in which a democratically elected parliament would govern, and he would become head of state with direct control only over foreign and military affairs.

As part of this liberal approach to government, he also reopened the ghettos and granted full citizenship rights to the Hebrews and Protestants in his domains. Among those rights was the possibility of admission to the university for all academically qualified applicants. Because the Collegio Foa and several other ghetto schools around Piedmont had offered an almost complete classical education, their recent graduates were eligible to enter the University. Leone Levi and most of the similarly educated coreligionists of his generation did so immediately. He enrolled in the Faculty of Law in 1851 and completed his studies several years later.

In 1848 the king took advantage of a popular uprising in the then Austrian-controlled Duchy of Milan[16] and marched his army into Milanese territory. After a few quick victories, Carlo Alberto's army was soundly defeated at Novara in 1849, and he sued for peace. The Austrians demanded reparations and Carlo Alberto's abdication as their price for ending the war. Carlo Alberto was then succeeded by his son Vittorio Emanuele II, who swore to maintain his father's government and social reforms.

---

16 [Control over the Duchy of Milan passed from Spain to Austria in the early 1700s as part of the settlement to end of the War of Spanish Succession.]

In 1851, Levi enrolled in the University of Turin's Faculty of Law. The prescribed curriculum included civil, criminal, constitutional, commercial, canon, administrative, and international law, and political economy. After his studies Levi began to practice law from offices in his house in Turin at via Garibaldi 10. By 1860 he was sufficiently well established professionally that he could afford to marry.[17] He married the twenty-year-old Benedetta Debendetti, who came from a well-to-do Hebrew family from Alessandria. Her ancestors had also been Renaissance bankers and earlier generations of her family had also lived in Nizza Monferrato. Presumably, she brought a substantial dowry to the marriage. In 1862 Leone's younger brother Samuele (1835-1908) graduated from the University of Turin also with a law degree and joined Leone's legal practice.

In 1867 Levi was elected to the *Società Filotecnica di Torino,* the society's initial year. This society grew to include among its members many of the leading intellectuals in Turin, itself perhaps the leading intellectual center in Italy at the time. Notwithstanding its technical name, it included writers, artists, scientists, engineers, doctors, and legal and medical scholars. Subsequently his younger brother Samuele and his brother-in-law, Cesare Lombroso, the celebrated professor of medicine and penology, were elected to the society. Leone also became a corresponding member of the *Società Fisico-Medico-Statistica di Milano.*

In the mid- to late-1860s Leone also began giving lectures at the Società Filotecnica, which were subsequently published in its journal. He also began writing essays which appeared in popular journals such

---

17 [In Italy at that time, men were generally expected to well-established professionally before marrying. That practice more or less continues to this day.]

as the *Gazzetta Piemontese*[18] and *Corriere Israelitico* of Trieste. His first full-length book was *Piemonte ed Italia–Saggio di Critica Storica* which appeared in 1866. Three years later he published *Lampi Sulla Società Contemporanea*.

Around 1871 Leone may have been offered a post teaching Hebrew in the Faculty of Philosophy and Letters. Because taking that position would have required him to devote more time to his academic career and to limit the amount of time he could devote to his legal work, he turned down the offer, citing his need for a larger income to support his rapidly growing family which by then already numbered eight children.[19]

---

18 [This Turin newspaper was started in 1867, and quickly became a leading newspaper in Piedmont. In 1894 its name changed to La Stampa, a paper that continues to this day and is noted for, among other things, its publication of many essays by Primo Levi.]

19 [There is a Levi family tradition that Leone was offered a post teaching Hebrew at the University but that he had turned it down because its salary was insufficient to support his large family. While we have found no documentary support for this claim, it is remarkably consistent with the following situation. During most of the 1800s, the Faculty of Philosophy and Letters included a broad mix of liberal arts subject areas, including languages and archaeology. The university owned and still owns a world-class Egyptology Museum. As such, it almost always had a professor of Semitic languages and an Egyptologist on its faculty. Because the ancient Egyptian language had a Semitic-like grammar and shared numerous words with early Semitic languages, these two positions were always closely allied. In 1871, Luigi Calligaris, a specialist in Arabic literature died and Pietro-Camillo Orcurti, a famous Egyptologist, had to retire on account of ill-health. In addition, the government was pressuring the university to eliminate its Faculty of Theology, which had a chair of Hebrew and Sacred Scripture, on the grounds that a government-sponsored institution should not be in the business of training Catholic priests, particularly at a time when the Pope had just excommunicated the king for the third time. Conceivably Levi was offered a post in Hebrew at that time to fill the resulting void in Semitic languages. In late 1871, Rodolfo Vittorio Lanzone, an Arabist, and Francesco Rossi, an Egyptologist with deep knowledge of Semitic languages were appointed to the two open posts in the Faculty of Philosophy and Letters. Theology's incumbent professor of Hebrew and Sacred Scripture retired in early 1873, when the Faculty of Theology was finally disbanded.

Nonetheless, his interest in Hebrew scholarship continued and over his lifetime he assembled a small library of antique Hebrew books, of which the oldest was the 1542 edition of a rabbinic Machzor, which contained all the prayers and Bible readings for the annual cycle of Sabbaths and holidays, along with commentaries from Medieval and Renaissance rabbinic scholars. This two-volume set had been censored twice by the Inquisition though the passages the censors had blacked out have since begun to show through the censors' ink.

In 1872 he published his first book of *Maxims* followed in 1874 by a second book of *Maxims*. These two books were meant as a legacy for his children and subsequent generations of his descendants. Translations of these two volumes constitute the core of this book. His final book, *Il Tempio Israelitico Di Torino*, was serialized in the *Vessilio Israelitico* in 1876.

As one can imagine, after he and Benedetta produced twelve children in sixteen years, exhaustion set in. Leone Levi died on November 24, 1876. His widow subsequently married Leone's younger brother and law partner Samuele and they had two more children, fraternal twins, in 1879. Their son was named Leone in honor of Benedetta's first husband, Samuele's older brother. The younger Leone also grew up to be a lawyer, working initially with his father and one of his older half-brothers, Israele Levi. Samuele lived to 1908, and Benedetta survived him by an additional twelve years.

The older Leone's collection of antique books passed to Samuele upon his death. Samuele then passed them on to his son, the second Leone, who safeguarded them while he hid from the Nazis during World War II. The younger Leone then passed those books to his son, my uncle Ruggiero Levi, who left them to his daughter Jeannette. Shortly before Jeannette died of cancer, I purchased those books for my personal library.

Three final notes

The origin of this book was rooted in my discovery of a copy of the two volumes of Leone Levi's *Massime* in the Library of the Jewish Theological Seminary in New York City. After reading them I felt a strong urge to translate them for the benefit of Leone Levi's many American descendants, most of whom do not read Italian and have only a very limited sense of their ancestor's life and times.

In an appendix to Volume B, Levi included a longish essay to illustrate his Maxim 167:

Becoming illustrious is the most powerful revenge that one can have against others' insults.

This essay describes his rather insulting treatment as part of a committee to celebrate the unveiling of a statue in the town of Saluzzo to honor Giambattista Bodoni, an eighteenth-century typographer and printer and Saluzzo's most famous son. Levi's role was to write a tribute to Bodoni in Hebrew as part of a multilingual album in his honor. I found a copy of that tribute book in the Saluzzo municipal archives and have reproduced it in an appendix to this book with the permission of the town archivist. In memory of Levi's link to Bodoni, this book was set in a Bodonian typeface.

This book is organized in four parts:

- Translator's Introduction
- Massime, Volume A, together with Levi's index to it,
- Massime Volume B, together with Lexi's appendix and index
- Translator's Appendices, The Bodonian Album
  A partial bibliography of Levi's writings.

MAXIMS

BY
LEONE LEVI

VOLUME A

TURIN
STAMP. DEI COMP.-TIP. A. ODDENINO E COMP.

1872

For My Children

PREAMBLE

Where I explain to the reader how I was induced to write *Maxims*.

EFFORT EXPENDED–UTILITY PRODUCED–

When I first considered writing some of the maxims which ultimately came to be this book, I immediately thought of the foregoing double scale that Melchiorre Gioia[20] developed with which to measure the true value of a piece of work. I asked myself how hard could this be when the general public produces adages with ease. To write 100, 200, 300 or more maxims, wouldn't that be nice! Listen to the common folk, the second-hand dealers and basket makers! And, after all, has there ever been a writer who has not filled library shelves with his sayings? Everybody makes them up: "In the beginning there

---

20 [Melchiorre Gioia (1767-1829) was an Italian writer on philosophy and political economy, and an early advocate for Italian unification and republican government. He was one of the first economists to apply measurement and statistics to the formulation of government economic policy and for making estimates of economic damages in legal proceedings.]

was the word, and the word was with God and the word was God."[21] *Surely, I could find something with my brain that could, in the words of Francesco Domenico,*[22] *"flutter some little ribbon or a sweep cobweb from the wall."*

At the end of the day, there is always the same uneasy feeling that constrains you: Can you sing like a bird that was born to do so, or would you produce only tittle-tattle? Saying to yourself that you are constrained and weak could be fatal to your efforts, so you had better not look at the effort expended. And if you then speak of the utility produced, that is others' concern, do you hear? Remember that the above-named bird's own warbling often attracts buckshot or snakes. If you have the least crumb of a brain, you should listen to yourself as you repeat "This most true maxim will not please the most important people; it is worse than their parodies which you might receive in exchange for all your hard work."

Truly, truly after having given myself this warning worthy of seven sages I would have kept silent above all else, were it not for a blessed circumstance that pushed me to start. As everyone well knows, if you really want to do something, there is always some enabling circumstance. But let's not jump ahead to the maxims.

One day, as I was rummaging through some papers, I came across the last will and testament of a fine-spirited fellow, a will that I found so bizarre and original that I began to consider making one of my own along the same lines. As you will see, the fault lies in that silly habit of imitation that lives in all of us self-respecting humans, somewhat like the similar tendency in monkeys. This particular will was written by a

---

21 [John 1.1]

22 [Francesco Domenico Guerazzi (1804-1873) was a 19th century novelist and politician whose writings contain some of the foundational ideas of the *Risorgimento*, the reawakening and unification of Italy in the 1840s-1860s.]

man with a dozen children who was nearing death with not a farthing to his name.

He formulated his lists [of bequests] in an antiquated structure that I did not recognize, "Seeing that I came into this world as part of the undertaking of the Danaids,[23] *I am leaving no inheritance for my sons and daughters save for an empty bucket. This being as God wished, may his holy name be blessed, I thought I should dress up my last will and testament since I have neither gold nor silver for my children to divide after I leave this earth. To make up for this lack I leave you some of your father's precepts."*

This man then listed a series of advisories, a few of which were very commendable, and others for which it would be best to keep silent. Of these, I included the one listed as §70 in this book to give you an idea of its companions. Then he continued, "Remember, my children, Jesus the Redeemer of the world: (After which in the original document there appeared four dots making the sign of the cross. ⁞) "It pleased Him to leave behind various woes and evils after his coming; he did not want to protect the world from the law of the ancient Spartans who rewarded those who stole most skillfully. If it should occur to any of you to take things that belong to others, your only cause for being brought to justice will be if you do it artlessly.[24] *But you should remember this example that occurs in modern times, most often in the*

---

23 [In Greek mythology, the Danaids were the fifty daughters of Danaus. His brother, Aegyptus forced Danaus to compel his daughters to marry Aegyptus' fifty sons. On their collective wedding night, the Danaids all murdered their husbands for which they were condemned to spend eternity attempting to fill an empty, leaking bathtub with water using leaky buckets. The testator is describing his life as attempting to fill an empty fortune, but all the money he earned would leak out, so he will die penniless.]

24 [The Spartans taught their sons guile in war; part of their training including having them steal from others; those who were caught were punished for being detected rather than for stealing.]

form of those who seek to accumulate money working for people who manage others' assets; they must fairly share the illicit profits that come from what was promised but not done or not delivered. That approach is as simple as converting Giotto's "O" into a nine.[25]

"Truly you should remember the little fellows who speak openly outside of certain court houses of leveraging the real estate whose managers are accustomed to raking off so much from the sums meant to go to auxiliary bishops that they make Croesus appear to be miserably poor in comparison. And then they tell these auxiliary bishops about the troubles they ran into, the craziness of the losses, and so on, and so forth. And, in addition, you will see the foregoing gentlemen, who were once poor, given the respect owed to those who serve at the altar of the Holy Crucifix. What I am telling you, if you do not know how to act like a spider, don't become flies for lack of such knowledge. And so, my children, may God bless you."

I am not a patriarch, nor am I morally crippled. I will not make recommendations to my children along the lines of the above story, other than to advise them not to become flies in the mouths of spiders. But in the end, I said to myself that I should follow this man's example and leave a testament of advice for my children.

Said and done, I sat down at my table and began to turn my pen with my fingers, dipping it into the ink several times without writing a single word, precisely as happens when a writer's brain refuses his wish. Then I began: "May 4th, 1871" and then I began to doodle on

---

25 [The story of Giotto's "O": When Pope Boniface XI was seeking a painter to decorate the basilicas of St. Peter and St. John, he sent a representative to the studios of various famous Italian painters, including Giotto, to collect samples of their work from which the Pope could judge who would be selected. Instead of giving the messenger a painting from his workshop, Giotto took a fresh sheet of paper and drew a perfect circle freehand. Upon seeing the perfection of this circle, the Pope knew he had the ideal artist and awarded the contract to Giotto.

the edge of my paper. Next, I said to myself, I do not want to dictate maxims for a testament to my children that will be in a folder tied up on a notary's[26] shelf or in a public archive, forgotten right away by those to whom they were addressed. What if I were to print these precepts that flutter through my head! Either they will be deemed good and be sought for by the public as well as my descendants, or they will not be so deemed, and they would all be justifiably forgotten.

At this point I began to have doubts: Would the public be interested in me and my precepts and maxims? I paused for a moment, perplexed, but then I decided that I wanted to give birth to this effort, and I felt encouraged.

I said to myself, a maxim must be so brief that is does not have time to annoy, and if one or another would make people think, "No way!" they are not constrained to stick to it; they can dismiss this one and quickly run on to another.

And yet, I thought, that well-known uneasy feeling of speaking to the public, as I mentioned above, was pressing me at the bottom of my heart. Finally, I decided the reason for proceeding to be sound and I began to write maxims now and then as my brain suggested them.

EFFORT EXPENDED–UTILITY PRODUCED!

I have truly spent considerable effort to write these Maxims, whose rules have made them much more complicated than it might appear. Will they prove useful to those who might read them? My most revered Master, who has watched over all, please note that

---

26 [In Italy, as in much of Europe, the term "lawyer" generally refers to a litigator or barrister, whereas a transactional lawyer is generally designated a "notary" or solicitor. Notaries focus on drafting contracts, wills, and various other types of agreements and settlements.]

if I did not think 'yes,' I can assure you upon my good faith that I would not have written them, let alone addressed them to my children, notwithstanding the above concerns that I had voiced to myself.

MAXIMS

"Speak to me and be witty."
Purgatorio 13

"As with those who are so over-reverent
When speaking before their superiors,
That they can't drag their voice to their teeth
I began to speak without uttering any sound.'
Purgatorio 33

1.
Those who rise early live longer.

2.
Those who eat little think much.

3.
Few words, many deeds.

4.
Those paying great compliments often have little heart.

5.
Those who mind others' business neglect their own.

6.
Buying what you do not need is madness masquerading as reason.

7.
Hearty work heals poverty, but it is a medicine; because most people are children at heart and refuse their medicine, there are many poor people and few real workers.

8.
He who spends the time needed to keep himself and his attire tidy has invested wisely.

9.
Religion brings tranquility of mind, so misfortune seeks it out.

10.
There is religion and religion; the learned use it to enhance their understanding and the ignorant to show their brutishness.

11.
Those who invoke religious arguments in ordinary discourse demonstrate their ignorance, their mental weakness and often their barbarity.

12.
One who bases arguments only on his own opinions shows mental myopia; one who rejects sound judgments developed through rigorous study shows weakness of character.

13.
Many who preach tolerance do not practice it.

14.
To appear especially learned enhances one's self-respect but to merely go along with the opinions of all the others weakens it. Consequently, people use their expertise more often to criticize others than to praise them.

15.
Lowering one's voice reinforces his words.

16.
Overzealousness often raises suspicions. Therefore, the extra-goodhearted are often beset with woes and troubles.

17.
Feeling oneself superior to others is often an illusion of a juvenile mind.

18.
The desire to appear superior often pushes people to criticize others.

19.
Slowness in condemning the work of others shows maturity of judgment.

20.
Love generates love and loyalty, loyalty. Thus, these are both necessary elements for marital bliss.

21.
A sweet manner creates and protects all that one loves.

22.

In the misery of old age, it is a great pleasure to recall the good deeds done in the happy days of youth.

23.

Slander can seriously wound a person even if he is virtuous; therefore, it is the preferred weapon of treacherous people.

24.

Calmness in the face of misfortune shows strength of spirit, just as modesty among the rich and powerful shows sound values.

25.

People derive greater pleasure from speaking and lesser from listening.

26.

Those who forget others' favors show that they were not valued.

27.

An education above one's station in life only renders him unhappy with his lot.

28.

Marrying outside your religion will be difficult. Never do it unless you can keep a carriage in the coach house and horses in your stable.[27]

29.

Only shared pain can be fully felt; the best of friends can offer sympathy and try to alleviate the pain but cannot feel it.

---

27 ["You can keep a carriage ... horses in your stable," i.e., "You are well-off."]

30.

People like to see the suffering of others because it helps them feel their relatively greater happiness. Even more than fanaticism this perverse pleasure underlies religious persecution in many countries.

31.

Hate travels a long straight line, love a parabola, anger goes full circle, and pity occurs only at singular points.

32.

The most powerful sentiment is curiosity; the longest lasting is greed.

33.

Once faith is lost, reason cannot restore it, but fear can bring it back.

34.

Do not laugh at the foibles of another man's wife.

35.

A truly honest man is not insulted if he is suspected of thievery.

36.

Do not trust a person who constantly claims to have clean hands and boasts of his candor.

37.

I have never known of secrets successfully shared among three people.

38.

The best advice is not to give any.

39.

When you speak about someone else, always imagine that he is there to hear you.

40.

The best charity is one that helps the recipient with his work and not one that replaces it.

41.

Think of life as a journey whose end is unknown and learn from it how to determine the true worth of each and every thing.

42.

A genius often undervalues order, but he frequently needs its help.

43.

One will eventually have to pay for even the smallest oversight.

44.

Audacity is often rewarded but timidity never is.

45.

The only cures for a timid man's poverty are for him to win the lottery or inherit from a rich uncle in America.

46.

There are many types of courage, each driven by its own motives. Those types driven by noble causes are thought virtuous, while those with base motives are disdained. The courage of an assassin is often greater than that of a soldier not because of its inherent nature but because of what inspired him and how he explained his motivations. Thus, an act of courage can bring a man either fame or infamy.

47.
Risky ventures can result in either praise or blame for the same act of courage, putting a man either on a pedestal or the gallows.

48.
A man who appears devout in a secular society may be motivated not by religious conviction but by a desire to be admired for his courage, and similar logic can apply to a free thinker in a deeply religious society. In like fashion, a martyr is not always motivated by faith nor is one killed in war always motivated by heroism.

49.
A man is like a horse in that both like to strut their beauty, the man in elegant clothes, and the horse in a fancy bridle and saddle.

50.
A man is like a dog in that both undervalue a person they do not know.

51.
Each time you speak with a new acquaintance, always remember to be humble; he may turn out to teach you something.

52.
Do you wish to save time, effort, and money? Ask each person you meet about his work, listen well, and learn.

53.

Have you ever had the experience of responding to a warm greeting heard on the street and then feeling confused when you realize that the greeting was directed at someone else? This would happen to most rich people who, if parted from their fortunes, would realize that the honors and titles bestowed on them were really directed at their money.

54.

If it were true that we found toil to be a pleasure, each person would be happy with his lot; however, that is not the case. Constancy in wearisome labor is thus worthy of praise, no matter how high the remuneration is that motivates and supports it.

55.

Constancy is a strength that one acquires through training, and its opposite is a trait innate in mankind. It is the most essential element in marital bliss and family happiness and it appears especially between well-schooled spouses.

56.

Each generation revises the judgments passed by previous generations—the truly great people are those whose reputations survive such reviews intact. But fortunately, or perhaps at the will of the Chief Regulator,[28] it follows from this test, as dreadful as death, that everyone believes it to the extent that it occurs to them and they think about it.

57.

If someone truly believed deep down that he would die both bodily and in reputation, even a genius would languish, disheartened

---

28 [God]

and downfallen. But if you speak of death, you always mean that of someone else, and if you work, it is for it to be remembered and to survive even past the time when you say, "One day I will die."

58.

Your duty to proclaim truths of which you are convinced refers only to public matters and never to the personal qualities of an individual about which you might be mistaken.

My father once told me, "You would rue the day in which a rogue understood that you knew what he was. You would surely have made a mortal enemy for life." In response I asked, "Father, should I then lie?" My father then replied, "You should not condemn him to others so long as you can avoid becoming an accomplice in his knavery."

59.

Excellent doctors are rare, and great politicians are yet rarer, but they all claim to be so, be they doctors or politicians. One who diagnoses you with an illness without recommending an effective treatment or who carries on about a public problem without suggesting how a king, minister or governor should address it in this or that way shows you only that he does not understand the issue.

60.

The ancient sages said that beginnings are always difficult, and they were right. I believe that finishing is also difficult and also think that I am right. They were referring to work in general, and I am talking about a specific task. Certainly, on their first day with a chisel or paintbrush neither Michelangelo nor Urbinate[29] was a sculptor or a painter. The early sketches of *Night* and of *The Transfiguration* were far removed from the refinements of the final touches and brushstrokes that enable you to see the tranquil repose of the woman and of a heavenly and radiant beatitude created from canvas and paint. I maintain that for all the people who begin a work of genius, not one in ten thousand brings it to completion. Even Michelangelo sometimes lacked the infinite patience to achieve the final perfection of his works. Relative to this difficult task of completing things, one must always question whether he has the strength to bring something to fruition and must never, even to his most intimate friends, speak of a work in progress as one soon to be finished. You must always remember that many more travelers get lost in *the deserts of toil and patience* than in the sands of the Sahara.

61.

Free will is not a one-time act of the brain but an inherent and continuing part of its work. The only possible proof of free will, or at least the most difficult one to plausibly contradict, is the ability to change one's mind. The power to want or not want something indicates that one is capable of free will. To pretend that one is not capable of free will is absurd, just as it is absurd to imagine a paralyzed man walking on his own paralyzed legs. Instead, to deny that one is capable of free will is to deny the possibility that a sane person can change his mind.

62.

Sometimes our will is subject to the power of others and therefore the direct agent of a crime is not always the most culpable. This is

---

[29] [Urbinate is one of the common names of the great renaissance painter Rafaello (Sonzo), a native of the town of Urbino.]

the most difficult part of meting out punishments in accordance with the strict norms of justice. In addition, given that in each case the criteria to establish the free will of the accused and the degree of his responsibility vary, the sound foundation of the jury system requires that those criteria be weighed by specialized judges.

63.

The laws of sympathy and antipathy, of agreement or disagreement in opinions about religion or politics, or fear and other passions weaken the power of free will in mankind, while education and vigor of temperament help to develop and grow its power. Therefore, in regions where ignorance is prevalent and among weak and decadent people, the jury system produces terrible results.

64.

The response of the sworn witnesses in penal matters is a measure of the degree of vigor and civility of a country. Countries where witnesses' actions do not substantially mirror the public's sense of right and wrong, scientific education, or common knowledge are generally poorly governed. And in the contrary case, the opposite obtains.

65.

When you meet an established person, you might say to yourself, here is a painter, a sculptor, an architect, a doctor, a lawyer, a tailor, or a knife-grinder. But when you meet a youth, take care to say to yourself, this person might become a Shakespeare, a Franklin, a Napoleon I, or a Pius V.[30]

---

[30] [Pius V was pope from 1566 to 1572 and was declared a saint in 1712. He rose to the papacy through the ranks of the Inquisition and was responsible for implementing the recommendations of the Council of Trent leading to the Counter-Reformation. Among

66.

You must always aim to do praiseworthy deeds in all your work, and you should not fear the ridicule that often results in a fall. Imagine if Dante had announced that he wanted to write the *Divine Comedy*, perhaps his closest friends would have been the first to dissuade him from this wonderful work.

67.

Never insult someone who contradicts your judgment, even if he is wrong, if you do not want to lose his esteem and also the esteem of wise men who might hear you.

68.

To assert a noted expert's agreement with your opinion without giving any proof of the same does not help your argument. It only adds to your opponent's displeasure of your contradicting him, and of your explicitly or implicitly repudiating him.

69.

He who is pleased with nothing displeases everyone else.

70.

It is precisely the indecisive men who adopt the most imprudent courses of action because shame and impatience force them to decide on the spot.

---

other things, he forced all the Hebrews in the Papal State to live in the ghettoes of Rome and Ancona, and imposed censorship of their holy books, most notably the Talmud. He is curious choice as a paragon of greatness for a Jewish author.]

71.

Adultery is a path strewn with flowers and thorns that takes you to the heights of a steep cliff from which there is no return but to jump off and fall to the bottom.

72.

One day I asked an old man,
"What is the easiest thing in the world to do?"
He replied,
"The thing which I will do tomorrow."
"And the hardest thing?"
"To begin right away."

73.

What you long for is always better than what you get, and unexpected benefits are always better than what you desired.

74.

A good heart and imagination amplify the moral regrets of life. Movement and distraction can quiet those regrets only if they do not produce their sometimes-fatal results:

> All things fade in oblivion's night:
> .... and man and his death
> And their extreme resemblance, and the remnants
> Of the earth and the sky obscure time.[31]

---

31 [Translators note: This fragment comes from the 12th stanza of a long poem *Sepulchers* by the Italian romantic poet Ugo Foscolo (1778-1827). Foscolo was born in the Venetian-owned Greek island of Zante, the son of a Venetian nobleman and a Greek mother. As a Venetian patriot, he opposed Napoleon's conquest of the Venetian Republic and Austria's later annexation of Venice's empire after Napoleon was banished to St. Helena.

75.

Desire causes one to lose the ability to value good things once he has acquired them, and he reacquires it when he has lost them. Unhappy, he lives illuminated by three lights, those of desire and disappointment, which amplify their value, and possession, which diminishes value to the point that the owner can no longer perceive it. Experience alone can dissipate such illusions, learning through moderation in desire, the true value of what he has, and resignation for that which he has lost.

Curiously, Foscolo spent his last years as a political exile in England, exactly the opposite of what happened to Lord Byron, who was born in England and died in exile in Greece. The following is the original text:

XII TAB
All'ombra de' cipressi e dentro l'urne
Confortate di pianto è forse il sonno
Della morte men duro? Ove più il Sole
Per me alla terra non fecondi questa
Bella d'erbe famiglia e d'animali,
E quando vaghe di lusinghe innanzi
A me non danzeran l'ore future,
Né da te, dolce amico, udrò più il verso
E la mesta armonia che lo governa,
Nè più nel cor mi parlerà lo spirto
Delle vergini Muse e dell'Amore,
Unico spirto a mia vita raminga,
Qual sia ristoro à dì perduti un sasso
Che distingua le mie dalle infinite
Ossa che in terra e in mar semina morte?
Vero è ben, Pindemonte! Anche la Speme,
Ultima Dea, fugge i sepolcri; e involve
Tutte cose l'obblio nella sua notte;
E una forza operosa le affatica
Di moto in moto; e l'uomo e le sue tombe
E l'estreme sembianze e le reliquie
Della terra e del ciel traveste il tempo.]

76.

There are only a few absolute principles that apply in all aspects of social life, and there are even fewer people who observe them as a matter of course.

77.

You do not have virtue whose exercise is correct under all circumstances. Only with judgment, and not with indiscriminate passion, can you hope to distinguish between weakness of character and the strength of a good heart, and between disinterested generosity and that inspired solely by egotism.

78.

When a good deed is undertaken solely for the pleasure of doing good and with no other aim, then one can call it truly disinterested. No one can call another person to account for his innermost feelings that may offer explanations tied to personal rewards without delving into the deepest recesses of his conscience and changing how it governs that person's behavior. To say to someone, "You did a deed because you sought the pleasure of doing it." is like negating the influence, and indeed the existence, of one's love of his fellow man. Instead, it ascribes as his only motive for such deeds a desire to increase his self-respect. In truth, he who does not feel a love for his fellow man cannot find pleasure in doing good deeds. Thus, in such cases of disinterested good deeds, self-respect is more a reflection from doing those deeds than a motive for them; were it also a motive it could not be distinguished from his love for the recipient of the favor, and one needs to remember that this alone matters in social relationships.

79.

Heaven save you from a literary woman, and even more so from one who pretends to be so.[32]

80.

Writers must avoid the mistake of avoiding simple everyday words in daily conversation.

---

32 When I first published this maxim in the journal *Il Corriere Israelitico di Trieste*, I received several very courteous letters about it. I considered publishing the response signed *A Woman* in which she took me gently to task for contradicting myself because I had written another maxim which posited that the most essential element needed for marital happiness and family peace was an elevated level of education of the spouses, and then on this one I wrote "Heaven save you from a literary woman, and even more so from one who pretends to be so."

"My dear lady," I replied to her, "For me, the appropriate education a woman who is destined to be the mother of a family, is not as a scholar; if it happens that you value a more complete education, I would prefer that it reach the level where you avoid ostentatiously showing off your erudition.

"For a literary woman instead, or for the woman who pretends to be so, I meant specifically one in whom such showing off becomes a continuing habit, and who abandons the administration of her household, its economy, and the nourishment and basic education of her children to hired hands in constant pursuit of this hero, or that novelist, or to refine a sonnet which will be praised by a local newspaper.

"Thus, dear lady, the education of a woman that is important beyond any cost, is one that is solid and which permits one to say proudly of her, that she has raised her children as good as Tiberius and Caius Gracchus [The Gracchi brothers served as Tribunes of the Roman republic, representing the interests of the common people; they are sometimes considered the first populists or socialists], and here are my jewels (i.e. her children). It is not one of those who, loosening the reins of fantasy, permits herself to roam from book to book and becomes fixed on a single idea, that of appearing knowledgeable.

"Thus, making a great distinction between a woman who has been properly educated and a literary woman, or worse, one who pretends to be so, I avoid the contradiction that you seem to see those of my maxims which you have cited."

81.

In conversation, never discuss your personal affairs except in response to direct questions.

82.

Make sure that your silence can never be interpreted as a sign of haughtiness.

83.

Do not make up excuses to silence the one who is accompanying you along the way. Always listen well to one who is sharing his thoughts with you if you wish to be faithful to the doctrines of human equality and fraternity.

84.

Do not disdain untrained people who pretend to teach you about your own area of expertise. Rather, be tolerant and empathetic toward them.

85.

Americans do not say, "It is thus." But instead, they say, "It seems to me that it is thus." Or "It ought to be thus." They do well in speaking this way.

86.

Many years ago, I knew a man who entertained a lady at dinner with a tall tale and, to this day, she still laughs about the story. Always attune your conversation to the interests of your companions.

87.

Because human opinion varies widely and is very individual, you should avoid introducing a story with a statement such as "This is a sad story." or "This will make you laugh uproariously." as the opening statement tends to diminish the impact it promised.

88.

Of the many oddities I have observed in the world, I have never encountered a truly tolerant bigot. If you think you have such a person, try scratching him and he will begin to spew fanatical hatred; this goes to show that bigotry is a form of masked egoism, crass ignorance, false charity, and an evil heart, as all of these are attributes of religious intolerance.

89.

A hungry man is quick to anger. Therefore, continuous privation lessens his responsibility for his actions.

90.

Morality and general order are the results of progress.

91.

True correction is shown by example.

92.

The public recognition for the most learned people in the many fields of the arts and the relatively high rewards given for their work contribute more effectively to the collective national wisdom than the schooling required of everyone. This is because people voluntarily follow those who are esteemed and well paid.

93.

Always do as much and as well as you can.

94.
The shares of men and women incapable of lying are not the same because lies are generally a deplorable expedient of the weak.

95.
The most chaste woman loves to feel that she has the charm that her sense of duty constrains her not to show.

96.
In order to be able to legitimately say that a given thing is easy to do, it is generally best to have done it yourself.

97.
Conversely, in order to say that something is impossible to do, we should have tried to do it with all the means at our disposal and not been successful.

98.
One must believe in the justice of mankind, but not count on it overmuch.

99.
Often indifference and an easygoing nature are masks that are best not exchanged for the faces that they cover.

100.
If you are speaking with someone who listens kindly and poses his contrary observations in the form of questions which raise doubts, make sure of your facts or you will lose the argument. His method is the approach of the truly wise.

101.

Conversely, if you are talking with someone who interrupts you without hearing you out or turns to the others in the conversation and puts you down with comments like "What baloney are you telling us?" do not bother to respond—this fish is not worth the bait to catch it—and you risk wasting your time trying to set him straight.

102.

The lazy man and the striker often seek work to sooth their consciences; but, when they are offered jobs, they merely shrug and walk away.

103.

The truly industrious and those with active minds know how to find useful things to do in any situation. In the winter such a person in the Alpine valleys makes nails and tacks; one in the warmer places makes baskets and wooden clogs, and so on. On the other hand, a do-nothing just fritters away his time, yawns, and sleeps, saying "there is nothing to do here."

104.

One who begins by wresting control of his behavior from his own whims, ends up needing to gain control of it from the whims of others. Today he is a slave of his own making, and tomorrow of necessity.

105.

Men live in groups. Each person believes that his neighbor's group is full of joy and light, while his own is somber. But, as soon as he joins the neighbor's group, the somberness follows him, and the light fades out. The only happy ones are those who bring along their own light based on sound reason.

106.

Singing is not always a sign of happiness.

107.

Sometimes unwise and dishonest means can help one seek his fortune. If you are ignorant and impotent, claim loudly to be wise and strong and many will believe you and give you fame and fortune. However, you will be despised by the few who grant true glory. To achieve the goal, you will say "What does it matter? In the world at large, the rich are most respected." And your admirers will agree with you.

108.

People judge the happiness of others based on their own feelings. If someone else acquires something that you want, you will exclaim to yourself, "Oh, how happy he must be." However, since feelings are not the same in all hearts, that joy often manifests itself otherwise and is muted by hidden sorrows, so that exclamation is often accompanied by complaints about the unjust distribution of benefits. With great insight, the poet and philosopher Metatasio wrote:

> If your heart suffers pangs,
> If you read what is written before you,
> How many things that cause envy
> Should really result in pity.[33]

---

[33] [Metatasio (1698-1782) was an 18th century Italian poet and opera librettist. The original text of this aphorism of his was:
Se del cor l'interno affanno
Se legesse in fronte scritto
Quanti mai invidio fanno
Che farebbero pieta]

109.

The most ridiculous person is one who uses opiates, waxes, and rouge to try to hide the changes that time has caused in his body.

110.

There is no passion more contrary to your aims than jealousy.

111.

Jealousy is a particular type of envy that can cause violent rage, and therein lies its sin. Like all passions, it cannot be quelled except by well-enlightened reason, the only means of curing or at least cooling it.

112.

The illusion of discovering valued objects at low prices drives the mania for collecting things, a mania that appears incurable.

113.

All illusions lead one to false ideas, and it is the ongoing duty of human reason to fight against them and make them disappear. For good reason, he who best succeeds at this effort is called a wise and great thinker.

114.

Sometimes, as in the themes of religions of all types, in customs, in biased science, and the like, illusions share a common character, and one who can overturn them is termed a talented benefactor.

115.

Truth demonstrated on the basis of sound principles is the most important of all benefits, even when it turns out to be painful. In the latter case, it is like a surgeon's knife, dreaded but curative.

116.

Sometimes illusions are dear to us, and woe unto the man who destroys them or even only attempts to do so. History shows innumerable victims of such efforts.

117.

Frequently people see only one side of the truth and then try to mask this error by preaching falsehoods. This fatal mistake has cost mankind much blood and, in addition, only produces a slight change in passions and the need for further battles.

118.

A wise man never avows something as true that he cannot prove: for him, the similar is only that. He never confuses the possible with the impossible, when he does not know says simply "I don't know" without masking his ignorance with words and absurd stories.

119.

When an illusion is unique to an individual, touching only personal sentiments, and is not contrary to science, virtue, or justice, it is compassionate not to call it out. Who would tell a dying mother that her son had just died?

120.

Ingratitude is only a rebellion against the sense of duty.

121.

Curiosity brings a love of variation, and therefore inconstancy of affection.

122.

Once curiosity is satisfied, all sentiments derived from it diminish including love, of which it is the essence.

123.

The most curious man is, at the same time, the one with the strongest emotions.

124.

Curiosity among women is moderated by timidity. If it were not so, all other emotions would be overwhelmed by it. That is why in life's dramas, if the protagonist is a woman, she is always courageous.

125.

You should not conclude, however, that a courageous woman is always inconstant and the timid woman is always faithful on account of her timidity. Human reason, when well taught, is always the sovereign master of one's actions. And you should not confuse the brain with the heart or reason with affection.

126.

The exercise of the virtues is admirable and this presupposes a difficult internal battle in which it won out over emotions that were just as powerful.

127.

Work is man's best and most faithful friend, one beyond comparison. It encourages him in good times, it helps and consoles him in times of misfortune, making him happy all by itself. Oh, you Do-Nothings, if you could only imagine this true friend to whom you turn your back, you would be the first to decry your fate and would seek it out with a lantern.[34]

128.

Like all friends, however, work only rewards those who truly love it with all their heart.

129.

The idea of duty does not come and go like sentiment; when it is fully engaged, it becomes the foundation of all virtue.

130.

The lie is the route travelled by small and wicked passions to perform evil. You can never say or do enough against this hateful, deceitful, and abominable vice that can ruin the best of intentions and lead them astray. A single lie from a truly honest man can instantly destroy the reputation which he has toiled many years to cultivate. When you see a meadow covered with flowers, a single plant can indicate that beneath this multicolored carpet lies a wet and marshy soil that could be fatal to anyone who chances to walk upon it. The character of one who knowingly lies is like such a meadow.

131.

The truth can offend or not; it all depends how you present it. To warn someone of an impending danger can save him or cause his downfall.

---

34 [A reference to Diogenes, who reputedly wandered about at night with a lantern in search of an honest man.]

132.

Most would pardon a jester for his jibes but no one would do so for those of a talented man. The jibes of the former are entertaining, while those of the latter humiliate.

133.

Fear of punishment and the hope of reward are the basis of common people's religion. They engage in prayers, fasts, abstinence, discipline, submitting to martyrdom and the like to further their own interests.

134.

For the common man, religious practices arise from the sting of remorse.

135.

Those who seek to extend the boundaries of man's existence and intelligence, or, at least, who seek with all their might to improve the well-being of those around them, are doing good. Only they can believe that they are acting according to the commandments of the Supreme Ruler.

136.

The principle of the ancient sage Hillel, in which he summarized the entire Torah[35] as, "You should not do unto others what you would not have them do unto you" is incomplete only in that it does not include its active contrapositive; but it is remarkable because it implies that it recognizes freedom of conscience and imposes only the need to follow the moral laws, to the exclusion of the sanction of positive laws from dogmatic faith

---

35 [The five Biblical Books of Moses.]

137.

One of the most fatal aberrations into which human discernment can fall is that of considering the political leadership to be competent to regulate the public's conscience. From that is born the intrusion of religion into politics, and force as an argument of the superiority of an opinion, with resultant human slaughter as fierce as it is deplorable. Modern civilization has undermined that aberration but has not destroyed it and the book of blood remains open.

138.

Real truth is neither fanatical nor intolerant. It merely asserts that two plus two is four and not five. It may suffer martyrdom from whoever asserts it is five, but it continues smiling even in death or martyrdom and is satisfied repeating to itself, "And yet it moves."[36] Two and two, four!

139.

Recognizing one's own ignorance is the first step of true learning. All errors are born from the fact that the human spirit is willing to accept many false premises without question.

140.

No sentiment is the same from one moment to another during its duration. In us it follows a strangely curved path, higher or lower according to age, sex, temperament, health, or the circumstances of one's life.

---

36 [Galileo supposedly said this to himself after being forced by the Inquisition to recant his theory that the Earth orbits the Sun, contrary to Church teachings that the Earth sat still at the center of the Universe.]

Religious sentiments follow this same law as do all others. Thus, you can maintain without fear of erring, not only that no two people have exactly the same religion, but also that a given individual's religious thinking changes from day to day under the pressure of differing conditions and he will undertake different actions mandated by his religious convictions. In other words, his religious feelings will vary in intensity from one day to the next. Today he may bow to this altar, maybe tomorrow to another, the day after that to none, and yet on another day after that to all of them.

141.

Often the common folk, having won a fortune at the lottery or the stock market, will lose their God or patron saint.

142.

Do you want to live quietly and at peace with everyone?
- Never contradict anyone, verbally or in writing.
- If you are poor, stay that way.
- If you are talented, don't show it too often, and if you use your talents, allow others to benefit from and enjoy them.
- Whoever tugs on your clothes to get ahead of you, step aside and let him pass.
- Obey the evangelist's precept that orders you to turn the other cheek to the person who smites you.
- Hide your physical gifts.
- Do not choose a beautiful wife.
- Raise your children according to your own values lest the one who is brighter than the others breaks the eggs in your basket.[37]

---

37 [*Breaks the eggs in your basket*, i.e., makes things difficult for you.]

- If you learn that someone is praising you, plead with him for goodness' sake to swap censure for praise, or at least to keep quiet.

And even all this may not suffice.

143.

It is inevitable that all gentlemen will suffer from war during their lifetimes; but it is virtuous to not start one.

144.

Little by little our passions and vices become our masters. Pay careful attention to yourself and cleanse yourself of them when the first appear, for, once they have become rooted, not one person in a hundred thousand knows how, and is able, to defeat them.

145.

You can find a bad side in everything other than, perhaps, the love of parents for their children. Often it is better not to look for it, but to appear good-natured.

146.

Smiles, little words, oozing tears, and soft kisses may indicate equally a heart open to love or closed by adultery.

147.

Many times, artifice imitates reality so well that even the most wise and expert jeweler needs to resort to his file to distinguish the real jewel from the fake one.

148.
The passage of time will inexorably and surely uncover any fakery.

149.
The most powerful and faithful love is one which has ceased to be reciprocated.

150.
If you reach the age of seventy, you will have been many distinct people, all different from one another. If the passing of the last of these is grieved, it indicates that they were all good, as the apparent identity of their body causes them each to be judged responsible for the others.

151.
Know that people never pardon anyone. They may act as if they have pardoned, make pardoning a duty, and have even fooled themselves into thinking that they have pardoned, but the nature of memory is such that it impedes true pardon.

Therefore, learn how not to be blameworthy. The most profound regrets would be of little use to you. A whole life of good behavior, maybe even one illustrious in the sciences, arts, and letters or of great dignity would not erase others' basic fault-taking. It is like sprinkling plaster dust to cover spots on stained linens.

152.
To spend time wisely means to work to serve others. Work hard and become wise as did Aristotle; if you do not do or teach, your time will rightfully be described as wasted.

153.

Always pay serious attention to your enemies' criticism of you. You will often find sound advice buried within it.

154.

Before following the advice that your mind suggests today, let it mature during the overnight silence. In the course of that quiet time, the imagination tends to color everything with the good and the beautiful and it opens the suggestion to your dreams.

155.

It is said that women are the masters of pretense, and it may be so. However, the diarist who poses himself as supremely modest is even better than any woman at playing this game. As you might expect, you will find the greatest arrogance is that of such journalists because of their lack of wisdom.

156.

The carrying on of an arrogant person compares to true modesty like an imitation compares to the real thing.

157.

It is a great lie for a famous critic to curry favor with minor artists and praise mediocrity. While he loses his reputation among the excellent, he also perverts the taste of the common folk.

158.

Public praise for talented youths is like adding salt to food; it is necessary, but in excess ruins them.

159.

If the members of extremist parties were tolerant, the pen alone and not the sword would drive progress.

160.

All means that favor the developing and strengthening of the body are broadly consonant with the existence of human intelligence. Thus, exercise is not only a suitable discipline, but it is highly moral and therefore a duty.

161.

Arrogance is the coat that frequently hides cowardice.

162.

When the greatness of the danger and the smallness of the end justify fear, the latter changes its name to prudence.

163.

Unfortunately, he who sleeps is often a sinner.

164.

The honest man who takes on the management of others' business, sharpens the scissors of Atropos[38] on the thread of his own life.

165.

It may be that one day you might desire take into your carriage the wife of the street vendor of matches;[39] never take the one of an honest employee who has no resources other than his work.

---

38 [Atropos was the one of the three Fates in Greek Mythology. She rendered the decisions of the other two fates immutable.]

39 [*Street vendor of matches*, i.e., a street hustler.]

166.

Often, we wish for something which we are unable to do or accomplish.

167.

There is a wide distance between fame and glory.

168.

The living are alternately criticized and vexed, while the dead are praised and forgotten.

169.

Know how to judge yourself severely and tremble alone before your own sentencing; only that can give you the right to ignore the injustices done to others.

170.

Youth and the strength that accompanies it are always in opposition with the powers that be. Therefore, repression becomes the means of control of all types of political governments.

171.

A youth with great expectations was carrying on among a group of friends, expounding enthusiastically in favor of atheism. He was heard by a rich and philosophical old man who loved him and who motioned that he would like a private word. The old man said, "Look, I hear that you need money. How much do you want? Here is my purse. Help yourself." and he withdrew a large purse from his pocket.

As the old man spoke, the youth blushed and, feeling somewhat offended, he responded, "Who told you this, kind sir? I have entertained no such thought." The older gentlemen then responded, "Young man, normally, among people of your age, denying God means that either your purse is empty, or you have an untrue lover, or lack ambition, or have an unfulfilled wish. I supposed that the first reason was what inspired your speech. Please excuse me if I was mistaken."

172.

If the nobility of their race was the most admired in the world, the Jews would name their children Moses and Jacob instead of Maurice and James.

173.

The promise to give or do something in the future is discounted by hope. But keeping our word is a duty whose fulfillment in many cases does not depend solely on us. Thus, real transgression occurs only when we willfully violate our promise.

174.

Superior intelligence, whether real or only supposed, charms, and wit inspires love from your inferiors. Here they are devoted and there they become partisans.

175.

Different areas of expertise and mutual respect are the foundation of true friendship.

176.

Oversharing of your personal troubles is inconsistent with true friendship.

177.

When the common man does not feel valued, he tends to seek commiseration. Unfortunately, his parading of his personal miseries often results in others gossiping about him to all comers.

178.

Remember that a man of rare and elevated spirit is one who, if poor, does not talk about his poverty, and if out of luck, does not talk about his misfortunes.

179.

Many more people will sympathize with you to show off their own superiority rather than out of the goodness of their hearts.

180.

Those who blindly attack others give evidence of their own ignorance or prejudice.

181.

Human vanity is so blind that people imagine erecting monuments to oneself to be the same as erecting them to a man of genius.

182.

He who gives his children language, gives them bread.[40]

183.

The news of the world is covered by many talented people, and the daily press suppresses most of it.

---

40 [*Gives them bread,* i.e., provides for them]

184.

The common man sees nobility in a coat of arms, while the philosopher sees it in work.

185.

Only things of absolute beauty are universally seen as being in good taste.

186.

Adulation is the mother of bastards, unties the purses even of misers, breaks many bonds, displaces true merit, and opens every door, even those of academia. Many believe that it will open the doors of Heaven, and for that reason they daily recite praises of God.

187.

Civic virtues shine brightest and are most often seen in impersonal government, because there is little of the adulation on which false merit depends and few opportunities for it to emerge.

188.

Praise given to mediocrity is one of the means by which jealousy degrades true merit.

189.

Very rare is the merit that knows not to bow to the powerful.

190.

Behaving contrary to the laws of nature undercuts the finest of man's abilities and therefore his character. Therefore, a vow of celibacy is just as immoral as polygamy. It is unconscionable and goes against social norms; consequently, civil society has the right to weigh against it, and indeed to prohibit it.

191.

If you vowed not to eat, drink, or sleep you would be avoiding your duty to yourself and therefore be under sentence of death. Such happens also with a vow of chastity; other than in those very rare cases where such abstinence is motivated by fidelity, death comes, perhaps more slowly, through gloominess or mania which lead to self-hatred, faithlessness, or suicide. To those who have doubts about this sorry outcome, I say "Observe with an open mind, and you will believe."

192.

One day a group of men were discussing when human ingenuity was most quickly and sagely shown. One said it was in reciting poetry or in extemporary reckoning. Another said it was in successfully parrying misfortune in the midst of a battle against an unexpected and unplanned for incident. A third suggested that it was in protecting oneself during a fall. The fourth, the oldest and wisest reasoner in the group suggested that it was when someone who was caught in a sinful act instantly concocted the most plausible possible cover for his or her actions.

193.

When intelligence has reached a certain level in a genealogical line, it tends not to spread out to the branches.

194.

Men tend to deny the intelligence of others until it is proclaimed by their fame, but they bow before visible riches that cannot be denied. That is why the rich are better known and esteemed than modest sages.

195.

Everyone is judged by the many who know him, and the most inexorable severity influences those judgments. Often slander and betrayal derail a fair judgment which greatly embitters those who are unjustly condemned. The latter, even if they console themselves with their perception of their own clean conscience, cannot always remove self-doubts about their virtue, as happened to Brutus at Philippi.[41]

196.

People do not like to face their own wrongs. Even for the most just, disapprovals merely annoy them and do not correct their behavior.

197.

Making a great show of honors and distinctions received and to affect superiority in your words and deeds makes you obnoxious and hated. Be careful that true merit does not fall into such blunders, which suggest base and ignorant vanity.

198.

A good heart tends to involve itself too much in discussions, and this is not the least of its minor defects.

199.

Excessive zeal is another defect of a good heart.[42]

---

41 [Marcus Junius Brutus, one of Julius Caesar's confidantes, was one of the leaders in the plot to assassinate Caesar, which he justified as an effort to restore the Roman republic after Caesar's dictatorship. Prior to the battle at Philippi in which Brutus was defeated by the combined forces of Caesar's nephew Augustus and Marc Antony, Brutus was supposedly visited by Caesar's ghost who foretold his defeat and subsequent suicide.]
42 See Maxim number 16.

200.

Try to always remain neutral and fair and avoid the pressures of your sympathy or antipathy. Only an unjust man uses his influence to take from one person to give to another without any reason other than that he dislikes the former and likes the latter.

201.

It is exceedingly difficult to accurately judge those around us. It is possible that you will discover a most terrible and powerful enemy in one whom you thought you could attack with impunity and, on the contrary, powerful help from those from whom you least expected it.

202.

Do not judge the capabilities of others, except in comparison to you and your values, and above all, leave comparison to third parties to Plutarch.[43]

203.

Men of highly energetic or very weak characters, the two extremes, are the most vindictive. Between them, time will calm the former, but the second whose vendettas, though rare, are far worse; a weak man will not act except when he is highly confident of success, and his concentrated rage is exceedingly difficult to placate.

204.

Sometimes a man of weak intelligence will rebel against his internal voice that advises him of the strength of a superior mind and he will

---

43 [Plutarch was a Greek philosopher and Delphic priest of Apollo during the first century CE, whose best-known surviving work is a volume of biographies of numerous Greek and Roman worthies including Alexander the Great, Cicero, Julius Caesar, Marc Antony, and Marcus Junius Brutus.]

deny its power. In such cases, instead of submitting to this hated power he develops a jealous hatred that becomes ever more implacable the more he senses his own weakness.

205.

The best remedy to all errors is to avoid making them.

206.

The desire to remove himself from a current painful situation often clouds a person's reason. For this reason, he often undertakes bad remedies which only make the situation worse.

207.

For the wretched, tomorrow does not exist. Solving the problem of getting through today is his only thought. As for tomorrow, God will see to it.

208.

When you are both rich and wise, you can aspire to do many things. When you join riches and wisdom to an excellent pedigree, you can aspire to do anything.

209.

In many cases the reformer revives and protects while the conservative, with his impotent opposition to change, causes the destruction that he seeks to avoid.

210.

Public opinion follows a curve. When it is broadly shared, he who does not go along with it will remain isolated, impotent, and outside of its progress.

211.

The best recommendation in any situation is to have good reasons and know how to express them. But the pessimists say that in certain countries power and money still have the advantage over good reasons.

212.

No one is poor until he believes he is.

213.

Finding myself one day atop a hill where a yell was repeated three or four times by the echo, I asked loudly: "Tell me the secret to make my fortune? Do tell...Do!" and the waves resounded with "Do! Do! Do!"

214.

Anyone can easily be a prophet in his own house, comparing income and spending. But few are willing or able to become prophets in this way, and when the prediction turns out badly, they disbelieve the result rather than mend their ways.

215.

In the major cities, human thought tends to be much broader, passions stronger, and the virtues and vices are both much greater. In contrast, in the smaller towns the small passions are more venomous and longer lasting, and small glories are won with pompous and childish triumphs.

216.

There is no man driven by only a single passion, no matter how violently he holds his foremost one.

217.

A wish fulfilled or a passion that has faded or been superseded can often lead to regrets. To know whether the regrets are justified, if such were possible, one would need to place the individual in question in the same physical and moral context as he was at the time he acted to see if he would do the same thing. Most likely David would have given the same command to Uriah in order to have Bathsheba.[44]

218.

The ancient sages said that a man is best understood when seen in anger, under the influence of wine, by his purse, and through his pen. I say that it is faster and better to observe his eyes and listen to his tongue.

219.

When in the course of conversation, you constantly hear "I" rising to the surface, beware that you have before you a scoundrel, a balloon filled with wind, or one who is both at once.

220.

Not all killers, not even the most atrocious ones, end up in front of a judge. There are others that ride about in fancy coaches. Instead of fists or poison, they use pinpricks.[45]

221.

In order to become wealthy tiptoe around the edges of the penal code and be careful not to become ensnared in the clutches of its text. Once

---

44 [In the Bible, King David sent his soldier Uriah into the front lines in battle in order that he should be killed, and David could have his way with Uriah's beautiful wife, Bathsheba.]

45 [*Pinpricks*, i.e., they are character assassins who use innuendo and false accusations.]

you are wealthy, you will be considered a pillar of society, everyone coming after you will be derided as *nouveau riche*, and you will be revered as old money.

222.

It is said that everyone has a balance scale in his heart, in which above one pan is written Duty, and above the other Interests. It is also said that when a hundred purses in the second pan do not tip the balance, maybe you need a hundred and one, and if one additional does not tip it, try two. I believe this story to be a lie, at least in one in a hundred cases.

223.

The throat and avarice seem to dominate among the old. Concentrated in the former is the sensuality that has been blunted in other areas, while the second enables the illusion that the coffin is only a foggy, indistinct, and far off image, or does not allow us to see it at all.

224.

The man whom you find busy at his own warehouse and the woman that you find at the dance behave very differently when they are seen at home.

225.

Many who become apostles of public opinion when they are out and about, rebel angrily against it when they are in the privacy of their own homes.

226.

Do not believe in heresy, orthodoxy, in the character of politicians, the sincerity of speakers exhorting morality, or claims of disinterest put forward by promoters. Instead believe in your doubts about those who show themselves to be fanatics and intolerant of others' opinions or who make a show of being much more serious, temperate, courteous, or just than others.

227.

The justice and morality on which a civil society is based are a synthetic product based on behaviors of which you will find only hints here and there. What I mean is that while today's society as a whole is just and moral, but only rare individuals are so. Even though this sounds like a fundamental contradiction, it seems to be the case.

228.

The well-taught farmers, the teachers of letters and sciences, the artists and the workers are the totality of the worthies of mankind.

229.

Only believe those that have known extreme poverty when they cite themselves as examples that we should disdain the trifles which the powerful bend over to gather to adorn their gilded vanity.

230.

The more you study, the more you become aware of how small you are.

231.

A pen has two points, one to cause you to be praised and become immortal, and one to be hated and become infamous. The choice takes a great deal of effort but is always available to the wise mind. Moreover, the difficulty of making the correct judgment is greater than that required to master one's passions. For that reason, only a few are able to make that choice.

232.

If the pen is not warmed by the fire of genius, it does not make its mark and instead wounds he who wanted to use it to harm others.

233.

A Catholic friend of mine went with me to the top of a hill where there was a strong echo. Because he was troubled by a woman who had unjustly accused him of philandering, he yelled,

> "Who can help me find success if no one will give justice to me?"
> Echo answered, "Me! Me! Me!"
> "From whom should I seek help, the saints, Jesus, or the Virgin Mary, that holy woman?"
> And Echo responded,
> "Woman! Woman! Woman!"
> I observed to my friend,
> "The spirit who lives in these parts is rather perverse."
> To which my friend replied,
> "Wouldn't you agree that he has a point?"

234.

It would serve you well, my friend, to observe that failing to greet someone and having a stiff back are powers that you should never use toward a man does who not impress you. Courtesy, affability, gentility, and the use of words and acts of social conventions that signify respect for others do not detract from your self-esteem and decorum and are much more valuable than you might believe.

235.

The habit of meditating on or declaring one's ideas in public reduces a man's interest in private conversations and therefore joining others to attend plays, take strolls, and have chance encounters. Thus, while an author creates a desert around himself with his unsociable withdrawal, he pleases us with the power of his mind to create the illusion that this desert is really a delightful and magical garden.

236.

A clever idea that is not accompanied by hard work, merely exists, travelling alone in its own compartment, and dies unknown and uncomforted, merely sighing about this dream or that.

237.

The manufacturing industry is a true partnership created from tangible capital (gold) and imputed capital (work). To grant this partnership legal standing is one of the most difficult problems of our times. Unfortunately, this problem is not simply an abstraction; justice requires its resolution lest we suffer incalculable damages and undergo many difficulties. [46]

238.

Great ability has many different manifestations. It can liberate, work for its own benefit, constrain others, be wasted, misrepresent itself, rebel, or do nothing at all.

---

46 [This item refers to the issues surrounding the creation of modern corporations whose shareholders' liability is limited to the value of their shares. Italy did not establish a proper legal framework for such corporations until 1882, after Levi's death.]

239.

Many truths have produced and can produce great evils, because when they are combined with imposters, lies and errors, among other misfortunes, the product of that truth is its own negation.

240.

No one can know the precise limits of his intelligence. Bad teaching, lack of mental exercise, laziness and other capital sins can create the appearance and substance of limits to even the greatest intelligence.

241.

The greatest degree of perfection in a given activity is acquired only through repetition.

242.

Rich women tend to prefer the theater, balls, and travel to the duties of motherhood. Early aging, bad breath, false teeth, and sagging breasts are the lighter and more common punishments of this monstrous behavior of exchanging the proper role as a true mother for a false one. Some improvement!

243.

Nowadays there are many rich people who, being from a family with many children, prefer a life of constant ill humor, family discord, and risk of getting horrid diseases which are difficult or impossible to cure. This demonstrates that the unjust institution of primogeniture could also have a good side, at least for the rich and privileged for whom it was created.[47]

---

47 [Given that Levi had twelve children, he was perhaps concerned about inheritance fights among his heirs and potentially other family issues.]

244.

A woman is a true angel when she is next to the cradle of her child, by a sickbed, near the litter of an injured person, overcoming all miseries, and smothering her own concerns to offer loving comfort to others, or restrain her own desires in order to care for a loved one.

245.

A man can commit suicide over a hopeless love, but only a woman can die from its pain.

246.

It is much easier not to enter into a bad roadway than to exit from it.

247.

There is a big difference between being contented with one's lot and being happy with one's good luck. Only the former offers a ray of true happiness to a wise man in a wretched life.

248.

You *must know* in your profession, arts, or calling. You *may know* in other disciplines.

249.

If you reflect well upon the causes of your ill feelings towards another, you will almost always find your pride among them.

250.

One may suspect that racial differences underlie antipathy among people at least as much as differences of religion.

251.

The greatness of men for the most part is an illusion created by distance.

252.

Showing off in public and the elegant style of your clothes ordinarily have as much merit as libertines' boasts about their deplorable victories over maidenly virtue. Take off your fancy clothes and step down from the pedestal and you will see yourself unmasked.

253.

A reconciled enemy is a hidden enemy. A man never truly pardons another's transgressions.

254.

Reconciliation helps to temper the acute phase of hatred and to impede its open activity that always disquiets, pains, and poisons life.

255.

Your misfortunes and miseries can calm your hatred and render it only latent. Recover and you will see it rise again because it is a compound of anger and jealousy.

256.

There are differences among hatreds. The less culpable is hatred in response to others' provocations. Indeed, this is never true hatred, though it can become so through desire for revenge.

257.

It is not only just, but also highly expedient to control your antipathy toward a given person. However, because it is difficult to hide its first appearance, and further tends to be a reciprocal feeling, it is prudent to always be wary of those toward whom you have felt a strong dislike.

258.

If you call the bad things that might happen to you at the hand of someone who dislikes you foreboding, you are merely substituting a prejudice for the reasoning that teaches you that such evil might be produced by the same antipathy that responded to or was caused by yours.

259.

Learn the real facts and do not act upon your ignorance or superstitions.

260.

We do not always value things for what they are worth. Leadership roles, distinctions, and awards conferred by reason of birth or popular demand are generally valued more than the regard for scholarship, the one objective worthy of human intelligence in this short life.

261.

The liberal professions, honestly practiced, rarely result in riches by themselves. They can, however, result in accidental riches, such as the professor turned stock market speculator, impresario, broker, or even more so, as a member of Parliament or by marrying a rich and spoiled wife. But in these cases, it is clear that it is not the profession that made them rich.

262.

The esteem granted to scholars and that granted to the rich are not at all alike. The first belongs to the person and the second to his wealth;

this latter would be more precisely called credit, which can be granted even to moneyed scoundrels. The difference is not merely one of words as there are many millionaires who are despised because of their shabbily obtained fortunes. Only the latter are denied credit for their money, while lenders offer millions of lire of credit to the others. Overall, justice and public opinion recognize this difference, and that is a good thing.

263.

Today, the language-based professionals have become vague and airy in their studies. The so-called science of evidence-based law has become an occupation that can be carried out by anyone who can read. Progress can only take place through true advocates, those with law degrees who can quickly and clearly understand the private interests of their clients and those of their opponents.

264.

It would be of great benefit to the community if lawyers could rationally apply deep learning and the history of the law to its exercise. Unfortunately, the pressure of the legal profession blocks the fullness and depth of this practice, while in many cases, cleverness is used to achieve quick remedies; therefore, for the most part, what happens in these cases is like what happens to physical beauty: after a few years nothing remains except a reputation rooted in the past and the wrinkles of the present.

265.

Wisdom in any branch of study always remains incomplete and humble and uncomplicated in its manner, and therefore rarely results in fortune.

266.

It is frequently the case that the spoken language needs to be translated in order to know its true sense.

267.

Before putting faith in a fact that seems uncomfortable to you, study well the speaker.

268.

In most cases, to persevere is to succeed. Only in this sense can one say that wishing is power.

269.

A sincere person must hope never to be consulted on the value of the works of others, because, those who are inferior hope for, peers expect, and superior practitioners require praise, and cases in which praise is truly deserved are rare; therefore in most cases, person consulted must either lie or displease others.

270.

Knowing how to write or speak does not include knowing how to act.

271.

Ordinarily a person values above all else in life to earn higher respect for his ability than accorded to those who have disdained him.

272.

One never loses his religion in the middle of vast oceans or deserts.

273.

It is great foolishness to show a lack of confidence in those in whom one must trust.

274.

It is imprudent to trust or confide in others more than is necessary.

275.

Never abandon that which you may desire to reacquire tomorrow.

276.

It goes without saying that, for the supreme overall benefit to your descendants, you should seek a future spouse endowed with a body without physical defects and of medium height, with wide shoulders, a long neck, a thick head of hair, and beautiful teeth. Tossing over your shoulder any other consideration, even a most flattering appearance can spare both you and your posterity of many tears.

277.

There are misfortunes that all the gold in the world cannot remedy but that the most elementary forethought could have avoided them; all know this elementary truth, but few remember it.

278.

It is ridiculous and dangerous to boast of one's physical shortcomings. Only men of great merit or spirit can gracefully joke about their physical limitations.

279.

Sincerity is always a child, a lamb among wolves. To observe, to know, and to keep quiet are three verbs that can in many cases be one's guardian angels.

280.

If you are overwhelmed by love without a shadow of doubt, go directly to your doctor. This is madness, even in Torquato Tasso.[48]

281.

I do not know of any sound education that is separated from physical exercise; in a boxer, for example, exercise steels his heart against the emotions of the fight and thereby increases his physical energy and courage. Unfortunately, exercise has been abandoned by English scholars as a ridiculous practice.

282.

The Medieval focus on force of arms suffocated the cultivation of the mind. Modern arms tend to depress the vigor of the body. Therefore, then there was too much focus on famous knights and today too much on calculation.

283.

In barbaric or semi-barbaric societies, personal valor was the primary driver of public safety, predominating over laws and customs as a means for organizing society. In civil societies, where power is measured in proportion to wealth, laws are the principal means of

---

48 [Torquato Tasso (1544-1595), a renowned Renaissance poet wrote more than five hundred love poems. He is best known for his epic, *Jerusalem Delivered*, set during the first crusade. Tasso ultimately went mad in later life and died in an insane asylum.]

protecting rights. I would say, among the illiterate, Hercules rules; among millionaires, the consumptive and weak rule.

284.

I was listening to a discussion between two philosophers: The first said,
> "In the same way that the heart is the organ of circulation, the brain is the organ of intelligence."

The other then replied
> "We are in perfect agreement, but now let's search for the place from which the poet could have drawn his subject matter to organize it in his brain for his poem."

> "Oh, that is a good one ... from his memory and his imagination."

I was carefully listening to the words of those two sages, and at this point I spoke up, saying,
> "Memory and imagination, what are they other than a product of the brain? Thus, the brain can imagine things that *have not been physically sensed, that is, that no longer exist or never did exist!* Thus, creative brains that have many such miraculous ideas can create them out of nothing at all, drawing those ideas from their own substance, a substance that is always renewing itself and is never used up! If that is the case, I can imagine the possibility of Creation [as in Genesis]. Who knows, maybe the universe is the product of a great brain located in another solar system, perhaps in the constellation Hercules, to which we are attracted.

Thinking thusly, I came to the following maxim: Carefully study the facts that you have experienced directly and affirm those that appear free from personal biases, fears, and the intolerance of neo-apostles. If those facts that you recognize help to overcome superstitions, so much the better. But you must never presume to believe these facts without allowing for the possibility that they might be contradicted by others' experiences.

285.

I once asked a vigorous old man, a friend of long standing, "How do you maintain the luxury of your excellent health, and how come you are always welcome among those who know you?" He replied, "How do I know? Half the time I am a damn fool, and the other half I act like one."

286.

One day, another friend of mine said,
> "A person can voluntarily commit suicide without even thinking about it."

"How is that possible?" I asked.

"With his own words." he replied.

287.

A word can be made of gold, silver, bronze, iron, ice, or fire, and each of our mouths indiscriminately mints coins. We commit the greatest wrongs when we spend one such coin instead of another.

288.

Why is it that I can always correctly judge the actions of others, and yet I often go astray in my own actions? It is because I do not feel others' passions, but I feel and follow my own.

289.

Memory embellishes the past, loves the present and hopes for the future.

290.

Money is like health; one truly understands its value only when it is gone.

291.

Nowhere does there exist a man so wise that there is no subject on which he is more or less a fool.

292.

Given the truth of the preceding maxim, underlying a despotic government is a universal madness that sooner or later ends in massacre and ruin, since the cask gives the wine that it contains, in this case, dreadful woes on Judgment Day.

293.

If I were a great and powerful man, I would prohibit the erection of monuments to me before the hundredth year after my death.

294.

Glory is similar to music which has certain combinations of sounds that do not resonate with the taste of every generation. Therefore, true and deserved glory is based on great and beautiful absolutes whose value can only be judged over time.

295.

The human spirit proceeds by degrees; let us imagine a scale from one to a hundred with which we could classify sages and madmen, scoundrels and honest people. The beauty is that almost everyone would appear on that scale, even if measured by different traits. That is why most pessimists place mankind at one end of the scale, and find that all is bad, and the world is getting worse and worse as time goes by. But they are right not to believe in the existence of saints.

296.

Resign yourself to often mimicking others' manners if you do not want to appear ridiculous or worse.

297.

He who wants to please everyone ends up pleasing no one, and one can say that is because of committing the sin of oversweetness.

298.

A man must set his course in the direction of what seems to him to be the path of goodness. He must not turn away from it unless the hoped-for good end turns out to have been the edge of a cliff; in that case to continue on would have been foolishness. But, because it is difficult to make right judgments, the change in direction needs to be considered with much intelligence and in good faith.

299.

Listen to others' advice, not to follow it blindly, but to consider it and choose wisely what to do.

300.

A coin has innate value only to the same degree as a geometric figure. It becomes gold or silver when it has been spent wisely, and it will have been wisely spent only when your use of it was not merely to further the interests of your family or business.

ILLUSTRATIONS

ILLUSTRATION I

9. Religion brings tranquility of mind, so misfortune seeks it out.

28. Marrying outside your religion will be difficult. Never do it unless you can keep a carriage in the coach house and horses in your stable.

These two maxims are conjoined. In addressing them, I would consider the ancient proverb, "Pay attention what is done rather than what is said."

When you hear people speak about such themes, many of those who consider themselves liberal or excited by the concept of liberty, use the word "man" to mean a wealthy twenty-five-year-old, the type who thinks, "Misfortunes? For shame. I do not even concern myself about death. Who speaks of miseries? The loss of a loved one—Bah! Of growing old and bone-weary, of needing to reap the affection that they have sown in order not to become too soon food for worms? That is the stuff of novels." He who says "man" is thinking of Antinous,[49] a

---

49 [Antinous was a handsome youth from Asia Minor and a favorite of the Roman emperor Hadrian. When the youth died before his 20th birthday, the emperor decreed him to be a god to be worshipped in the entire Roman Empire.]

young, strong, handsome, and rich man. There he is with a cigar in his mouth, a riding whip in his hand, with riding boots adorned with silver buckles, who, between one cigar puff and another, whispers with a foreign accent. God? I do not know Him. Misfortune, where does she make her home? Upon my honor, I don't know, and if I did know, I would make every effort to forget it."

Thus would speak such men as think they can overcome nature and life's difficulties, confusing a single point in time, the present, with the full cycle of life. Their failure to see that the real point of liberty, to enable you to recover from difficulties, creates more problems for them.

Would you like to really know what one who rejects religion really does?

I have seen those cigar smokers, said to be superior, crying like babies over the open graves of their mothers, and on their knees praying for her soul to the God they have rejected. I have seen others who have had reversals of fortune, in church choirs, singing hosannas and assisting the priest at mass. I have observed yet others engaging in the crazy superstitious activities in order to be healed, seek relief from pain, or avoid imminent disgrace. And others... well I could go on all day. Which of you, my readers, has not seen such goings on every year among the so-called strong spirits whose youthful power is in their hot-blooded veins and not in their hearts?

Thus, if you watch what men do and not what they say, you will discover that, fundamentally, religion is latently in everyone; however, it comes out only when misfortune breaks the veil of arrogance, just like what happens to a proud seaman when he is overcome by seasickness and with the imminent sickness, he discovers that he is like everyone else. I believe I am on solid ground when I posit that religion is found deep in the hearts of most people whom you might chance to meet.

Imagine a poor Christian workman who married a Jewish woman. God blessed the family, to use the Biblical phrase, with children and they became comfortably off, even though they had to work and save to have money. But the woman would not work or cook on the Sabbath. On one side religion, and on the other necessity—Love and Need are brothers like Polynices and Eteocles[50]—it is an old story but true. When Mr. Need enters the house, Mr. Love runs off either before or after being assaulted. Thus, for the workman, for whom the Sabbath is less important than necessity, screams at and argues with his wife until either violence or discord prevails in their household.

Another story: A young Jewish man, perhaps a sergeant in the army, falls in love with a pretty young Christian woman and they wed. Come the war, and here is our hero with *tefilà* and *tefillin*[51] as amulets to protect him from the enemy's bullets. In the meanwhile, his wife having made him the father of a beautiful lively son, he asks for two days' leave to celebrate his son's circumcision.

First the mother cried,

> "Circumcision? I don't want anyone to perform an amputation on my son. Do you understand?"
>
> "My dear, let me have it done; do you want me to go back on a sacred duty imposed by God on my forefathers for centuries?"
>
> "What forefathers? What God? What centuries? By the Holy Virgin, I do not want my son to be cut! No! No! No!"

---

50 [In Greek Mythology Polynices and Eteocles were the sons of Oedipus. When it was discovered that Oedipus had killed his father and married his mother, he was driven out of ancient Thebes and they assumed joint kingship of that city. Oedipus put a curse on them, and they did not rule peacefully; instead, they killed each other in their battle to control Thebes.]

51 [*Tefilà* and *Tefilin*, his Jewish prayer book and phylacteries.]

The words "I want" and "I don't want," sobs, shouting, until finally "To operate or not to operate" turns into a rage that never ends.

Or the wife brings her priest home on *Yom Kippur*[52] or she pleads with you day and night to save your soul and be baptized, or they have problems with the marriages of their children, or religious devotions interfere with daily life, or his private business is shared with her priest, or he prohibits her from attending church services, or ... or ... or. These issues might be small miseries among the well-to-do, but for the common people they become intolerable, as for them religion is a source of personal joy, consolation, and hope.

I said small miseries among the well-to-do, because wealth can result in greater tolerance, and for this reason, mixed marriages are more likely to work among the wealthy. The worst that can happen between rich people in mixed marriages is that one of them, say a Jew, finds himself on his deathbed, surrounded by his children and sees one of them to make the sign of the holy cross over his body, and asks himself if he will be reunited in the world to come with those whom he has so deeply loved in this one. And further, assuming he is still conscious, he will be unable to bless them in the name of the Lord God in the way that he was taught from earliest childhood.

I repeat. Judge a person not by what he says but by what he does. If he says he does not recognize God, come the storm, he will adore Him because that adoration will calm his distraught spirits. It is fine to preach the equality and fraternity of a mixed marriage, but this runs up against the most intimate thoughts of one's private life. To create elements of discord in marriages beyond the usual ones does not contribute to social virtue or civic wisdom.

True comity among people cannot be achieved without common principles. You can discuss the principles which appear absurd to you

---

52 [The Day of Atonement, the holiest day in the Jewish liturgical calendar.]

honestly using the liberty of thought and the weapons of reason; if your arguments are strong enough to bring you victory, you will be seen as having benefited mankind. But if momentary passions arise between two people who are married to different principles, the result is two unhappy people, and nothing more. Today's passion and tomorrow's reason: if two people differ on their fundamental beliefs, the result is to create discord. Now how would peace take root amid such discord?

ILLUSTRATION II

17. Feeling oneself superior to others is often an illusion of a juvenile mind.

Why is this so? Because there is never enough time to discover the infinite pile of things that you do not know. Many times, I have heard youths of the age at which one reads Virgil for the first time[53] dismissing stories in the daily press, saying that they, good Virgilians, would know how to set the press straight. Indeed, they criticize Manzoni[54] for having produced a single flower and say that Foscolo's *Sepolcri*[55] was a minor work relative to *Paradise Lost*,[56] that Guerazzi[57] lacks imagination and that Giusti[58] was a silly fellow. And heaven help

---

53 [In the classical Italian education, one studies seven years of Latin over the span of what we would describe as middle and high school. Virgil was most likely studied in the fourth year, so these would be students in their mid-teens.]

54 [Manzoni (1784-1873) was author of the greatest 19th century Italian novel, *I Promessi Sposi* (*The Betrothed*).]

55 [See the footnote to Maxim 74.]

56 [Epic poem of John Milton (1608-1674).]

57 [Francesco Domenico Guerazzi (1804-1873)– See note 23.]

58 [Giuseppe Giusti (1809-1850), Italian poet and satirist, whose satires on the Austrian rule of much of northern and central Italy built popular support for the overthrow of Austrian rule and the unification of Italy under Italian leadership.]

those authors just beginning to attract attention from the criticism of these beardless youths for whom a missing comma, an audacious neologism, or a single incorrect date are sins unworthy of mercy.

In daily life, do not be surprised if your son, having just completed his legal studies, reviews a draft contract of yours and responds by citing Horace and Cicero, or if the contract is already signed, he tells you that you should have done A and B differently, or that you were wrong to say C and D. People behave like this: Those without experience do not value their lack thereof, many of them die before they learn that those who stick to the facts should be respected, and that finding fault with the work of those with well-established reputations comes across as simply nit-picking.

ILLUSTRATION III

52. Do you wish to save time, effort, and money? Ask each person you meet about his work, listen well, and learn.

The world is an encyclopedia open to anyone who wishes to read it. The question is simply one of leafing through the pages. The pages will be told to you by your peers if you wish to listen. Have you ever met someone who does not enjoy being seen as wise? Whatever your science, art, calling, or custom, you can add the basic principles of others' professions to your knowledge by conversing with them. Everyone likes to speak about what he knows, and indeed he is attracted to disciples who humbly ask him questions. Unfortunately, the hard part is to remain humble, which is something that few can do, most especially the most scholarly among them, who are able to pretend to be experts in fields in which they know absolutely nothing, such as the great Newton and many other mathematicians who wish to be considered profound theologians.

ILLUSTRATION IV

65. When you meet an established person, you might say to yourself, here is a painter, a sculptor, an architect, a doctor, a lawyer, a tailor, or a knife-grinder. But when you meet a youth, take care to say to yourself, this person might become a Shakespeare, a Franklin, a Napoleon I, or a Pius V.[59]

It is rare that your familiars include world-changing people. When one meets truly eminent people, he should speak with hat in hand. With lesser eminences he speaks after a tip of the hat. With others, a simple nod and handshake will do, and with yet others, he stops briefly to listen to what they have to say. And finally, with others a quick glance and simple "hi" will do. Why should you bow to a truly great personage, and tip your hat to the rich; why shake hands with your peers, an odd behavior, like that of certain islanders who rub noses? And with inferiors, why do we deign to hear them? After all, such a person does not limit himself to working for another, but instead serves the other and wears a servant's livery, which makes him appear dough-faced and therefore worthy of being looked down upon.

Really, this is no laughing matter in that society is organized that way. Good God, I would not claim to want it any other way, and even less would I want to reorganize it. Indeed, I have observed it in my own behavior. I have had visitors at home whom I accompany to the door when they are about to leave and bid them farewell with a bow and warm smile, dancing like a ballerina. For others, I may rise when they

---

59 See the note to Maxim 65.

are about to leave, and may follow them for a few steps. For yet others I merely wish them goodbye while remaining seated, while perhaps raising my voice a bit awkwardly.

Sometimes, I confess, I misapply the word democracy, in that I do not push it to the point of believing that I hold no person to have more or less importance than another. In holding this position, I occasionally I hear a voice within me that grates at my conscience, but I still believe in the idea that I am obliged to bow before my superiors, and that I have a right to address my inferiors by raising my voice.

So be it! I and everyone else know what we do under similar circumstances. If a prince comes to visit, we hang tapestries from the balconies, we play great music on the occasion, and we shout hurrahs; we do not raise our voices when speaking with a marquis, and we do not bow to our domestic servants. In short, our actions and our words are adjusted to others' rank, power, titles, and clothing because we recognize who they are and one has to behave with them in accordance with the rules of human society.

Why are you mistreating that child?[60] You never know what sort of man he may turn out to be. When I think that in almost every family, there is a child who lives in Procrustes' bed.[61] The mothers of these unfortunate little ones pull on their feet, while their fathers cut off their legs. (I beg your pardon for this rhetorical figure of speech, but it contains a metaphorical truth.) When I think about such situations,

---

60 [Levi was particularly concerned with the ill-treatment of children, who were by definition, the social inferiors of their parents.]

61 [In Greek mythology Procrustes was an evil innkeeper who promised travelers that he had the bed that fit them perfectly. He would then show them an old iron bed. If the traveler were too short, Procrustes would stretch him on the rack to fit the bed, and if the traveler was too tall, Procrustes would surgically shorten his legs. Thus, the term Procrustean has come to mean to force a situation to meet an arbitrary standard.]

they do not cause my hair to stand on end, because I hardly have any, but they do sadden me greatly.

> "What is the matter with that child, so sad looking, with a bowed head and his little thumb in his mouth?"
> "Tonight, he was sent to bed without his supper."
> "Why was that?"
> "Because he knows nothing, he never studies, and he does not care."
> "But he is only eight years old!"
> "My dear sir, nowadays eight years old is like being fifteen twenty years ago. Mr. X's son was studying rhetoric at eight years old."
> "Rhetoric?"
> "Absolutely rhetoric, and this one, that jackass, prefers to turn somersaults, fill my closets full of paper birds, and to chase his hoop down the street, rather than to study and become a man. Well ... tonight no supper, and he is going to get it, and how he is going to get it!"

At this point, the mother joins in as the father reaches the end of his comments, punctuating her husband's speech with shouts and by boxing the boy's ears in ways that cause him to sob all night.

What happens after three of four years of such treatment in which the mother pulls on his feet and his father hacks at his legs? The son, whose studies have become a terrible plague, if he has any spirit answers by sticking out his tongue at his mother's sermons, kicks her and becomes a general pain in the neck. On the other hand, if he is a sensitive child, he becomes a wet hen for the rest of his life, or a terrible coward, a veritable punching bag. What a fine outcome that would be! And, yes, I am not speaking of parents who resort to locking their children in closets, subjecting them to nasty tricks or barbaric beatings. Those parents, even if they do not kill their children, which happens more often than you might believe, raise candidates for the prisons and gallows.

Again, I beg your pardon for my classical references, but all this brings to mind the Spartans, who sought to instill strength in their children, beginning at birth, and who placed the education of children under the strict control of the state. We do not do such things, but it is our habit to treat children as if they were nothing, or worse. Their parents and then their governesses sharply pinch the innocent children if they witness a young woman's tender love for a soldier, professed openly under a tree in the public park.

And ... children's innocent little hearts absorb their lessons deeply. Look at how many old parents are abandoned or abused by their children in revenge for the abuse heaped upon them in earlier times! How many protectors were lost because of a punishment meted out to a child in those times, how many sorrows today from past actions. Instead, we should think of what they may become: Mr. N, let me introduce you to the Senator! Mr. G, I present to you the commanding officer! So young! And to think how many times I beat him when he was little!"

ILLUSTRATION V

79. Heaven save you from a literary woman, and even more so from one who pretends to be so.

Faith! I would have preferred to illustrate another maxim, and I would have done so, but the fear of appearing insolent toward the fair sex forced me to address this one. The traditions of gallantry are still so embedded in me that I feel a need to justify myself for a statement that could cause me to be accused being ill-mannered in these times in which women's emancipation is the order of the day, and the story of Bradamante[62] is becoming a practical day-to-day reality. How many things have been written against literary women, and against the *basbleu*,[63] if you will pardon my French, a phrase I dare not translate and will leave simply as "blue stockings."

Old curiosities and commonplaces are what one well knows: today a woman must act like a man, a mother's role is confused with that of the family's father, the weaver's shuttle is confused with the sword. The goddesses Astria and Hygeia[64] may have their priestesses and the ministers of the latter no longer wear the veil or need the serpent as their symbol.

Children will be raised by their nursemaids when these are not in the front ranks among the militants. Shopping, cookery, linens, and laundry, in sum, the supervision of the entire domestic economy of the house and its attics will take care of itself—I wish it well.

But that which I do not wish is for me to eternally find my woman with a book in her hand. I would not want to hear from her very mouth citations from this or that author who wrote thus and so. Likewise, if she accompanied me on a visit to one of my friends, I would not want to see her screwing up her mouth and, after every few words, hear her naming such a multitude of authors as there are days in the calendar. Women have great tact in all cases except in that of wishing to appear learned.

---

62 [Bradamante was a fictional female knight who was memorialized in several Renaissance epic poems, notably *Orlando Furioso (Orlando's Frenzy*, and *L'Amore di Orlando (The Love of Orlando)*.]

63 [A rude French idiom referring to pedantic or pretentiously literary women.]

64 [Two minor Greek deities, the former the virgin goddess of justice, innocence, purity, and precision, and the latter the goddess of cleanliness and long life. Hygeia was one of the daughters of Asclepius, the god of medicine; she was often depicted as feeding a snake.]

One day my dear friend Scipione Giordano,[65] a man who illuminates medical science with his head and society with his heart, said to me that he once found himself at a dinner many years ago in a great house, accompanied by various illustrious people, among them Carlo Botta.[66] A woman took to discussing the Italian language with the illustrious historian. Botta made an observation and the woman responded in a professorial tone, "But then Corticelli[67] in his grammar said...." At the raising of the subject of grammar, Botta and the then young Giordano smiled disdainfully along with all the others. I do not want my wife to be subject to such smiles, because I do not enjoy the feeling of getting goosebumps.

I adore a good housewife, who can rock an infant's cradle with her foot and sew him a cute little shirt with her hands. She who can keep her house in order is like the conservator in a museum of rare coins. She, who personifies order and neatness, understands well the value of work and the household economy which does not exclude decorum, but avoids miserliness. She does not advise but with her actions, by her diligence, love, and tolerance, she teaches her husband the value of productive activity and savings. Oh, but unfortunately, even back to the times of King Solomon who knew many women, such a woman has been a rarity.

---

65 [Giordano (1817-1894) was an obstetrician and personal friend of Levi.]
66 [Carlo Botta (1766-1837) was a surgeon and historian . His life was upset several times owing to his involvement in politics, in which he sided with the French during the Napoleonic period, and later became an Italian nationalist, and among other things sought to purge the Italian language of French expressions.]
67 [Salvadore Corticelli (1690-1758) , Italian grammarian whose definitive grammar of the Tuscan dialect, published in 1745, contributed heavily to the ultimate acceptance in the subsequent century of that form of Italian as the "pure" form of that language.]

ILLUSTRATION VI

90. Morality and general order are the results of progress.

Ai! Ai! Ai! Recalling the rarity of strong women in our society has put me in a bad mood, even if I console myself with the thought of how often husbands say: my wife is strong even if such women are rarities. Even as I console myself with this thought, this is the absolute truth: not only do I take Hebrew women as my ideal of a good housewife, but good homemakers are more common among Hebrews than among women of other faiths. Moreover, this thought has made me so serious as to make me illustrate a philosophical maxim. In this way, even if this illustration has no other value, it will have that of putting my reader to sleep, if he has not already nodded off.

Let me start with some definitions: by the word *moral* I am expressing the *totality of good practices*. By the term *free will* I mean *conscience,* be that of the spirit or the brain. In this discussion we will set aside all the complications of the latter.

Returning to our subject, I contend that morality and general order are the results of progress. Mr. Giulio Simon[68] discussed at length the idea that free will is a fundamental law of our existence. I cite him not to show off my erudition but because I happened by chance upon his book *La Liberté*. He is neither the only nor the first person to propound the idea of a law of free will and I must confess that my stubborn brain cannot comprehend the idea of being *subject to* a law of free will. This must be a deficiency of my ability to understand things.

---

68 [Professor Giulio Simon (1814-1896) Author of *La Liberté de Conscience*, among other works in both French and Italian. He was a religious Catholic, and his writings on free will align closely with Church doctrine.]

For me, one who thinks about things a bit more simply, I will leave it to these exalted personages to tear out their hair over this subject. I say to one side in this debate, that the moral laws were dictated by God the Creator, and we must measure our deeds by them. It is only by this standard that we can be good and upright.

To the other side I cite writings of my dear friend and close relative, Cesare Lombroso[69] in which he talks about how physiology became a science via the work of Schiff,[70] Tyndall,[71] and Helmholtz,[72] when they measured the speed with which the brain directed voluntary motion, and the amount of heat given off by neurons when the brain thinks. Let me repeat, I stand firmly on the ground when I say that if a person has any conscience at all and if he is not influenced by the planets or by the *cells that think,* then his actions are shaped by norms and usages common among those around him.

Once it was thought that God would be glorified by subjecting other people to burning at the stake, mutilation, inserting needles under their fingernails, oiling their feet, and then forcing them to stand on a grate over burning coals and other similar gentle treatments. The *free will* of the judges who ordered these tortures was shaped by the social environment in which they lived that caused them to believe they were committing acts of extraordinary justice and love of their fellow men. When certain islanders eat their fathers in their old age, they think that is extending their lives. Their liberty to eat this or that was

---

69 [Cesare Lombroso (1835-1909) was an Italian physician and criminologist and also Levi's brother-in-law. He was a member of the faculty at the University of Turin.]
70 [Moritz Schiff (1823-1896), a German Jewish physiologist who developed the first experimental techniques in physiology.]
71 [John Tyndall (1820-1893), an Irish-born physicist who among other things, studied how the ear perceives sounds.]
72 [Hermann von Helmholtz (1821-1894) A German physiologist and physicist, who made early discoveries into how the eye perceives light.]

defined by their sense of filial piety that, in turn, was driven by their social milieu. Thus, the entirety of good morals, or what is believed to be such, follows from the degree of progress in a given time and place.

Thus, it seems to me that the main aim of human progress is to improve people's lives and understanding. There is no doubt that mankind's practices have a great influence over the results achieved. Hand in hand, we advance over time. The broad fields of science are helping us to understand which usages are most consistent with excellence. Therefore, the rule by which humanity progresses is to eliminate every principle that is inconsistent with the breadth of human existence and individual knowledge. Our progress in our lives increases in relation to scientific discoveries. Good social practices enable progress by removing obstacles that are inconsistent with science, and those practices are shaped by progress, eventually becoming a consequence of it. Bit by bit these practices endow principles with their true value.

ILLUSTRATION VII

91. True correction is shown by example.

Many times, I might have seen a schoolboy take out a long sheet of white paper and then draw upon it a rough rectangle with crooked lines, representing an apartment house, with smaller lines above representing windows and longer ones centered at the bottom representing a doorway. To one side he drew an animal with an oval for its face with two dots for eyes and an inverted capital T for a nose and mouth:

Perhaps I also saw that boy showing his work to his friends, and perhaps get busy correcting it, touching up or overwriting the lines. Soon the rectangle that was supposed to be a building became a hay rack, at the foot of which was a manger, made from what had formerly been the lintel of the doorway and, the animal which perhaps had been a cat emerged as an impossible chimera. I would have seen that boy and smiled, thinking, "Look, at that!" Well, in many cases that boy could have been you, dear reader, or me.

To do and to correct, that is quickly said; but this verb, "to correct," is not understood in its true sense if it does not lead to improvement. Now, do you understand the word "improvement" or do you only understand in each thing whether or not it is beautiful or good?

With regard to the education of his son, for a strictly devout man, it consists in teaching his son to regularly attend to his prayers, abstain from the prohibited foods, and not to work on the on the religious holidays. Instead, for a more lenient father, "improvement" consists in having his son immerse himself in his studies, and for a banker "improvement" means learning to stand behind a teller's window and calculate discounts, rather than composing music, writing poems, or painting; and for a farmer, "improvement" might mean teaching his son how to recognize superior lands or livestock; and for a tavern-keeper, "improvement" might mean having his son become expert in the selection of wine; and similarly for a father who would like son to become a lawyer, a notary, a doctor, or a clergyman.

Everyone thinks, "I am doing thus and so to teach my son and, in this way, I am correcting his tendencies for the better." But this idea is just as laughable as when you go to hear a sermon. Look over there, at the end of the great building, in the pulpit, that man talking about purging, oneself [of sin] with more or less appropriate figures of speech, saying to the public, "My brothers, follow the path that I suggest to you and it will be for the better!" That will be as effective as Demosthenes preaching to the Athenians to prepare for war against Philip of Macedon.[73] I would expect to see you among the first to walk out.

"Improvement!" I confess that that is a word that causes me to think deeply. Even if this word is too profoundly abstruse to pin down, there exist few principles that correspond to habits that are universally recognized as *good*, and among these is the notion of *true* correction. For example, it would be wrong to force your son to rise with the sun while you are under a warm downy quilt. One does not teach love of effort, work, or economy with his feet under the gaming table or walking arm in arm with Messalina,[74] nor in smoking a cigar with his arms folded, or in playing the lottery. Getting out of bed at dawn, good habits, and a love for work and for saving money, are not abstruse notions in which to seek *improvement*; they do not require a lantern[75] but are obvious factors in the progress of one's prosperity and which it is important to teach by your own example.

Why is it that so many do not grow up corrected for the better? Because it is one thing to say and another to act. I knew a father who was in the habit of ordering his children to do something, and when they did not do it immediately, he would get up and do it himself. "But Father, I am here to do as you ask," hurriedly responded the son. "Perhaps another time, my son. This time I am here and I have shown more energy and assurance of a job well done than you. Woe unto you

---

[73] {Demosthenes, an Athenian orator and statesman, tried in vain to rouse his countrymen to prepare for war to defend themselves against the imperial designs of Philip II of Macedon. Ultimately, Philip conquered Athens and much of the rest of Greece.}

[74] [Messalina was the third wife of the Roman Emperor Caligula; she was noted for her promiscuity.]

[75] [Levi here is referring to Diogenes, a Greek contemporary of Plato, was said to have gone about at night with a lantern to search for an honest man.]

when these are missing or are there only hesitantly. You hesitated, and I was here." answered the father, as he worked relentlessly while his son looked on in vain, mortified and ruing his lack of prompt action.

ILLUSTRATION VIII

92. The public recognition for the most learned people in the many fields of the arts and the relatively high rewards given for their work, contribute more effectively to the collective national wisdom than the schooling required of everyone because people voluntarily follow those who are esteemed and well paid.

It is universally agreed that it is in the public interest for the state to require that children be taught and that it is not just an arbitrary government order. The liberty to raise one's children and wards[76] as illiterate fools would be a freedom to damage the entire nation. Therefore, the government has a right to ask that all its citizens be taught at least to the level that can serve as a stimulus to enable potential great talents to emerge, and also for ordinary citizens to communicate their ideas by means of reading and writing and to carry out simple numerical calculations on their own.

Even though the requirement for public education of all citizens has not yet been fully implemented,[77] this is not the place to discuss this issue broadly. However, you should not be surprised at the need to examine very carefully claims that people have the right to consider

---

76 [Remember that Levi was writing in Victorian times when many parents died young, leaving small children to be raised by their relatives or in orphanages.]

77 [In 1864, not long before Levi was writing this book, Pope Pius IX issued a Syllabus of Errors, a listing various doctrinal issues that Catholics had to avoid. Among those "errors" was public education not controlled by the Church.]

this optional. We hope that soon any hesitance to public education will disappear, and in the future, we will look back in wonder at these times in which so many people regard writing as so much indecipherable hieroglyphics.

However, the risk of *forcing compliance* will always remain. This intrusion into family governance on the part of the political regime will be the lesser of two evils, this requirement and crass ignorance of the multitudes, but an evil it remains. In other cases, coercion *for the public good* can become a pretext for inquisitions, for slavery, when the claimed *good*, the object of the requirement, was erroneous or perhaps evil.

I cannot forget that the martyrs of our ancestors and their immeasurable tortures over many centuries that were inflicted in the name of the public good, which, according to the torturers, required a country with a single religion, and a single form of worship in that religion.[78] Its victims were people who were not of the appropriate religious convictions, beliefs that they could not accept without violating their own convictions. Nor can I omit memory that all the most monstrous and tyrannical laws were always imposed in the name of *the public good* and were enforced with sanctions as fearful as the angel Michael attacking Hell.[79]

However, these good reasons to be wary of laws *for the public good* do not apply in cases where there is near unanimous consent, such as in the case of public instruction, because of the extraordinary support for the law itself. This situation is just like in the cases of the

---

78 [It is not surprising that Levi had strong opinions about the Spanish Inquisition; both his mother and wife were Sephardic, i.e., descended from Spanish Hebrews who had been forced into exile lest they become subject to its gruesome tortures and public burnings at the stake.]

79 [In the book of Revelation in the Christian Bible, the archangel Michael is expected to lead the forces of God to victory in the war against the forces of Satan.]

extraordinary measures taken during the times of epidemics, such as requiring the use of disinfectants within a given city, provisions that must end when the high mortality period is over. But when you discover a provision which accomplishes the same benefit as a coercive law without the risk to personal liberty, and better yet, is also longer lasting, you should advocate strongly for it, because it brings the desired benefit without the defect of which laws are justifiably accused.

Now in the case of public education, in my opinion this law consists in raising the salaries of teachers and giving them an honored social position. I recall that in the days when the parish priests were the only power here in Piedmont, in every house of even modest means, one would find at least one tricorne[80] hanging on the coatrack. My God! How much youth was wasted in the reciting of blessings, in the idleness of choruses of hosannas ... and who knows what else. The fathers of those families thought they were improving their lot by making their sons into priests, and I think they were right in that judgment in those times. From the moment that they had learned enough to be ordained and authorized to wear the cassock, off came everyone else's hats ; any door on which they knocked was open to them; they became trusted advisers in every matter; so I repeat, those fathers reasoned that, given these facts, what faithful Christian would not want his son to be a priest?

So, instead of comparing this situation to that of the much-despised differences among social classes which affect both people and businesses, compare this situation to people's tendencies. If

---

80 [The tricorne hat originated in Spain in the 15th or 16th century as a priestly head-covering; it then spread to France and Italy. The French King Louis XIV adopted it during his long reign from 1643–1715 and it spread all over Europe as a style, especially for the propertied classes. Levi here uses it as a symbol of the clergy, i.e., he suggested that any propertied family would have sons in the priesthood.]

mankind's teachers were revered to the same extent and that their honorable work were rewarded with pay sufficient to cover the needs of their daily lives and to give them a level of comfort, then fathers would encourage their sons to engage in any type of study that would give them dignity and honor.[81]

Certainly, to be called *a teacher* of science or art would entail more difficult training than is currently required. However, all fathers would be beguiled by the intellectual distinction that they wish to amplify in their children. If the career of teacher were well paid and viewed as worthy, even those who do not succeed in this path would end up better taught, and this would contribute to an advantageous increase in the national level of learning. Of course, it is not possible that all children be directed toward a single career path. On the other hand, attracting better minds to teaching would have a strong effect on all careers in both the arts and the professions, and yield great improvements in public instruction.

Returning to the model of the priesthood: in Italy, as a result of a few well-publicized examples about ordinary lawyers being elevated to seats in Parliament, and in turn members of Parliament promoted to ministerial roles, the law faculties are overrun with students. While surely not all such students will be elected to Parliament or become government ministers, all those students have hopes of following this path, and that is enough to induce them to study and to become, if not part of the national government, at least capable of becoming leaders their local community or family.

---

81 [We must remember that some years before writing this book, Levi may have had the offer of a teaching post at the university. Because of its low pay he opted to focus on his law practice for the greater pay that would enable him to support his large family.]

ILLUSTRATION IX

131. The truth can offend or not; it all depends how you present it. To warn someone of an impending danger can save him or cause his downfall.

This is all a question of tact. There exist people who know how to say and do everything with particular grace. You would see them seated on a high-backed Chiavari chair,[82] moving on it in all senses without the least squeak, when you think that if it were you in his place, all would go to the dogs. Never a bump, never any stupidity or vulgarity, never a word other than one of precisely measured courtesy, even when they tell a hard truth, a truth that could potentially offend someone.

Such people exist, although they are very rare, and to imitate their model is an extremely difficult art. I think that they are born thus, and this good nature of theirs which makes them welcome everywhere, was sucked in at the breast of a mother who must have been a kind and noble woman. Sitting, eating, drinking, leaning, moving, riding astride a horse, speaking a good word, modulating the tone of voice, and smiling, these are all actions or capabilities we all have, but none of us use them as such people alone know how. I do not understand it, even after a night of dancing, their yellow gloves[83] seem so clean that it seems as though they had studied how to stop up their pores. The best part is that they have not studied anything, and it all seems to come naturally to them.

---

82 [A particularly elegant and comfortable type of easy chair.]
83 [In the 1800s, all fashionable people wore gloves, with special types for different activities, be it driving a carriage, serving tea, or twirling around the ball room.]

Such people, dear reader, if they end up fighting a duel over their words,[84] it is because they wanted it so; furthermore, they understand the art of calling the next fellow a buffoon in a way that causes him to laugh as well, for fear of appearing impolite, vulgar, or intolerant, were he to take offence.

Aren't they lucky! Though I am bound to say that such people are generally rich and belong to the upper classes.[85] However that may be, this talent for always saying and doing the right thing is a precious gift for dealing with the everyday practicalities of life. Thus, when offering counsel or advice, it is always a matter of tact.

There is a story about a famous painter, who stood one day on a high scaffold after painting a magnificent ceiling fresco. While painting he was visited on the high scaffold by an amateur who was passionately admiring the just-completed part of the fresco. Having admired it in detail, he backed up on the scaffold to better view the image in its entirety. The painter was continuing to paint while the amateur kept on backing up to the point that he was about to fall off the edge of the scaffold—one more step and he would have fallen to his death. Just then, the painter, with a large brush in hand, turned to glance at the amateur, and began furiously to paint over part of the fresco. "What on earth are you doing?" cried the very upset amateur. "Nothing, really" replied the painter, "I have just saved your life."

A person warned by a shout would have instinctively taken a step back instead of taking a step forward and would have fallen to the floor. How often have there been times in your life in which a less insightful

---

84 [I.e., their insults never result from speaking rashly, but are carefully considered.]

85 [Levi is careful to distinguish the difference between those who are rich and those who have class. Those two categories are overlapping but not congruent. Giuseppe di Lampedusa's novel *Il Gattopardo (The Leopard)* paints a very finely drawn contrast between a rich peasant and a financially embarrassed nobleman.]

or less friendly painter might have shouted a warning to you, risking your life, instead of covering over a bit of the picture?

ILLUSTRATION X

133. Fear of punishment and the hope of reward are the basis of common people's religion. They engage in prayers, fasts, abstinence, discipline, submitting to martyrdom and the like to further their own interests.

Who would say to a man that, in a few days[86] would be saying the words of *Teshuvah,* of repentance, upon seeing him sheathed in splendid *Taled*[87] trimmed with artistic embroidery in gold and silver thread, facing the holy ark bowing devoutly, with a grand prayer book printed in Holland or Bologna,[88] intent on accompanying the cantor in reciting the sacred psalms and poems: (I chose the example of an Israelite, but could as well have chosen someone kneeling in church participating in the *Intemissesto.*[89]) Indeed, you will see him with bowed head, carrying the scrolls of the sacred Pentateuch and assisting with its reading, refraining from work, and fasting completely

---

86 This essay was written a few days before Yom Kippur, the Jewish Day of Atonement

87 [The Hebrew word תלם (the Jewish Prayer Shawl worn by men during services in which the Bible is read) is transliterated into Italian as *Taled* and into English as *Talit*]

88 [Levi owned a beautiful *Machzor, a* prayer book covering the annual cycle of weekly services and holidays complete with scholarly commentary from Renaissance and Medieval rabbis) . This two-volume book, printed in Bologna in 1542, standardized the Italian rite for Jewish religious services. His copy is in my library.]

89 [A made-up word referring to the Catholic mass taken from a satirical poem in the February 3rd, 1853, issue of the humor magazine *Il Fischietto.* The poem conjures up the image of the carryings-on of various government ministers in costume during the pre-Lenten carnival, including one dressed as a priest who pretends to officiate at a mock mass.]

for twenty-four hours; who would say to him, "Kind sir, desist from this foolishness, because, you see, your ceremonies are just that; stop doing them, kind sir. And what? You think that today you are adoring God, the supreme intelligence, with your masquerade of clothes and chest beating?"[90]

"But you are adoring yourself, my man; your hopes and fears stand at the top of your thoughts: you are attempting to quiet your apprehensions, satisfy your desires, and ease your remorse. Your bowing is to increase your fortune. Your quiet recitation of the psalms is for your future happiness. In short, your prayers are directed toward a minor God created in your image who presides over the stock market to cause it to rise or fall, over the clouds that they should not cause a tempest to damage your vineyard, over your health that you should remain corpulent and strong, and finally over your trade, that He should despoil Titus and Caius,[91] in order that you should profit thanks to their misfortunes."

Ah, but I am not the Prophet Isaiah to declaim in these times, "To what purpose is the multitude of your sacrifices unto Me?"[92]

God, my God on High, forgive me, and you too, Dearest Reader, forgive me as I surprise myself in preaching a sermon. A sermon? For shame! It is not a sermon that I am making, but a rhetorical figure to describe a true situation as it appears to me.

You, Dear Reader, might say to me that I am just being crotchety. The world has always been thus. I should become devout for whatever purpose. Meanwhile, my devotion will show my faith and fear of God;

---

90 [During the Yom Kippur services, the recitation of the community's sins is traditionally accompanied with chest beating.]
91 [This appears to be an obscure reference to the classical story of Titus Andronicus.]
92 [Isaiah Chapter 1, verse 11. One of the traditional bible readings for the Day of Atonement is from the first chapters of the Book of Isaiah.]

if were to pray, it is natural that I should pray for something. Ever since Moses, whose prayers asked God to pardon the people even unto us, everyone has prayed for his own people. And in the end, praying is better than denying [God].

The world has not always been as you say, Dearest Reader. It was not so very long ago that people sacrificed themselves and their affairs in support of their faith. Was that good or bad? It was noble, this I can say for sure. In those days, banks closed on the Sabbath, and people did not just fast and pray on the Yom Kippur. You would have found millionaires at their prayers in the morning to recite the Kaddish[93] in memory of their ancestors, not for gold, nor for a carriage, nor for a bauble. You would never have seen them do something which in their mind would have offended their beloved God, and thereby delegitimized their prayer. Thus, in the end, they were making personal sacrifices for their faith. Today they do not sacrifice, may God pardon me, for so much as a slice of *prosciutto*.[94] Now, what sort of faith is this, and where is he that dares to pray?

Once, when one said the word *religion*, he meant love of God and of his fellow men, self-denial, charity, peace, amity, submission, granting of pardon, raising up those in misery, helping others in this world, and having hope for the next. Today, we have nothing of the sort, no such ideas or sentiments. Then, if one made errors in his ways, they were sublime errors. Today religion has become little more than a balance sheet, of assets and liabilities. Don't you hear people saying,

"God, vanquish your enemies (meaning *my* enemies) and you will be sanctified. God, overthrow the world, destroy their country, let a thousand heads fall in great battles, and here am I, prostrate and

---

93 [A prayer glorifying God recited in memory of the departed.]

94 [*Prosciutto*, an Italian ham is generally served in paper thin slices. This choice of image is particularly ironic for an observant Jew, for whom the eating of pork is prohibited.]

genuflecting before you, and I will pray unto you. For Your sake, may the sun stand still over the city of Gibeon and may the moon stop in your honor, so that its light will not bear witness to night-time slaughter in the valley of Ajalon[95] and you will be glorified."

Why glorified? And suppose such a prayer had been uttered in the empire of the Turks, and they would have answered, "Because Allah is the only God, and Mohammed is not only His prophet, but also his Caliph, his supreme Caliph." And thus, Dear Reader, are the prayers that today come from on high.

Quiet, quiet, you writer! The sun will not stand still, nor the moon, and Mohammed is dead. Such enthusiasm today makes you downcast. And have you per misfortune become intolerant? Let everyone pray for his own interests: the king for the protection of his reign, the miller, for his flour.... Enough already, I will stop speaking on this theme.

ILLUSTRATION XI

142. Do you want to live quietly and at peace with everyone?

- *Never contradict anyone, verbally or in writing.*
- *If you are poor, stay that way.*
- *If you are talented, don't show it too often, and if you use your talents, allow others to benefit from and enjoy it.*
- *Whoever tugs on your clothes to get ahead of you, make yourself small and let him pass.*
- *Obey the evangelist's precept that orders you to turn the other cheek to the person who smites you.*

---

95 [A Biblical reference to Joshua's conquest of Gibeon and subsequent night-time defeat of the Canaanite kings in the nearby valley of Ajalon.]

- *Hide your physical gifts.*
- *Do not choose a beautiful wife.*
- *Raise your children according to your own values lest the one who is brighter than the others breaks the eggs in your basket.*[96]
- *If you learn that someone is praising you, plead with him for goodness' sake to swap censure for praise, or at least to keep quiet.*

And even all this may not suffice.

I must confess, if jealousy, ambition, greed, lust, or treachery no longer existed, my maxim would be a slander upon mankind. However, it is clear that I do not wish to give it as a maxim to follow; rather I want to show the price one can pay to achieve relative peace from others' words and deeds in the broader society in which he lives. Those who wrote that war is the natural state of society[97] were probably motivated by reflections suggested by this maxim since there is surely no one in the world that would follow it

However, I would like to add a few thoughts about the first condition listed, that of never contradicting anyone else verbally or in writing. People will more easily put up with disagreement shown by others' actions than by their words. Thus, one may say that most alienation has as its starting point a verbal argument. The acrimony among the various political parties in countries with democratic governments has its origins in differences of opinion which result in strong disagreements. Those disagreements arise from our own sense

---

96 [*Breaks the eggs in your basket*, i.e., makes things difficult for you.]

97 [Here Levi is referring to the English political philosopher Thomas Hobbes (1588-1679).]

of power that seeks to impose our opinions on others. There is no one who does not suffer inwardly from hearing himself contradicted.

Education helps you tolerate the evidence and logic that defeat your position, but the argument and, even more, the defeat hurt you internally to a degree inversely proportional to your importance. Because the overwhelming majority are anything but important, you would be wise to contradict people as little as possible.

Sometimes, a client wishes to undertake litigation with arguments which to you seem totally wrong. You try to convince him that this litigation will be fruitless. He will insist on pursuing it, and you will insist otherwise, and then he will walk away, still firmly convinced of his position. You will think that the issue is settled, but six or seven months later you will hear that the court has published a decision indicating that your client lost his case, and that you have lost your client.

I could cite many other such situations but suffice it to say that the man best received in any given place is the one who is least argumentative.

ILLUSTRATION XII

150. If you reach the age of seventy, you will have been many distinct people, all different from one another. If the passing of the last of these is grieved, it indicates that they were all good, as the apparent identity of their body causes them each to be judged as responsible for the others.

151. Know that people never pardon anyone. They may act as if they have pardoned, make pardoning a duty, and have even fooled themselves into thinking that they have pardoned, but the nature of memory is such that it impedes true pardon.

Therefore, learn how not to be blameworthy. The most profound regrets would be of little use to you. A whole life of good behavior, and maybe even one illustrious in the sciences, arts, and letters, or of great dignity would not erase others' basic faultfinding. It is like sprinkling plaster dust to cover spots on stained linen.

These two maxims by turns complete an idea of mine. To say that over seventy years, one becomes a succession of different people may seem paradoxical, but it is true. You can verify this for yourself by comparing who you are now to the person you were many years ago. You will see that the only thing that binds the two together is your memory. The physical changes we call "aging" and in the moral domain we call them "disillusionment."[98] Your habits, principles, passions, desires, and knowledge all change over time; you could have been dissipated and learned to moderate your behavior, delinquent and become virtuous, or wearing a Phrygian cap[99] at twenty and died fighting for the king at sixty. Our memory, the one faculty that attests to our being a single entity and that eludes analysis, I beg the forbearance of the materialists,[100] does not immediately enable us to perceive these changes, but they occur, nonetheless.

---

98 [An adage that has been variously attributed to Winston Churchill, John Adams, Thomas Jefferson, and/or Georges Clemenceau is that a man who was not a liberal in his youth has no heart, and one who does not become conservative in maturity has no brain.]

99 [Phrygian caps, also called Liberty caps, were the symbols of revolutionaries in late 18th century France.]

100 They say that every molecule in our body is replaced every four to four and one-half years; so, which is the molecule that preserves a fact from eighty or ninety years ago, given that there are centenarians with splendid memories? One day, I doubted this persistence

Human society is like each individual and demonstrates this fact every day, even if society will not admit to such a similarity or believe in it. Therefore, woe unto you if one of your successive selves falls short. The person in you who succeeds that one, no matter how hard he works at being virtuous and beneficent, will be followed by the bad reputation of your previous self.

I recall having read a story of a knight who bandaged one of his eyes in the presence of his lady and vowed upon his love for her that he would not unbandage it until he had completed a difficult quest in her honor. In due course, he fulfilled his vow but had the misfortune that his bandage fell off in battle and he lost the eye. Full of love, he threw himself quickly at the feet of his lady; but it seemed that a man with one eye was not to her taste, even if he were a knight. She said to him, "Sir, now bandage the other eye and go look for the one you lost, and then come back." The knight was changed and the lady's judgment was justified.

But such a judgment would not be justified in the case when a man has changed for the better; and yet, people generally will not believe it. They will neither accept the change as fact nor pardon him for his past misdeeds. Imagine finding a thief at your door and receiving him with open arms because he had sincerely repented of his past. The world simply does not work that way.

Enough on this weighty discussion!

---

of memories without being recalled periodically and sought a proof of it, I began to recite the *veahafta* [one of the prayers that observant Jews recite daily], something I had not read for more than twenty-five years. I had to refer to the prayer book only three times to remember the first word of individual verses. The rest I could recite from memory, and it runs for several pages.

ILLUSTRATION XIII

167. There is a wide distance between fame and glory.

183. The news of the world is covered by many talented people, and the daily press suppresses most of it.

One has to see what happens to you with those who claim to be world famous; how seriously do they greet you, how are you received when you meet them? Indeed, with what honor they greet you, do they stand up with their hats in their hands, or do they pick up, their hats and look at their watches!

Don't be shocked; they are in a hurry. On such occasions they can only give you a minute. They will tell you that they are sorry, but they are over-burdened with obligations, requests, and cares. If at that moment another famous and powerful person enters, they will ask you to please wait, and that brief minute that was all they could offer you, becomes so long as to outdo the miracle of the night of Alcmena;[101] so long that most often, if you are a humble type, you make note of your lesser importance, smile and move on. From the celebrity dentist to the well-known journalist, all those of cheap fame behave like that. Unhappily, not long after, when they are gone, people will not have the least memory of their existence.

It is true that fame is the way to the temple of glory. That way has such beautiful avenues, with Elysian rest areas where it seems to you

---

101 [In Greek mythology, Alcmena was seduced by Zeus in what seemed to her to be one night, but that actually lasted three nights; the product of this union was the hero Hercules. Hera, Zeus' wife, in a fit of jealousy, caused Hercules to go mad and kill his wife and children. In punishment for this deed, the gods sentenced him to undertake twelve great labors that were thought humanly impossible, though he completed all of them.]

that your laurel-crowned statue is the center of everyone's gaze, and you are besotted with thunderous applause all around you. Just think how many lose themselves is such dreams without thinking, without saying to themselves, "Wake up! Wake up! This is not the temple of glory. *Ars longa et vita brevis.*"[102]

One can die with such dreams, mister famous dentist, mister accredited journalist, and, unhappily, such death is forever. In truth nothing about them matters; those that matter do not get lost along that way and are seen as eminent geniuses from an early age. Desiring public esteem, they study both day and night to learn how to enter into the road to fame.

One morning or one evening, Mephistopheles causes them to bathe in a fatal idea. What if I wrote an article and brought it to Mister N, the editor of the newspaper X, and by some luck he were to publish it ... ? Then, my name would be on everyone's tongue, and I would be on the way to becoming famous. Oh, and why not? Didn't this colleague and that become famous in just this way even after having suffered some disaster or have had the misfortune of needing to retake their school exams because they had failed the first time? I will get on with it immediately.

And so, the potential great man of the country works hard writing and rewriting, fine tuning, reading, and rereading, touching up the piece until finally the article is finished. Should I take it in to the editor? Oh ... no ... no; I should write a letter to him. And so, he sits down at his desk, carefully avoiding any grammatical mistakes, "God help me!" to distill the perfect letter, a task that took two hours but was worth only about five minutes.

Now the letter is sent along with the article, and daily he anxiously awaits the newspaper. He buys it, and nervously scans it

---

102 [A Latin proverb: Art endures, but life is brief.]

from beginning to end. "Is it there? It isn't. ... It isn't." Four days pass ... then five ... and finally on the eighth day when hope of seeing the article in print is all but gone, you leaf through the newspaper, hurriedly, discouraged, when suddenly you shout, "Good God! It is there!" In the initial moments, our young man rustles the precious pages with his fingers, while being careful not to fold them and rushes home with the great excitement of a lover who has just received a long-awaited letter from his beloved lady.

"Good God, I thank you. The article really is there," and with a heart palpitating with joy, spreading out the page, and repeatedly reading and rereading the beloved article. "By Jove, they skipped a comma here, and why did they put a T there instead of L, and why did they change 'syringes' into 'strings'? Ah me! There are enough typos here to make me laugh for a year. Oh well, anyone who reads newspapers understands this problem. The Devil with it! The article is there, and I want to write others."

Mephistopheles laughs at this point, and the Muses and Athena begin to cry, and in the meanwhile, our beardless youth endeavors to propose laws to the government, here and there criticizing both monarchies and republics, the postal service and the ministry of transport, and dust gathers on books of physics, chemistry, geometry, law, and who knows what else, and the man and his country are poorer for it.

If I were the editor of a daily newspaper, and such a person happened to be my colleague, was under thirty years old and was not already a bit famous, I would say to him, "Sonny Boy, go and study, and if today's mania to write was still affecting you in the future, come back to me or to another newspaper editor when you are forty years old, when you will be universally accepted as a learned man, or recognized as an arrogant idiot, then, but only then, will you be able to make your career as a journalist. Today, however, love of my country constrains me to show you to the door.[103]

ILLUSTRATION XIV

181. Human vanity is so blind that people imagine erecting monuments to themselves to be the same as erecting them to a man of genius.

In the month of August 1870, I found myself in Genoa. After seven years, I wished to revisit the metropolitan cemetery with its superb marble gravestones. Reader, if perhaps you have not seen the marvelous necropolis, you should call to mind all that you have read about those of the Assyro-Chaldean or Egyptian civilizations as recounted by Arab story tellers, and you would have a pallid image of Genoa's cemetery. Imagine a gently sloping hill, illuminated by the sun which nourishes palm and orange trees, which was converted into a stupendous museum in honor of the dead by the best architects and sculptors. Facing the entrance, halfway up the hill, beyond the flowered tombs you come to a stupendous round building in which you will find the bones of the most illustrious Genoese. It is shaped like the Pantheon with a peristyle of black marble columns. Turning to the left and entering a long arcade, you will find a series of terraces rising one above the next with ornate mausoleums which are adorned with superb marble sculptures. If you then climb up the main staircase you arrive at a regal palace, the palace of the richest cadavers. There, surrounded by marble dovecotes in grandiose rows, your heart will tighten as you think about all of the poverty-stricken masses struggling through their daily existence.

---

103 [Levi believed in a freedom of the *responsible* press.]

I found myself there, as I said, one day in August of 1870. The splendid sunlight and the light reflected from the whitest of the marbles illuminated the shining arcades. But the solemn silence of that place, interrupted only occasionally by the footsteps of a few visitors, inspired an inner melancholy as happens among those who walk alone among the tombs. I began to think about that sublime worm called Man and about the proclamations of fraternity and equality, against which people rebel, even in death. There, below this zone sleep the poor and here under all this marble, the rich, both reduced to skeletons.

I kept walking until a reached a corner where I saw an angel that guarded the entry to a crypt. That pale and very beautiful figure so shook my already distressed imagination that he seemed not to be a marble sculpture but instead a living figure who was smiling at me. "Angel" I said to him, "You appear to have a spark of genius in the little flame that burns before you. Speak to me; what is your name?" "Cevasco" was the answer from a nearby voice. I noticed the name next to that of Santo Varni, and two or three other illustrious people, and I paid heed to nothing else.

ILLUSTRATION XV

182. He who gives his children language, gives them bread.

Certain philosophers have noted that life (and what is life?) adapts itself into various forms because of mutations that succeed on the earth's surface. Science has shown that there was a geological period in which there were frequent floods and the earth was damp and marshy. At this time, life took the form of colossal lizards,[104] some of which were supported by membranes in the shape of wings

---

104 [i.e. dinosaurs]

which helped them move about. When giant continents formed with luxurious growths of vegetation, life transformed itself into an age of large mammals that survived while many earlier life forms disappeared. When mountains rose up as the continents separated or intersected, flowers appeared to beautify the earth and animal life appeared in the form of bees and butterflies that fly from flower to flower. Under the influence of man, life forms continue to perfect themselves and their size changes in proportion to the reduced space they can occupy, and the giant animals of ancient times were replaced by ones suited to the new era, something which intelligent life forms will study in the future.

Now man has shrunk the earth's size thanks to steam power, the telegraph, tunnels bored through the mountains, and canals cut across isthmuses. In this novel and rapid cycle of change, will the human form be changed? Will we become taller or shorter? Will our skins be black, yellow, red, or white? I certainly don't know, but I believe that common usages and social conventions are sure to change to conform to the new relationships that are daily reaching the various countries and their peoples.

In a world undergoing such changes, the first necessity is for people to listen to each other, and it will not be far off when the most essential and foundation of any civic education will of necessity the study of spoken languages. It is especially important for wise people to know many languages in order to foresee these changes, understand these times and adapt to them.

Today, even if a father who has taught his son to express his ideas in the Italian, French, English and German languages, is on his deathbed and as poor as Job, he can die assured about his child's future, and say to him: "Your facility with languages will be your magic wand; you need only wave it to achieve any of God's benefits; learn to use it well."

ILLUSTRATION XVI

193. When intelligence has reached a certain level in a genealogical line, it tends not to spread out to the branches.

Dante wrote, "How rarely human worth ascends from branch to branch."[105] But Charles Darwin and his many followers were not yet born when this was written.

Who does not know that intelligence and virtue always increase, as Mother Nature applies the law of natural selection through the mating of men and women? But, as one who has a light brain and speaks superficially about things, I say to myself and others like me, this model bodes ill for those who are humble, and beyond that I say nothing.[106]

I will only allow myself to add two further observations. The first is that it seems to me that certain systems that are said to be derived from experimental philosophy are in fact based on reasoning about things which are, in short, possible, probable, supposed, or ideological; such systems smell of the condemned metaphysics[107] from a mile away. The *natural selection* and *survival of the fittest* which long ago changed my ancestral monkey into me can be called hypothetical and not at all founded on observation and experience. Let us hope that one day we will find the remains those who died in the desert, of whom *Rabbah*

---

105 [Dante, Purgatorio, Canto VII, Line 121: *Rade volte risurge per li rami l'umana probitate*]

106 I do not wish that my comments in this illustration reflect badly on me or cause a suspicion that I claim to have low regard for the work of a man whose name will be among the greatest of these times. In this note I am merely concerned with certain observations that I wish to draw from his work that are without question very important.

107 [Levi is referring to Kant's *Critique of Pure Reason*]

bar Chana[108] told, whose skeletons will negate the impressions produced by heretical human skulls, and that we shall find in the caves of Lahr, Engis, Eguisheim, Neanderthal, and other sites with jawbones of such dimensions as to cause an aged countess tremble with horror, a countess who is obsessed with the divided escutcheons of her noble ancestors.

Unfortunately, there were no collectors or museums in the days of the good Rabbah. He told the story that one day while he was riding on horseback on a voyage in the desert, the ground gave way beneath him in such a way that both horse and rider fell into a deep pit. As soon as the man stood up, he found that the pit had sides of ivory, so steep and smooth that it was impossible to climb out. Honestly, I do not remember whether the poor traveler died in the pit along with his horse or whether someone came in time to save him; it has been many years since I have read that true book. However, I can tell you what the huge hole was ... can you guess? It was nothing less than the eye socket of the skull of one of those ancient Israelites who died in the desert in the time of Moses. Compare that to the skulls of Engis and the other above-named sites! And now they tell me that my ancestor was a giant monkey!

The other observation that I want to add is that I am not convinced of Mr. Darwin's theory; I continue to believe in my maxim No. 193, *which to this day has not been disproved in the world in which we live, neither by natural selection nor by survival of the fittest.* Aha! If I could only arrange to marry Alessandro Manzoni to Vittoria Colonna,

---

108 [Rabbah bar Chana was a Jewish Talmudist from Babylonia. Among his writings were descriptions of fantastic voyages he claimed to have had in the desert and on the sea. In one of those voyages in the wilderness of the Exodus, he claimed to have seen the huge bodies of the Israelites who had died in the desert during the Exodus from Egypt, lying face up.]

or Gaetana Agnesi, or Novella d'Andrea.[109] Who knows what people would have been born from such a marriage? But blessed Nature is blind. And if it is not blind, if by any means one supposed Darwin's theory to be true, that Nature knows how to choose the fittest, if indeed it came to pass that that a snail should create steam power, at the end of the day, what is Nature? A chance occurrence? When great scholars say it is so, we must bow down and say that it must be so. But at some point, we are dealing with accidents that happen to be of benefit.[110] From the moment when a creature improves, from Adam the great monkey and various similar Adams came many great and beautiful people.

I would remain silent on this subject, if we were only talking about certain people who have been condemned to a lifetime of eating capons, sturgeons, and sweetbreads because of a whim of their barbaric monkey sisters. But to start from an orangutan and produce a beautiful woman or one worthy of entry into the index of a universal biography, upon my honor, this Nature-accident would have had to sweat over millions of years, and what is more, to have found a helping hand to succeed.

This (Darwinian evolution) is at best a metaphysical conjecture of value equal to many others which in the end have the value of being

---

[109] [Alessandro Manzoni (1785-1873) was the greatest Italian novelist. Vittoria Colonna (1492-1547) major Renaissance poet and close friend and quasi mother-figure of Michelangelo; Gaetana Agnesi (1719-1799), an Italian mathematician, philosopher, and theologian; first female mathematics professor in Italy. Novella d'Andrea (c. 1270-c. 1348) was a noted legal scholar and professor at the University of Bologna whose academic chair had been previously held by her father.]

[110] [Unbeknownst to him, Levi seems to have stumbled on the notion of random genetic mutations, some of which endow various creatures with capabilities enabling them to survive and reproduce better than others. Unfortunately, the world had to wait for almost another century before the mechanics of genetics and mutations came to be fully understood.]

dressed in more fashionable clothing. Some people may note that these issues are matters for books and athletics, rather than more or less for flashes of intellect.

Fine News! Didn't I say so right from the beginning? But what use is it? One hears many bad proofs from these gentlemen who put forward their reasoning in lieu of examining the real, though little understood, world. I must be permitted to state a few of my counterexamples to the rigidity of those who claim that the undeniable progress toward the better is necessarily a product of accidental events, that the drive toward perfection has always been and still is the product of accidents, of the very slow and necessarily good taste of benevolent accidents!

ILLUSTRATION XVII

208. When you are both rich and wise, you can aspire to do many things. When you join riches and wisdom to an excellent pedigree, you can aspire to do anything.

209. In many cases the reformer revives and protects while the conservative, with his impotent opposition to change, causes the destruction that he seeks to avoid.

210. Public opinion follows a curve. When it is broadly shared, he who does not go along with it will remain isolated, impotent, and outside of its progress.[111]

---

[111] It is my intention to write a piece which I am struggling to make worthy of being shared publicly. This essay is necessarily limited by the extent of my talents and also needs to be true to my personal convictions. I do not intend to offend others, nor do I wish to portray myself as being superior to other men who are noted for their rank or doctrine; I simply believe that which I affirm and I do not wish to, nor am I capable of, deceiving myself.

The first of these maxims is very general, and therefore I grouped with the other two, whose application I want to discuss specifically in the case of religion. Even here, one can see serious ills that could for the most part be prevented, if people did not act like the person who is ill with tuberculosis, but does not examine the causes of this fatal disease[112] and instead obstinately maintains the lethal conditions that cause it, and worsens his condition, leaving him without any possible treatment.

The Mosaic religion has the great advantage of professing as essential dogma the existence of a single, omnipotent God, master of the universe. The Supreme Being not only fills every heart with himself throughout life, but also acts to promote all goodness and avoid many evils.

What is the nature of our dispute (between myself and the rationalists, Voltaire and Hobbes)? Who offers comfort for our unhappy existence, you or I? You yourself confess that faith in God has drawn some men back from the edge of sin; this confession suffices for me. Even if this opinion has not prevented ten murders, ten slanders, ten evil judgments on earth, I believe that the world ought to embrace it.

You say that religion has produced thousands of misdeeds; say instead that superstition, which reigns in our unhappy world, is the cruelest enemy of the pure adoration which we owe the Supreme Being.

You hold that the adoration of God quickly becomes superstition and fanaticism. But should we not fear that in denying God, others

---

112 [In the 1870s when Levi was writing this book, tuberculosis was thought to cause one-seventh of all deaths in Europe and the United States. Until 1882, when Robert Koch discovered the tuberculosis bacterium, people ascribed myriad causes to this disease from parental inheritance to environmental issues such as bad air, unclean living conditions, and/or urban congestion.]

will abandon themselves to the most atrocious passions and horrible sins? You claim that there is only one small step between adoration and superstition. In fact, there is an infinite gulf separating these for those of properly formed spirit, and today there are a great many such people. They are the heads of nations, and influence public behavior, and year by year, we see the gradual removal of the fanaticism that used to cover the earth.

In addressing the doubts that we both share, I do not advocate Pascal's position that "You should keep to the more certain position ... because nothing is certain in areas of uncertainty ... nor do I propose that you believe in strange things simply to avoid embarrassment ... But I say to you, continue to cultivate all the virtues, to be benevolent, and consider all superstition with horror and pity; join me in adoring the beauty manifested in all of nature, and consequently its creator, the beginning and end of all. Hope with me that our discussion concerning the Eternal Being can be amicable and something over which we can disagree. You cannot prove His impossibility, much as I cannot mathematically demonstrate His existence.[113] You and I can only talk about probabilities, swimming in a sea in which neither of us can see the shore. Woe unto those who swim themselves to exhaustion. Let those who can reach the shore do so. As for those who shout to me," You are swimming in vain, there is no harbor!" They merely discourage me and sap my strength.

These stupendous words that I have abstracted from writings[114] of one of the greatest and most skeptical minds of the last century[115] could not be refuted even by the most orthodox Israelite. After all, the

---

113 [Notwithstanding this comment, in Illustration XX in the second volume of Levi's Maxims, he attempts to do just that.]
114 Voltaire: Dict. Philos., Dieu, sec. V.
115 [I.e., the 1700s.]

Jewish Great Legislator is defined as an incomprehensible Being, who proclaimed himself God by saying "*I am who I am.*"

But if these words of Voltaire are consistent with the overbearing concept of God that enters into every heart, willingly or unwillingly, from one instant to the next, and for one's entire life, they do not answer perfectly to scientific analysis. One might imagine that there could be a school in which religious arguments could triumph over the tradition of empirical proof. In such a school people would analyze every minute detail of the empirical tradition and by so doing reinforce common habits and preserve the faith. But, of course, there is no such school.

Neither one side nor the other can win this argument, even though their weapons are poorly matched. To the degree that I use the Holy Book as a valid argument against those who concern themselves with material things, forces, and the life cycle, I feel like the Chinese who covered the walls of their fortresses with monstrous grotesque figures to protect them from the cannons of the English and French armies.[116]

Mine is the method of [Biblical] criticism, which can preserve the consoling ideas concerning God from the attacks of dispassionate scientific criticism, the product of incomplete human reason. The weapons can be more or less equal, and therefore the heart should win out, given that such a victory will always be a great benefit and comfort in the sense expressed above by Voltaire.

Today it is useless to deny it; history teaches us that each age brings with it its own colors,[117] and those of preceding ages must pale by comparison. Today human reason colors our times with facts

---

116 [Levi is alluding to the antiquated arms used by the Chinese against the English during the first Opium War (1839-1842). In that war, China's weapons technology was thought to be several centuries behind England's.]

117 [Colors in the sense that artistic styles reflect the social styles of the age.]

and its methods and analytical approaches. It behooves us to bend with the times and demonstrate that these methods are incapable of destroying deeply felt *Truths* if we are unwilling to end up in a place where the multitudes find the penal code to be the only brake upon their nefarious tendencies.

Anathema, affected contempt, insults, mystical and ascetic affirmations and immobility, and worse, are weaknesses of prejudiced minds. They merely inspire pity for the person who launched, taught, or commanded them. With such and other equally blameworthy approaches, one poorly defends the value of an idea and other equally praiseworthy notions deduced from it. The only defense against reason is better reasoning, from which new

Oh, what a miserable spectacle! While all the ancient rites languish, abandoned, while the leading minds, those that lead the nations and have the greatest influence over morality, are split into two philosophical camps, and try to develop their doctrines from spirit and substance. Those who believe in a single God, hold forth on this faith: Do not touch the Queen! As if! I fear that this is a sham and will crumble to dust at the slightest touch. Then the sham will be disrobed of its torn and soiled vestments, and perhaps we shall see true faith shine forth in its ancient lost splendor from this same human philosophy.

A venerated idea does not need to be defended with weapons other than critical reasoning, but it needs to be freed from the fetters of its past whose means and approaches were so different from today's. It will always be the case that those doing good works will find hope and courage in proclaiming one Supreme Being, no matter what might be said to the contrary. Such declarations will strongly curb feelings of sorrow, resignation, and all manner of human excesses. Aside from faith in Him, we would have to create a new foundation for morality based on human imperfection, and therefore we would be forced to renounce the triumph of justice. Such a triumph could never be based on a purely human morality which is *necessarily* imperfect.

Oh, idea of an immortal God, who remains as a solid bastion that does not crumble, if only I could ever see you freed from the vile wrappings that make you appear curdled or mummified![118]

I have experienced human dignity, needs, biases, and all manner of fears, knots that fatally bind men's talents and render them impotent. When your influence, so fatal to human amity, is displaced by the strong voice of human duty among society's leaders, then even the most orthodox Jews will believe that the Messiah has arrived, after which God will truly reign over a just and civilized world.

ILLUSTRATION XVIII

227. The justice and morality on which a civil society is based are a synthetic product based on behaviors of which you will find only hints here and there. What I mean is that while today's society as a whole is just and moral, only rare individuals are so. Even though this sounds like a fundamental contradiction, it seems to be the case.

---

118 [Levi is trying to separate the moral teachings of religion, things that he thinks are absolute goods, from the supernatural elements which do not square with empirical observation and logical reasoning based on those observations. He views the latter as corrupting the image of God. The great Italian renaissance scholar Azaria de Rossi established this approach to religion in the 1500s in his book *Me'or Enayim, The Light of My Eyes*. Thomas Jefferson did the same thing when he took a pair of scissors to the Bible; he excised all the bits about supernatural beings and events and retained only the parts describing historical events, scientific facts, and moral precepts.]

Sea water can appear different depending on one's viewpoint: here, colorless as a crystal glass, there greenish or sky blue. And air, when seen through the atmosphere is sapphire blue, but when looked at through a drinking glass, is colorless. Here are my images of justice and morality when considered in relation to all of humanity or to a single individual. There they are unbreakable and inexorable like the rectitude and virtue of thousands of generations of ancestors of today's living. Here we find them pliant, bendable like the character of the individual who seeks to satisfy his own passions, one who cheats or is cheated. Collective judgment comes from the wisdom of the ages and is immortal; it ends up being identified with justice when the facts of the case are laid out. An individual's judgment is a weak spark that appears occasionally, clouded by the woes, weaknesses, and errors that he has experienced over his life, even when he has good intentions and seeks to act justly. And that is how it is!

ILLUSTRATION XIX

250. One may suspect that racial differences underlie antipathy among people at least as much as differences of religion.[119]

This thought comes to us intuitively even before we present the facts that corroborate this unhappy suspicion.

Young Hebrew, why do you seek to hide your name, borrowing the names Caesar[120] or James in place of Abraham or Jacob? Why do

---

119 [Recall that Levi was born and raised in the ghetto and was of the first generation free to live and pursue his full adult life and livelihood outside of its constraints.]

120 [While Caesar is a relatively unusual given name in the United States, its Italian equivalent, *Cesare* is quite common in that country.]

you try to modulate your voice to mask its timbre or your thinker's accent born of your racial background, lest your name or accent reveal the Semite in you? Would you refuse to recognize your ancestry with such acts if you were not afraid of the ill-will that people of a different race might show even if you have Jesus, the Madonna, and the saints in your pockets?

You hear the philosophers preaching the fraternity of all mankind, be they black, white, red, or yellow, but you know that individuals rarely honor that idea. I will not absolve you Abraham-Caesar or Jacob-James, but I do understand your concerns, and I will add the extenuating circumstances to my condemnation.

When I see the vapors of the past hatred, veiled anger, disdain, ill-will, and slander toward the Hebrews from such a great man as was Voltaire, and when I see the great distaste toward elevating Blacks to full equality in a democratic country such as America, I am right to search for the roots of such hatred in matters other than religious convictions.

And I sadly say to myself: if the descendants of peoples who were either fierce or martyred are not burdened with the barbarities or martyrdoms of their ancestors, there is nonetheless an undeniable hatred toward them that now and then turns into horrifying incidents executed upon the weaker ones, as happens today on the shores of the Black Sea.[121]

The Dacian-Romanians have still not overcome their hatred for the ancient and bloodthirsty Pannonian Avars[122] to the degree that they

---

121 [In the 1860s-1920s, there were a series of large-scale genocidal attacks upon various minority peoples of the Caucasian region, Ukraine, Turkey, and Romania culminating in the Russian pogroms against the Jews in the late 1800s and the Armenian genocide during World War I. These were principally instigated by Czarist Russia and the Ottoman Empire.]

122 [The Avars were a Turkic tribe that occupied much of the Balkans in the early post-Roman era.]

continue to kill or banish the Avars in their territory. Also, we should reflect on Spain, which should be regretting its fanatical banishment of the Jews in 1492. Imagine if the energy, industry, sagacity, wise counsel, entrepreneurial spirit, mental acuity of Spain's Jews had been brought to bear on that country in the times of the galleons and conquest of the Americas. Then Spain would have continued to this day to be the most powerful country in the world. Instead, it has been reduced to a second-rate power, and Count Montalembert has contrasted Spain's weakness with the commercial and industrial strength of England.[123] But the Dacian-Romanians are not convinced by this and other similar examples that one could add. Even if they do not expel the Jews outright, it will not be for want of desire to do so.

Now, is this hatred based on religious difference, is it based on race, or are they both hatreds that all of the judges of an entire magistracy have condemned as an attack upon innocent and honorable people? For what blind rage, for what sort of hatred, do people profane graves, even as they claim to be, and in principle are, civilized.

ILLUSTRATION XX

270. Knowing how to write or speak does not include knowing how to act.

How many people are there who, like Demosthenes after he led the pro-war party to victory,[124] turn and run away at the first skirmish? How many penniless orators and writers are there and how many

---

123 [Charles Forbes Conte de Montalembert, The Political Future of England, London 1856, Chapter XVII, p. 258 and ff.]
124 [Demosthenes, a fabled Athenian orator, argued for the city to prepare for war to defend itself against Philip of Macedon.]

others are there, who make their names as small-time writers but never become millionaires? It would be better if Mr. Brain abandoned the pulpit and engaged his hands and arms if we would like to see the isthmuses and mountains cut with canals and tunnels, buildings built, millions earned and every task undertaken and completed.

But yes, when he is on the speaker's rostrum, Mr. Brain would much prefer to speak as a learned professor than to than to move his muscles and undertake the arduous work that takes all of his strength, which demonstrates the proverb, "From Said to Done, there is a wide space."

"What a fine article Mr. X has written!"

"And have you heard how well he speaks?"

So, what did Mr. X do? Woe unto him if he could not answer this question!

LEVI'S INDEX[125]

A
Ability, 166, 248, 258, 268, 270; Ill. XX
Action, 270; Ill. XX
Administration, 5, 164
Adultery, 71, 146
Advice, Advisor, 38, 153, 154, 299
Affability, 234
Ambition, 208; Ill. XVII
Anger, 218
Antipathy, 63, 200, 250, 257, 258; Ill. XIX
Apostles, 225
Appearance, 224
Arms (Appropriate), 282
Arms (Force of), 282
Arrogance, 161
Artists, 228
Artifice, 147, 148, 155
Atheism, 171
Avarice, 32, 223

B
Barbarity, 11
Benefaction, 26, 78, 135
Benefactor, 26, 78, 135
Bigotry, 88
Blood, 137
Boasting, 197
Boxer, 281
Brain, 12, 284
Bread, 182; Ill XV
Business (Others'), 5, 104
Business, (One's own), 5

C
Calm, 24
Calculation, 282
Calumny, 23, 195, 222
Capital Crimes, 240
Capricious, 104
Character, 24, 190, 203, 226
Charity, 40
Chastity, 191
Celibate, 190
Centers, 215
Civility, 64, 137
Cleanliness, 8
Coin, 300
Collectors, 112

---

125 [Levi's original index numbers point to the maxims addressing the particular index term or issue. We have followed his model. I have added the corresponding illustration numbers as appropriate]

Commiseration, 177
Company, 237
Compliments, 4, 234
Condition, 27
Condemn (Slowness to), 19
Confidence, 273, 274
Conscience, 64, 78, 102, 136, 169, 195
Constancy, 54, 55
Conservative, 209; Ill. XVII
Convenience, 234, 180
Correction, 91, 196; Ill. VII
Courage, 46, 47, 48, 281
Courtesy, 234
Credit, 262
Criticism, 18, 153, 157, 168, 180
Curiosity, 32, 121, 122, 123, 124

D

Decorum, 234
Death, 57, 191
Defects, 278
Deeds (Good), 22, 78
Descendants, 193; Ill. XVI
Desire, 75, 217
Despotism, 292,
Devotion, 174
Difficult, 72, 96, 97
Diffidence, 36, 273, 274
Dignity, 234
Disappointment, 75
Disapproval, 196
Disdain, 14, 50
Disinterest, 77, 78, 226
Dissimulation, 99, 106, 118, 224, 225
Distraction, 74
Doing, 72, 93
Duty, 248, 129, 222

E

Early-Riser, 1
Earnings, 92; Ill. VIII
Easy, 72, 96, 97
Eating, 2
Education, 27, 64, 160, 281
Educators, 92; Ill. VIII
Egotism, 77, 133; Ill. X
Emotion, 123
Emotional Pain, 29, 74, 176
Ending, 60
Enemy, 58, 153, 201, 253
Energy, 281
Envy, 111, 188, 255
Equality, 83
Error, 117, 139
Esteem, 67, 92, 130, 177, 260, 262; Ill. VIII
Example, 91; Ill. VII
Exercise (Physical), 160, 281
Exercise (Moral), 240
Existence, 135, 160
Eyes, 218

F

Facts, 3, 259, 267, 284
Faith, 33, 48, 267
Fakery, 147, 148, 155
False Merit, 187
Falsehood, 242
Fame, 56, 57, 167; Ill. XIII
Fantasy, 74, 283
Farmers. 228
Fault, 151, 22
Felicity, 30, 108, 247
Felicity (Marital), 20, 55
Fiction –See Artifice
Fidelity, 20

Fight, 281
Flattery, 186, 187
Foreboding, 258
Forethought, 246, 275, 276, 277
Force, 137, 170
Force of Arms, 282
Fortune, 107, 247
Fortune (Making One's), 107, 213, 233, 261, 265
Fraternity, 83
Freedom of Conscience, see Conscience
Friendship, 29, 127, 128, 176, 177

G

Genealogy, 193; Ill. VXI
Generosity, 77
Genius, 42, 57, 114, 181, 232
Gentility, 234
Gifts, 233
Good Deeds, 22, 78
Glory, 167, 215, 294; Ill. XIII
Good Faith, 226, 298
Good-Natured, 99, 145, 285
Good-Hearted, 16, 74, 77, 179, 198, 199
Goodness, 73, 75, 135, 150, 160, 298; Ill. XII
Good Reasons, 157, 185
Good Taste, 211
Government, 170
Greatness, 251
Greed, 32, 223
Guardian Angel, 279

H

Happiness (Marital), 20, 55
Hatred, 31, 204, 254, 255, 256
Haughtiness, 82, 155, 156
Hearing, 25
Heart, 4, 28, 284; Ill I –See also good-hearted
Health, 290
Hercules, 283
Heresy, 226
Heroism, 48
High-Spiritedness, 178
Homicide, 220
Honesty, 35
Hope, 289
Human Spirit, 295

I

I, 219
Ignorance, 10, 11, 130
Ills,
Illusions, 17, 105, 108, 112, 113, 114, 116, 149, 154, 223, 251, 252; Ill. II
Imagination, 74, 283
Impression, 87
Improvidence, 207, 214
Inconstancy, 55, 121
Indecisiveness, 70
Industry, 237
Infidelity, 34
Ingratitude, 120
Injustice, 169
Insolence, 101
Instruction, 52, 55, 64, 75, 92, 240; Ill. III, Ill. VIII
Instructors, 92 Ill. VIII
Intelligence, 135, 160, 174, 194, 204, 208, 240, 248, 260, 265; Ill. XVII
Interest (Private), 222
Interest (Public), 58
Intolerance, 88

Ire, 31, 88, 188, 255

J
Jealousy, 110, 111
Jester, 132
Journalism, 183; Ill. XIII
Journalists, 155
Joy, 30, 108
Judgment, 12, 19, 56, 67, 77, 169, 195, 201, 217, 231, 288, 298
Jury, 62, 63, 64
Justice, 62, 98, 108, 257, 262

K
Kindness, 83, 100
Knights, 282

L
Language, 182, 218, 266; Il XV
Lawyer, 263, 264
Laziness, 102, 103, 163, 240
Legal Science, 263, 264
Level, 86
Libertine, 252
Lie, 130
Life, 41, 150, 151, 243, 254, 260, 271, 287; III, XII
Lightness, 11
Love, 20, 21, 31, 122, 146, 149, 244, 245, 280, 289
Love (of one's fellows), 78
Love (Paternal), 145
Love (Of variety), 121

M
Making One's Fortune, 107, 213, 233, 261, 265
Malevolence, 249

Manner (Sweetness of)), 21
Marital Happiness, 20, 55
Marriage, 28, 243; Ill I
Martyrdom, 48
Maternity, 242
Memory, 284, 289
Merit, 188, 189, 197, 229, 236
Merit (False), 187
Method, 85, 100, 101
Millionaire, 283
Mimic, 296
Mind, 215, 231
Misadventure, 9; Ill. I
Modesty, 300
Money, 290, 300
Monument, 181, 293
Moral, 90, 136, 262; Ill. VI
Moral Exercise, 240
Moral Liberty, 61, 62, 63
Motherhood, 242
Movement, 74
Music, 294

N
Nature, 190
Negligence, 43
Nobility, 184, 208, 228; Ill. XVII

O
Obligation, 129, 222
Offended, 67
Operate, 72, 93
Opinion, 12, 63, 68, 87, 225, 226
Order, 42
Ostentation, 36, 177

P
Pain (Emotional), 29, 74, 176

Parallels, 202
Pardon, 151, 253 ; Ill. XII
Partisans, 174
Passions, 63, 111, 117, 130, 144, 215, 216, 217, 231, 288
Paternal love, 145
Patience, 60
Pen, 218, 231, 232
Perfection, 241
Persecution (Religious), 30
Perseverance, 268
Pity, 31, 119
Physical Attributes, 276
Physical Defects, 278
Physical Education, 160
Physical Exercise, 281
Pins, 220
Pleasing (Oneself), 69
Pleasing (Others), 297
Polygamy, 190
Political Parties, 159
Politics, 59, 137, 170
Posession, 75
Posterity, 276
Poverty, 7, 45, 177, 178, 207, 212
Practice, 264
Praise, 158, 168, 188, 269
Pretense, 107
Pride, 249
Primogeniture, 243
Principles, 76, 115
Private Interest 222
Professions/Professors, 228, 248, 261, 263
Progress, 90, 159, 263; Ill, VI
Promise, 173
Promoters, 226
Prudence, 162, 257
Public Interest, 58
Purse, 211, 218

Q
Quiet, 142; Ill. XI

R
Race, 172, 250; Ill. XIX
Reasons, 105, 113, 125, 259
Reasons (Good), 211
Recommendations, 211
Reconcialtion, 254
Reformer, 209; Ill. XVII
Remorse, 134
Regret, 151, 217; Ill. XII
Religion, 9, 10, 11, 28, 33, 133, 134, 137, 140, 141, 272; Ill. I, Ill. X
Religious Persecution, 30
Remedy, 205
Removal, 206
Repetition, 241
Repression, 170
Resignation, 75
Respect, 234
Revenge, 203, 256
Revision, 56
Rewards, 92; Ill. VIII

S
Saints, 295
Satisfaction, 69
Secrets, 37
Self-Esteem, 14, 78, 234, 271
Sentiments, 140, 210; Ill. XVII
Silence, 82
Sincerity, 226, 269, 279
Slander, 23, 195, 222
Slow-to-Condemn, 19

Society, 227, 264, 283; Ill. XVIII
Speaking, 25, 39, 81, 270; Ill. XX
Spirit (Human), 295
Spouse, 276
Stain, 151; Ill. XII
Stature, 230, 251
Suicide, 286
Superiority, 17; Ill. II
Superstition, 250, 284; Ill. XIX
Sweet-mannered, 21
Sympathy, 63, 200

T

Talented Person, 132, 183, 192, 193, 194, 264; Ill. XIII, Ill. XVI
Taste (Good), 157, 185
Tears, 276, 277
Thinking, 2
Throat, 223
Time, 148, 152, 294
Timidity, 44, 45, 124
Toil, 54, 60
Tolerance, 13, 84
Tranquility, 142; Ill. XI
Transgression, 173
Treachery, 23.195
Trifles, 229
Truth, 58, 115, 117, 118, 131, 138, 239, 277; Ill. IX

U

Unhappiness, 69

V

Valor, 283
Value, 41, 234, 260, 294
Vanity, 49, 109, 181, 219, 229, 278
Variety (Love of), 145

Versatility, 12
Vigor, 63, 64
Vices, 144, 215
Virtue, 77, 126, 187, 195, 215
Voice, 15

W

War, 143
Weakness, 12, 77, 94
Wealth, 53, 194, 208, 221, 261, 283; Ill. XVII
Wisdom, 247
Wishing, 166, 268
WSillingness, 61, 62
Woman, 34, 79, 95, 124, 125, 155, 233, 242, 244, 245; Ill V
Word, 3, 80, 234, 286, 287
Work, 7, 93, 102, 103, 127, 128, 152, 165, 184,
Workers, 228
Works of Art, 60
Writers, 80, 235, 270; Ill. XX
Wrongs, 196, 205, 206, 258, 287

Y

You, 81
Youth, 65, 170; Ill. IV

Z

Zeal, 16, 199

MAXIMS

BY
LEONE LEVI

VOLUME B

TURIN
STAMPERIA BORGARULLI
Via Montebello 22

1874

To My Children

BORN A HEBREW, FEBRUARY 7 MDCCCXXIV
A PILGRIM
ON THIS PRECIOUS EARTH
THAT MY FIRST CRY GENERATED
ALAS
FANATIC, FIERCE, AND IMPLACABLE ZEAL
THAT PROHIBITED IN THIS LIFE
ETERNAL BLESSING WITH
THE LIGHT OF KNOWLEDGE
TO A POTENTIALLY HIGH MIND
OR
MEN TO BE HONORED
INSPIRED BY TRUE CHARITY
WHO EXTINGUISHED
THAT EVIL ZEAL
WITH THE DECREE OF JUNE 19 MDCCCXLVIII
I DEDICATE
TO YOUR IMPERISHABLE NAMES
THESE TWO SERIES OF PRECEPTS
THAT I HAVE COLLECTED
AND ADDRESSED TO MY CHILDREN
AS THEIR MODEST INHERITANCE

Literary Property

PREAMBLE

> *"My dear friend, it seems to me that there
> is a winged spirit in your writing..."*
> F. D. Guerrazzi[126]
> *Letter to the Author of the*
> Massime *of 21 June 1872*

It is commonly said that humanity has finally achieved maturity. In this matter I grieve for mankind, but I see it as I glance through all of the phases of an individual's lifetime. Will it end one day? Well, I would almost swear to it. Perhaps it will cease to exist in the same way as the elderly, gradually producing less and less. But the perpetual duty to preserve and embellish life while it endures applies equally well to individuals as to communities.

Today mankind has achieved maturity. Do you remember, dear reader, when you were a child? What fun it was to stand before the puppet stage and watch the buffoonery of Pulcinella, laugh at the follies of the Doctor, and delight in the songs of Fasolino?[127]

---

126 [Francesco Domenico Guerrazzi (1804-1873) An Italian lawyer, politician, and writer, who was repeatedly imprisoned by the Austrian Grand Duke Leopold of Tuscany for his republican politics, and who ultimately served in the Italian parliament after Tuscany was absorbed into the Kingdom of Italy in 1860.]

127 [Theatrical characters from the classical Italian *Commedia dell'Arte.*]

> When my father beat my mother
> Out came sins and scandals.

Fasolino, the righter of wrongs, who beat Pulcinella because she beat her husband, What a hero! Were you satisfied dear reader? Indeed, you were! The fellow who made the puppets dance on the stage, sing their songs, engage in their fanciful discourse, and recite their poems became famous. When you grew up, you looked indifferently upon that shabby puppet theater, and yet you smiled a bit when you vividly remembered your youthful enjoyment of it.

Humanity has finally grown up. There was a time when any excuse sufficed to burn books in the piazza, and a crowd would surround the spectacle. And many such volumes which sleep eternally in the grave of hatred were the occasions for tears and blood to the delight of their contemporary children's puppet stage.[128] Having achieved adulthood, humanity has become studious. Its current higher status has opened its ears to many voices. No, it is not impatience that distracts humanity's attention, but the enormous difficulty of a book earning attention amid the voices of so many contending works.

Today we can divide all literature into two vital categories, that which pleases, and that which teaches. Aside from these two categories, you can achieve momentary interest or success if you have a famous name, distinguished family lineage, high office, or memorable achievements. But if your work does not have intrinsic value, it will soon be forgotten on account of its total lack of substance.

---

128 [Levi is referring to the Counter-Reformation which resulted in the censoring, banning, and burning of many books, including the works of Galileo and the Hebrew Talmud. He owned a copy of a two-volume prayer book (and which I now own) which was published in 1542 and whose rabbinic commentaries were censored by the Inquisition.]

Pleasing! It is very difficult to write five pages without your enemy, boredom, appearing and eliciting an orgasm of yawning from your reader's jaws. It is even harder to write ten pages without causing the foregoing mandibular orgasm to reappear ever more frequently, causing your reader to leave the remaining virgin pages and allow them to turn into eternal dust or something even worse.

In earlier times, travelogues and novels were deemed pleasing. In the world of years ago, when travel was by slow and dangerous sailing vessels, the world was much bigger relative to what it is now with steam power. In their youth, our fathers enjoyed hearing tales about the lives of wild savages and louse-infested barbarians. When they were children, our parents were entertained by huge tomes, products of the pen and engraving, which described the beastly daily lives of these peoples, their rude huts, and their crude boats made by burning out the insides of tree trunks. Today instead, we ask for details about the navigability of their rivers and the region's geology, descriptions of its flora and fauna, and the nature of its major products. As for the local inhabitants, we seek precise information about skulls[129] and skeletons, and many details about their daily habits and practices.

The art of saying much with few words requires those who seek to address us to be mature adults. It does not take much for us to find these collections of alphabetical symbols too long relative to our need to know. Other writers cover the substance of their ideas much more briefly. It improves our life when we can reduce the amount of time it takes us to learn and accomplish things.

At one time novels pleased us. When society was divided into rigid castes, it included a small number of privileged people who were encircled by barriers that were insurmountable by the masses; all sorts

---

129 [Levi's brother-in-law, Cesare Lombroso was a doctor and penologist who propounded many theories about the importance of phrenology.]

of goods and honors fell to those privileged ones by reason only of their birth or the fervor of their faith. All the others had to make do with hopes for Paradise after their deaths. Mothers and daughters delighted in stories giving fantastic accounts of the triumph of human equality. They dreamt that in such a triumph perhaps their children would rise up in the world. Or, in the case that the hero fell victim to the prevailing system, they wept at his fate, hoping that his failure would lead to better times.

But the arrival of political and civil equality eliminated for the most part the conflict among people from different life stations. The novel now has no other resource to draw upon than the poet's imagination. With the greater maturity of mankind, human experience is much more uniform across society; mothers and daughters expect stories to be based on true facts and yet also be ever more inviting. In this way, the field of novel writing has become rather restricted.[130] *Society is no longer divided between nobles and commoners; the special power and privilege of the clergy is no more; and the battles between people of different faiths are no longer. In the mind of a mature mankind, the only legitimate faith is in the power of science to aid in making sound judgments; science has smashed the power of myths and myth makers. Today's true nobility is limited to those who are learned or valorous.*

There is still the potential clash between the rich and the poor and the poet can exploit the differences in their relationship. But I cannot easily guess how much ingenuity it would take to create an image of such a compelling character, that is a fair imitation of the truth, and yet is enough of a marvel to be worth the cost of printing. I leave it to those who dare to confront this difficult problem to find the answer. To me is not worth the effort.

---

130 [I am left to wonder what Levi would have made of today's huge current consumption of mass market paperbacks.]

If others wish to bring us back and paint a scene from the past, they might be successful, provided that they can faithfully reconstruct not only history, but also the period's customs, usages, and thoughts. In short, he would need to know how to truly identify himself with a long-gone era and bring it back to life with his words. Under these terms he could please a mature public. This would be a work that would require the intuition of a genius together with the patience of a naturalist. On the one hand such literature pleases by having become scientific[131] but on the other in its decline it is reduced by degrees to merely supplementing the daily press.

Daily journalism is the one modern type of literature in the hands of mankind that the people of today know and are willing to consume. It can range from buffoonery to wisdom. It reports on the foundations of partisan passions and interests and can agree and support them.

I have said nothing about poetry. Certainly, in every time period, people have been and will be pleased by the splendid images dressed up in rhythmic words. Poetry has always been and will ever be youthful. But the truly great poets of any one people, those still remembered today and valued across the different social classes, can be counted on the fingers. I will add no more than necessary on this topic. May it please those who know how and can write in this way. Certainly, I find that most people prefer to earn eternal praise by singing in a choir rather than seeking glory by reciting verses.

There remains theater which is customarily considered both a fashionable entertainment, and also as a form of serious literature. It can succeed up to a certain point in either the first aspect but not

---

131 [i.e., fact-based]

the second or vice versa.[132] *Giambattista Niccolini*[133] *would not have approved of a staging of his works as histories. He is among the few authors of this sort who has pleased the public in our times and whose work should survive him.*

But I will not elaborate on theater as entertainment; this is not the proper place for such a discussion, I will only add that as literature, theater is a form of poetry. It adds further complications to the general difficulties of writing poetry. Specifically, it also needs to add sublimely conjoined reality while avoiding becoming commonplace, a natural development of the story line, believable actions that appear to be fact-driven and must lead to, and end with, an educational moral. And all this must be accomplished simply with dialog. This is what is required for an excellent play in which art imitates life.

It is well and good that the young are reminded in a book of maxims of the extraordinary difficulties that authors of all types of literature encounter in order to earn people's future attention to their modest accomplishments. They very cautiously commit their own reputations knowing that they have only one chance in a million of success and are otherwise wasting their time.

And I say to those who feel within themselves the holy fire of a genuine drive, a drive whose character can be recognized by its expansive force that will tolerate neither a yoke nor a brake: be careful. Other than the usual obstacles, which are in themselves quite large, I see some among you being broken by an inevitable rock, that

---

132 [Levi views theater as either an entertainment, i.e. as a popular art form appealing to the masses, as or serious literature which in his mind's eye puts it beyond the ken of the masses. Consequently, a play needs to be one or the other but cannot be both.]
133 [Giovanni Battista Niccolini (1782-1861) was a liberal Tuscan playwright who wrote a series of romantic-style tragedies on historical themes. He was also a literary and artistic critic. Politically, he favored Italian unification under a republican government that would be independent of the Church.]

of your first public praise. Whoever is satisfied by this has received a death sentence.

It would be best to recall that in the fullness of time, each literary work is comparable to a picture done in pastels that cannot be judged by examining it close up. Viewed from a distance, the colors of such pictures harmonize, and the figures take on character, and the rough strokes of the pastel sticks fade into a unified image that represents real art and turns out beautiful and admirable. And this is natural, in that to succeed as a writer of historical fiction, you need to discover the timeless truth, beauty and justice, and not only of a single period.

In most cases, the clash between the new author's work and the people then living cannot explain why certain works that were famous in their day are now forgotten. The judgment of those who hear you, O naïve ones, is simply judgment at first glance. That praise will encourage you, but do not be satisfied with it, just as you should not be disturbed by indifferent reviews. Within yourself you have just as powerful an ability to judge your own work. Your own capacity to judge is the best one that I know. He who believes that every author is satisfied with his own work is making a big mistake. You have worked, studied, and tired yourself out over many years and produced a book. After it has been published, you feel intimately tied to it, and rereading it for the first, second, or third time, an internal voice will tell you, "This isn't true," or "It is not right," or "This is not well written," and yet you would not be wrong in saying to yourself, "Bravo!" But to make it more accurate is difficult, and I would say that you will never find a more exacting judge than yourself.

Today's mature public prefers to focus on literature that teaches. That is not to say that that they dislike jesters, buffoons, and people with sad tales. Indeed, in times of idleness, they pay for stories about hunchbacks and crippled people, and I put in evidence that the public *will pay excellent writers even when they have nothing of value to say, only to weep when they are placed in their graves. The public will continue to pay them even when they put on a vaguely serious look and whisper, "This is my Italy" much to their own great amusement.*

But, in serious moments after having paid for them, the public condemns them to be forgotten. If in life they had the unhappy privilege of the court jester, to hate and be hated, in death they find the oblivion of the common grave. Contemporary passions or the manic need and eagerness for talking about themselves create sad illusions, air bubbles as it were, that pop leaving a droplet of water. These illusions drag men who could otherwise exhibit valor and gain public esteem into a bog.

But aside from these somewhat evil entertainments, the public's attention prefers instructive writing. To teach, a writer must have in his mind great acuity, strong intuition, a keen sense of observation, deep knowledge, and the capability to push science forward or at least to render it understandable by the public. Hail to the sublime people who know and can teach! You are the true leaders who stand at the top of the pyramid whose base is all of mankind. You are the brightest sapphire at the top of the pyramid. By virtue of your works, you have received the privilege of driving your splendor down into the lower social strata as time goes by.

Hail O Men for the public benefits you deliver to your fellow men. You sweat during the day and stay up at night to help improve their lot or teach them how to make good use of their intelligence. I will not erect an idol to you as I am unable to do so. But I will address you with admiration.

I admire you when you drive away ignorance with your light, when you learn to measure the true worth of things, when you dispel any pretense of superiority of one person over another, and when you do not seek personal gain from others who have approached you.

You should be granted control over your life as an individual, as a member of your family, as part of the broader society. You should be the one to establish the moral laws, those which teach people to work for the general good for the sheer love of doing the right thing. You should be the ones to determine what is possible or impossible. You should discover the true history of mankind and drive out false legends. You should be in charge of leading your fellow people in the present and teaching them how to move toward an even happier future.

Oh, youth of the future! It is good that this is first brought to your attention in a book of maxims. It is well worth taking one one's most essential duty, that of knowing how to teach people to recognize the ineffable joy of life above its problems and misfortunes.

As I reread this preface, it seems in the end to be a bit impulsive and here and there and somewhat juvenile for a man of my age. But I do not wish to change it, as overall it does not seem bad to me.

But I do have one small concern that I wish to clarify, and I have been asking myself, "If perchance a reader asked me, now that I have described the great difficulty of succeeding as an author and teacher, why did I write this new series of maxims? What do you hope to accomplish? In what way do you expect success?"

I would answer as follows: "I have studied mankind in depth, and I am laying out my personal values. With the first series of these maxims, I received the applause of intelligent people and to a lesser degree, also from the public. I hope to receive more of the same."

Turin, June 26, 1874.

MAXIMS

Not even perverse minds and barbarian peoples with absurd customs can change natural law, which we have shown to be universally based on reason, and when change is seen, it is not the law that has changed but the facts.

Giambattista Vico[134]
Universal Law, chapter 48[135]

1.

Excessive fear of an inevitable danger tends to increase it and sometimes creates new ones.

2.

Today's civil marriage laws contradict true morality in that they do not recognize the role of physical beauty and are contrary to the breadth of people's ideas.

---

[134] [Giambattista Vico (1668-1744) was a Neapolitan philosopher and jurist, generally seen as the inventor of the philosophy of history and cultural anthropology.]

[135] [Vico's original text: *Perturbationes animorum, vel barbarum gentium absurdi mores, nihil quicquam jus naturae demutant, quod demonstravimus constare rationem. Et si quandoque mutari videtur, ibi non jus sed facta mutantur.*]

3.

Do not worry about having excessive progeny. Remember that there have been only a few children who have become great men.[136]

4.

Those who teach learn as much about the good as about the bad; this implies that the ability to communicate ideas leads to developing related concepts.

5.

Those who marry close relatives become doctors' annuities.

6.

Any society in which people who wish to express their personal opinions on public issues must veil their thoughts and words is not a mature society.

7.

In substance, originality consists in deducing new ideas from known ones. When the new idea is true, it serves to extend knowledge. I would say that originality forms the indefinable part of beauty that consists of real or imagined truths that are elegant, clear, harmonious, substantial, and instructive; it makes you think, inspires you, moves you, and induces you to admire it, curse it, and laugh or cry about it.

8.

Philosophy does not distinguish between the ideas of *correct* and *useful*. Unfortunately, there are not many philosophers.

---

136 [Levi certainly did not worry about having too many children. He and his wife, Benedetta Debenedetti, had twelve, nine of whom survived into adulthood.]

9.

Frequent tears indicate either mental instability or excessively sensitive feelings.

10.

Excessive confidence or diffidence in your own intelligence both render it sterile.

11.

Deep study is not useful to the impatient ambitious person. Thus, you will find intelligent people and even geniuses among such people, but rarely are they truly wise.

12.

Public offices teach their holders, but it is a teacher paid by the government, even if the office holder does not learn anything. But woe unto the ambitious office holder who does not learn from it.

13.

You can recognize a truly ambitious person in that he is driven by a single and constant idea, to be seen by the public and to do so on every occasion and at any cost, in order that he rises ever higher on the winding staircase of his career.

14.

A focus on making money is an undertaking that can lead to a quiet ferocity in which throats are cut politely or even while laughing. How many nooses have been hoisted with gloved hands? What does it matter if the acquired money is minted from mud? It is picked up any way. You do not even see their money lust which masquerades as

Thalia[137]. In fact, the respectable public drunkenly cries "BRAVO" to the teacher as his money banishes their perception of his evil deeds.

15.

Do not abuse your powers because the time will come when a raveled hole in your life can no longer be mended and you lose your life on account of that hole.

16.

It takes many years to have solid proof that you no longer stumble with the usual foot.

17.

Each time that the government functions necessary for life are artificially impeded, freedom of action ends, and volition becomes the slave of the need to go on living. Therefore political, civil, religious, and economic leadership must have a strong influence over the proper actions of the judicial system.

18.

Fear can be an important part of education, just like the cases in which various poisons can serve as medicines for certain diseases.

19.

The desire for the esteem of others and the fear of losing it create a certain feeling called *honor*. It is the duty of future society to grant or remove praise according to each person's actions. Today there are still people who scorn the victim of a swindle, instead of the swindler.

---

137 [In Greek mythology, Thalia was the Muse of comedy and bucolic poetry.]

20.

True virtue is that which fortifies the good, which in turn is none other than the application of human intelligence to the world in which we live. All other virtues are relative to people's opinions and the times in which we live. For example, you might view constancy as obstinance, religious devotion as idolatry or ignorance, and a saint as a fanatic. When speaking of a virtuous act you should ask yourself to what extent it was supportive of a life of good works or mankind's collective wisdom. If you answer the question based on the facts and repute of the situation you can correctly judge its value.

21.

Everyone needs love, but to be loved is often a matter of good luck, which can have little or no connection to merit.

22.

Making a quick decision as to a coherent plan for the future based only on your feelings or the words of your close associates is the result of a good heart and poor judgment. It is always better to consider it for an additional day, especially if you fear a painful disappointment.

23.

People are motivated to act either to further their own interests, for pleasure, or on account of duty. When it is for their personal interest, the result can be riches; when it is for pleasure, the effort will be to keep it, to produce more of it and sometimes it results in loss of life,[138] and it can produce great works or abominations. Only when it is done for duty is it always virtuous. A person is better off if he can recognize

---

138 ["loss of life" as for example in thrill seeking.]

which of these three motives applies to the words and deeds of those who approach him.

24.

An act or its avoidance that is dictated by duty and also serves one's personal interests or pleasure is virtuous, because the duty that motivates it is not contradicted by other larger motives that might prohibit it.

25.

Every lie derives from a duty avoided in order to satisfy personal interests or pleasures. A person of rare esteem is one whose conscience fails only once a month.

26.

True duty is best measured by the recognition of true virtue; all other criteria can be fallacious.[139]

27.

Morality, that is the collection of good habits, keeps the body healthy, the brain robust, and the heart tranquil. It produces the essential good. This rule is easy to say and difficult to follow.

28.

In general, people are judged more or less in proportion to the values of their leaders. But leaders whose minds are capable of offering wise leadership and guidance grow ever scarcer, as the number of followers and the scale of their society grow ever larger.

---

139 See maxims 20 and 27.

29.

Pride, rustic timidity, an ineffable desire to isolate oneself, or an ambition to increase the number of one's followers through deeds rather than words, divert many powerful minds from active politics; this is the reason that there are so many weak-minded leaders.

30.

A powerful mind is so attractive and strong that when it speaks, it blocks the ideas of all weaker thinkers. That is why one should judge people not only by their words, but also by their deeds.

31.

In all situations be aware of your own strength. Indigestion and sleep that is interrupted or disturbed by nightmares are all warnings that you need to adjust your habits or seek a change of scene. If your thinking becomes labored and slow, you need to rest and set aside the means by which you translate thinking into action, lest you develop an early weakness or die.

32.

People are designed to walk, not to run nor for inertia. Thus, those who sit still go nowhere, and those who run wear themselves out and frequently fall by the wayside before reaching the midway point of their life's journey.

33.

Never have I heard a wise and mature person say, "That scam or that misfortune could never happen to me."

34.

People oscillate between their love of truth and the pleasure of their dreams. When they are close to both reality and poetry, they love the illusions that calm them and hate the truth which disturbs them even as they excitedly pursue it, spurred on by a mysterious urge. Wise is the strong person who avoids the stumble stones of the passions as he pursues truth. Only with truth and not with ghosts and illusions can mankind make progress.

35.

He who looks forward to poverty in old age has not known true misery.

36.

I find beauty to be the strongest positive attribute and deformity to be the worst crime, a crime which human injustice almost never completely pardons.

37.

Look at the young woman, whether pretty or ugly, who pretends to take great pleasure in your kiss. This is the strongest means at her disposal to enslave you, and all women know it.

38.

I have found judges who are unjust as a result of their excessive efforts not to be so.

39.

Even rarer than wise people are those who know how to contain and correct their own tendency toward malevolence, a true poison of the human race which results in treachery, twists judgment, and destroys good will.

40.

Slander is the mistress of malevolence. At one time she travelled nakedly but today the knife often cuts when it has been clothed in praise.

41.

Almost always severe judgments of others find their initial impulse in a hidden and malign pleasure. Also, when people criticize others in the name of the public good, there frequently is a bit of nastiness or jealousy that plays a small part in the impulse to criticize. And in so doing, what a triumph there is over a rival!

42.

People may outwardly curry favor with a powerful person with acts that may benefit him or cause them to tremble. But in their hearts, they tolerate the former and detest the latter.

43.

Schemes to obtain offices and honors are perhaps less common than those to obtain money. But of these two, only the latter are punished; and yet they are not always the more damaging or culpable.

44.

I have seen many people rise up to high positions by standing on the backs of their wives, all the while not looking back, as explained in the fable of Pluto and Orpheus, when the latter sought to bring his love, Euridice, back from Hades. Once they have reached a high station, I have often noted the public laughing at them, while they, in the livery of office, laugh at the public.

45.

Two disillusionments can wound you more than any others. The first, when the learned deem a work of yours unworthy, and the second is when circumstances cause you to lose faith in a friend or lover. In the first case you can console yourself with the hope that you will succeed with another try. For the latter, just as with the death of one whom you dearly love, there is no consolation except the passage of time.

46.

Better a carriage for my body than a monument on my grave. He who pays his debts and loses the shirt off his back loses his credit, but not so with he who goes bankrupt with his savings hidden away. The cynical voice that I sometimes hear in my head reminds me of the fact that today's society is still not at its best with respect to justice and admirable self-denial.

47.

One is a real businessman if he can translate his feelings to mere calculations assigning numbers and values to them. This idea produces money, and therefore has value; that one does not and is therefore worthless. In contrast, dreamers want to introduce feelings into all aspects of their lives, to the point of composing idylls at the feet of Phryne.[140]

---

140 [Phryne was reputed to be a courtesan in ancient Greece who grew very rich from her trade, owing to her great beauty. When she was being tried for the capital crime of impiety, she was supposed to have bared her body, dazzling the judges with her beauty, and causing them to acquit her. The great sculptor Praxiteles is said to have used her as the model for several of his nude female statues.]

These two extreme forms of the human spirit in turn hate each other to the point of madness, though even lunatics will laugh at each other's follies during their occasional periods of lucidity.

48.

If curing oneself of his depravities were as independent of his free will as engaging in them, virtue would not have a name.

49.

To state known facts and deduce from them the likelihood of a future event is said to be foresight and wisdom. On the contrary, predicting future events from present circumstances without any natural cause and effect linkage is said to be prophesying and is idiocy. Indeed, it is idiocy and malevolence when you predict another's misdeeds because you must know that predicting bad events in this way is a form of wishing for them to happen.

50.

If you make a good faith effort to avoid a problem, but it happens anyway, it is unreasonable to regret its occurrence. However, it is not in good faith to hold a public office for which you do not feel qualified.

51.

Ignorance and cowardice are unfortunate traits in a private person, but they are crimes against the public in politicians and soldiers.

For this reason, the people detest those who misgovern the country or are weak military leaders.

52.

Poverty is not a sin, but it is a plague that causes revulsion in those who see it.

53.

People do not like to make irrevocable commitments and when they must do so it is with the secret hope to be able to get out of them.

54.

The difference between an *opinion* and an *understanding* consists in the latter being based on proven truths, and the former only on beliefs. People will fight to maintain their opinions, but for solid truths there can be no discussion by virtue of the evidence supporting them.

55.

It is permissible for people to confuse their own opinions with true understanding, but it is not permissible to impose that confusion on others.

56.

An uneducated mind silences the heart and leaves little room for pity; a single passion can cause such a person to act cruelly, even if he is not cruel by nature.

57.

To continually make a show of your happiness can enrage others or cause them to laugh at you. Neither outcome is desirable.

58.

It is a difficult art to verbally call people out for their errors or deficiencies without offending them. It is extremely difficult if not completely impossible to do so in writing. It is possible that they can hide their feelings of being offended, but you will see it burst forth at the minimal provocation. It is sometimes tolerated from the rich and powerful; from most of the others, it is not at all.

59.

Few people can make the painful calculation of the future gains that will compensate for today's loss or deferred gratification. Most find it easier and prefer to waste their money in exchange for immediate gratification.

60.

In our own imaginations we all pretend to be better than we are; and when we hear someone speak of a personal weakness, it is said with the secret desire that you take it with a grain of salt.

61.

The human spirit can rise so high and fall so low, that if we could predict the future, many of us would end up either in an insane asylum or as suicides.

62.

Blind eye, man lost. People, like all other animals, fear the staring eye. The fury of a blind man entertains cruel children, and people naturally close their eyes when kissing, to avoid disturbing the sweetness of the moment.

63.

One day I was reading a column about the annual toll of suicides in a major city. I thought about it and then said, "Who can count how many of these were truly suicides? Could we all be wise and strong enough to sensibly control our impulses throughout our lives?"

64.

There exist heartfelt loves that can be measured in lire. Ten thousand for a hundred degrees of love, a hundred thousand for a thousand degrees. If your house should burn down, your love for it ends with the fire. The odd part is that when this is explained, everyone takes such love as a mark of integrity. I do not decry this state of affairs, I am just observing it, and sadly, I laugh about it.

65.

The marriage between an old man and a young woman is an unnatural experiment. It succeeds through tyranny or else it fails. In either case it leaves at least one victim.

66.

Much of the intensity of pleasure or pain depends on the type of organism experiencing it and also on greatly exercising and developing the imagination.

67.

The human spirit produces a type of paint which colors every word and deed. What in truth is called *hypocrisy*, is *convenience* when it has been painted. If someone does not use this paint, he runs the risk of martyrdom and then, after death, being adored or admired, as happened to Socrates and other sages. Paint, my brother, and you will live.

68.

It is much easier for the dead to rise again than for the injured to remain down.

69.

Do not declare yourself to be a friend of someone to whom you would not lend money.

70.

In your youth, risking your public reputation on poorly planned projects is like starting a large business with no capital. For each one that succeeds, there are millions who end up bankrupt.

71.

A youthful pen that curses this or that is like a green ember that hisses in the wind and goes out. Study what you learn from facts and the precepts of great men, Write and throw drafts into the fire until the mist of youth that colors everything around you, either rosy or dark and gloomy, has cleared. Allow yourself to be irradiated by the light of reason until you can measure your true strength against the terrifying sea before daring to sound your mighty trumpet with any hope of not ending up in oblivion. It seems to me that this is the right way to proceed.

72.

"Did you really enjoy seeing Aristides[141] honored with his triumphal parade? Speak truly to me."

---

141 [Aristides (530–468 BCE) was an Athenian general and statesman who led the Greeks to victory in several major battles against the Persian invaders, resulting in the Persians renouncing their ambition to conquer Greece.]

"No."
"Then why did you help to pull his chariot and shout "Hurrah!""
"Because I saw everyone else doing it."

73.

Jealousy often contributes to the delivery of true justice and the improvement of public morality because it can expose hidden facts about the accused more effectively than the mere love of Truth and zeal for the Good.

74

Because of the wide disparity in intelligence among people, only some of them are honored for their contributions to the overall progress of civilization. This is done notwithstanding our contemporary duty to fight against inequality among people. For this reason, honors are not distributed to everyone, and why those honors that are given out only rarely continue to be merited over time.

75.

Men tend to deny that other men are more intelligent than they are, and women deny that other women are more beautiful. This is the foundation of the different attitudes of the two sexes. The first proclaims the strength of his mind and the latter her form. But the problem is this: it is undeniable that there are effeminate men and mannish women.

76.

There were three women who were asking each other what an ideal husband would be. The first, an eighteen-year-old woman said, "Above all else, I would want him handsome." The second, a noblewoman a few years older said, "I would want him rich." The third, a young widow, said, "If I were to remarry, I would want him wise."

As I overheard this discussion, I said to myself, "Beauty is sought because of natural inclination, riches by calculation, and wisdom by experience."

77.

Approaching physical perfection has a scale similar to that of minds approaching genius. The higher you rise, the farther apart are the rungs. In the same way that study refines the mind, and develops and adorns intelligence, exercise of the limbs and cleanliness beautify and preserve the body.

78.

Few women can resist being seduced by compliments on their beauty, even though it is a gift of nature that comes at no cost and with no effort to those so adorned. Even so, it is admired and prized to a high degree, and it is this admiration that matters. They tend to love those who truly admire their beauty.

79.

Hearts of stone tend to be long-lived.

80.

You should always prefer a working jackass to a sleeping beaver.

81.

Talking about the defects of others is a poor way to burnish your reputation, but there are few people who avoid following this route.

82.

Think twice before acting. Remember that only a mind working alone works well on first impressions.

83.

Know what it is possible to do in your life situation and accept it without either arrogance or meanness. Keeping to your place avoids the embarrassment of being put down.

84.

Society weighs the act against the capability. It would be a laughable farce to see a poor man in a fancy carriage.

85.

I find the fear of death and the waste of one's life to be one of the worst and yet most common contradictions of life.

86.

As a poor man was being assaulted by three young men, I hear him shout, "May God strike you for your three Ls!" I chased off the three miscreants and then I asked to please explain the three Ls, because I did not know what he meant by them. He replied, "Laziness, liquor, and luxury."

87.

If you seek to squeeze too much production from your mind or your land, you will render them infertile.

88.

The daring can best deal with life's trials if they also know when and how to avoid them. Boldness is a gift that can work only up to a certain point, and you can learn that limit by exercising the mind and the body.

89.

Promising payment for good deeds and punishments for evil ones turns every action into one tied to personal interests. This approach has resulted in many dark pages of history because it induces actions for the wrong reasons. Philosophy teaches us that one should do good for the simple love of it.

90.

There are many saints who sought to earn their place in Heaven by sending others to Hell, for which, according to God, one should not envy them their place in the calendar or history. And do you think that all the people who would like to imitate them are gone from this Earth?

91.

It seems that everyone starts out wanting a fancier carriage to boost their self-esteem, and they work to earn it. But the reward from on high is only a simple supper of soup and good cheese. Even here, those who closely examine the full range of society, beginning with the very highest ranks, will laugh at all this, although with tears in the corners of their eyes.

92.

If someone preaches to you his disdain for good lands, ask him how well he has dined. If someone tells you that God wished that those in authority among men should not necessarily be the most intelligent, tell him that this is probably just his idea and that, if it were implemented, it would be to teach us a lesson.

93.

Have pity on those who think that opinions can be bought with gold. Such an exchange works only for those who wish to be swindled and are seeking out a swindler.

94.

People who seek to raise up those who can no longer stand on their own two feet are working in vain.

95.

In Venice, certain magistrates masked themselves when they were rendering judgments. I would prefer that the accused be masked in that appearances can often pervert the facts of the case, and therefore it is justice itself that is masked, and not the judges or the accused.

96.

How often it occurs that inertia or negligence causes us to lose things that we later pay good money reacquire. Temperance, good humor, emotion, and blood enriched with the oxygen from pure morning air all serve to preserve one's youth which, in vain, we later seek its parody version with cosmetics and dyed hair.

97.

Just as we condemn orators who love the sound of their voices and never come to the end of their speeches, we should also condemn those who choose to live their lives by passing many hours with a seeming gentleness that is really nothing but infinite inertia. I generally find that the hidden cause of this fatal gentleness is a combination of sluggishness and laziness.

98.

The love of others carries with it the difficult virtue of self-denial. The love of self, when followed to its end, destroys the soul and creates the illusion that one can live forever.

99.

He who tries to use words to change another's passions becomes his enemy.

100.

Entreaties and flattery are the two passports used by cheaters.

101.

When you need to count on people to help you, remember that there will be fewer than one in a hundred who will act.

102.

I say that tact is that capability with which you can cause others to listen to you without either words or deeds. Many are born totally or nearly without this faculty, with the result that from time to time they come across as either ridiculous or obnoxious. There are others who do not cultivate their tact because of their foolish pride. The former are unfortunate by reason of birth. The latter instead prefer to walk wearing blinders. For you it should suffice to note that even emperors need this capability.

103.
Unless forced to, people will not tolerate that which hurts their sense of justice. Therefore, in prosperous times, you may eat, drink, and sleep without fear of offending others.

104.
Everything is connected. Denying the existence of free will carries with it the total non-responsibility of mankind, and this in turn leads to the denial of the existence of justice. Accordingly, power usurps human rights. I claim that the first denial can therefore be considered a scientific error. In any case, even if you doubt it, you should choose justice over power.

105.
Small heads have small thoughts; it is only natural. Do small thoughts only come from small heads? That is up to you.

106.
You must remember that in human affairs, a "yes" or a "no" may last for only one day, and sometimes not even that long.

107.
When Nature sometimes invites us to enjoy it or to suffer from it, it is pointless to follow the precept that orders you in absolute terms not to enjoy or not to suffer. In a fight between the precept and Nature, which is more likely to win the battle?

108.
Hurried and excited words indicate hot-headed feelings, and this can destroy your life. A long-lived person should speak soberly, slowly, and quietly.

109.

People who are ill-intentioned and eager for scandal will often share semi-secrets to stimulate others' curiosity and to promote the intrigues and clashes that they find so entertaining. Young people often fall into these sorts of traps.

110.

Save me O God from a bossy mother-in-law, gossipy sister-in-law, and a complaining wife.

111.

There cannot be good judgment in the absence of ideas and acquired learning. You will hear people speak freely about religion, medicine, and politics because each of us is quasi-certain that he is not speaking with someone who is truly learned in religion, natural sciences, history, economics, or finance. Therefore, you can almost always be certain that the speaker's opinions are merely drawn from tradition or that he is simply repeating someone else's words.

112.

As people age, they perceive the world to be getting worse, even though it is their age and not the world which is changing. It would be terrible if their energy and strength remained as their perceptions aged. Their increasing weakness detracts from any virtues, including tolerance, which dies when their hair loses its youthful color.

113.

Knaves often claim sham rights to exploit others' excessive good will, and the more benefits they are given, the more they believe they have a right to demand. This singular habit among debtors with respect to good-hearted people is the worst of all because instead of repaying their debts, they let them grow into a huge pile.

114.

Human virtue is mostly the result of collaboration, but with vices it is the opposite.

115.

Beware of small debts. By incurring them, you may start an avalanche that can drown a great fortune.

116.

I strongly recommend that my descendants pay careful attention to how others build their public image over the course of their lives. It is precisely with such image building that many crows dress themselves up in peacock feathers and succeed in living on in history even though there is not a shred of evidence that they are worthy of it, while many noted and deserving minds remain in unmerited obscurity.

117.

Small passions are exhaled and expire via the written word, while great ones are aroused and burst into flame by the same means.

118.

Use leads to abuse, and abuse leads to painful boredom; for this reason, we love variety. Always remember that the visitor on the seventh night is expected for the preceding six.

119.

Conscience is built largely upon what one has been taught: one's knowledge and one's experience. To believe that everyone's consciences are the same is like confusing the universal natural human feelings with the knowledge of one's duty, or the wild ignorant passions with morals illuminated by knowledge.

When we yoke together equality before the law, and the necessary training, we replace ignorance with serious analysis in dealing with the issue of injustice; conversely, if one transgresses in favor of ignorance in dealing with this issue, he succeeds in making injustice the norm. Thus, education is a necessary and canonical part of justice.

120.

So long as there are mysteries, there will be minds that incline toward mysticism.

121.

You are allowed to believe in unknown facts, but you are not permitted to force others to have faith in them. And yet, some people claim that others should follow their beliefs, and those who do not do so are hated, derided, and insulted.

122.

Experimental philosophers have not done experiments to explain why human intelligence, which they claim is a product of the brain, habitually gives itself over, by its very nature, to fantasy and mysticism. And, in a quiet moment, some of them forget that they should deplore this *natural* aspect of the intellect which appears to be voluntary and correctible.

123.

When the existence of an *idea* takes the place of *reality* in all of its forms, the terms *idea* and *reality* become one and the same.

124.

It is not always the case that dying and settling up are the final steps.

125.

In modern society, there are many orators and few doers who espouse the principles of liberty, equality, and fraternity.

126.

Some people's feelings tend to create spaces within which they grow, and outside of which they die.

127.

It helps to have a broad reputation as a superior person to be accepted as such by any given individual.

128.

In the majority of cases, democracy and demagoguery are masks for personal ambition and greed. Appoint a demagogue as a minister of state or give a million lire to a beggar and you will see.

129.

A person's daily waking time comprises sixteen hours. Of those, I would believe that fourteen are spent on all manner of passion, anxiety, and pain and the remaining two are divided among various hopes and a few joys. Between them, I think I have misspent my time today. It is true that with better training we could move the stars on this front.

130.

Beauty is a conspicuous asset, and wisdom can become one also.

131.

A lavish-spending woman often marries a timid man and is lost with an audacious one. Because they tend to prefer the former, for each one who rides in a coach, a thousand end up miserable and abandoned in the gutter.

132.

Virtue is never so strong as not to concede a bit to the desires of triumphant vice, and not to ask itself sadly from time to time in front of him, "Tell me, what are you?" Never!

133.

A man will say to you, "I ate ten loaves of bread" when there were two, and a woman "I ate some crumbs." when there were two loaves. The former pretends verbally to be a satyr, and the latter, a Dantean she-wolf[142] pretending to be a Roman Lucretia.[143] Those statements illustrate, at least intuitively, wherein lie the distinct powers of men and women: with the man it is in his strength, and he pretends to have much, and with the woman in her delicacy and restraint, and she pretends to these.

---

142 [In Dante's inferno, the she-wolf symbolizes the sin of avarice]

143 [In Roman history, Lucretia was the beautiful and virtuous wife of a nobleman. Her rape by the son of the tyrannical Etruscan king, Tarquinius Superbus, led to the revolt of the Romans against the Etruscan kings and the establishment of the Roman Republic.]

134.

Birth, marriage, and death are not always legitimate joys or sorrows. Enjoy them today without intoxication, or cry over them without excess on account of what tomorrow may bring.

135.

It is more difficult to walk on the straight and narrow path than to recognize it.

136.

People continually try to present their good side, and from this comes mankind's universal comedy. Forbear when this fiction reveals cheating, seduction, surprises, dramas, or tragedies.

137.

It is much more possible to predict the future than is commonly believed. Many in fact can see what is coming but instead of pulling hard on the oars, they allow the boat to drift, even as they tremble and hope that some saint or other will descend from Heaven to help them, even though they know that Heaven does not exist and they should instead say "descend from the air."

Many others, even if they do not believe in saints, when they foresee gloomy events or probable storms, despair at their ability to avert them with their own strength and lie quietly in their boat, like the legendary man who was pathologically attracted to Niagara Falls, closing their eyes and letting themselves be swept to the expected catastrophe and drowned. Such an approach represents total cowardice of spirit and renders certain what was only probable.

It behooves us to always remember that energy and courage can help to avoid the greatest dangers, because they find great strength in reason which remains sound when propped up by them. On the other hand, inertia and fear destroy reason, darkening and neutralizing it, and turn the feet of those who are drowning into stone.

138.

A pregnant woman doctor, lawyer, engineer, magistrate, member of parliament, government minister, or ambassador makes a jolly show as she seeks to evade ridicule for her state. However, in the case of a pregnant woman who is a good mother to her family, that ridicule is exchanged for a crown.

139.

There are minds that understand synthesis, others that are analytical, and yet others having both skills. The first have talent, the second ingenuity, and the third genius. They first see things in their entirety, in their broad outlines, and often know how to judge things correctly without delving into the details. The second ones are attentive, perspicacious, patient, and precise observers and are correct in the details but are myopic and incapable of stepping back and contemplating the entirety of what they are seeing. The third group tend to analyze, coordinate and abstract from the details and the entirety understandings that enable them to then discover principles underlying truth and progress.

140.

A young man came to me, offered his hand, and said, "Guess at what my future will be." I replied, "You are handsome, industrious, active, economical, and bold. You will become rich."

141.

In no case should words replace the prompt actions dictated by reason. When you talk instead of doing what reason says you should do, it is your feelings that are fooling you, making you think that you are reasoning when instead you are listening to your passions. If you look, you will discover the root of your major troubles in this fault.

142.

It is a bad doctor who only offers anatomy lessons to his sick patients.

143.

It is easier to be cured of a chronic disease than of a habitual vice.

144.

I have seen marvelously precocious minds suddenly go sterile and descend to below average levels. Others remained sleepy until maturity, awaken suddenly and soon rise to great fame, as happened to Isaac Newton. His youthful misuse of his mental and physical faculties led to intellectual impotence; and later, quiet study and temperance led to major strength.

145.

When you have chosen your path, think carefully before allowing yourself to be stopped or deviating in response to someone behind you shouting "Stop" or "Turn off."

146.

Do not trust a cobbler who offers to make you a suit. This is an old saw, but always true.

147.

An ignorant person will frequently begin his work in the most difficult way. It is for this reason that certain assemblers of sentences start off on the path to literary glory with a poem, novel, or comedy. Their best works are noted for their use of arcane or obscure words culled from the dictionary, around which sprout semi-digested or insipid ideas saturated with who knows what or loud belching over obscure principles.

The knights errant who fight for *My Italy* do so with the sole purpose of swapping this image for that of a vague Phryne[144] in their deranged imaginations. They expect to be praised when they die merely for espousing commonplace ideas that they did not know or understand.

148.

He who is reputed to be wiser above all others in his own time is the person whose works jibe with the central passions of the society in which he lives. Those are the restorers of ancient parchments, the collectors of old gold coins, the producers of the finest wines, etc.

He who is reputed to be wiser than everyone else for all time is the one whose works are and remain absolutely beautiful or beneficial over the ages.

149.

There exist words in the spoken language that are never heard in educated, honest, and polite conversation. Always remember that such words reveal rough and ignoble speakers to the ears that hear them.

---

144 [See Note 140.]

150.

A young man tends to take care of his body and clothing to please others. The old man takes the same care so as not to displease others.

151.

The power of an emperor is not of a fundamentally different nature from that of a cobbler. It is just of longer duration and extends over a wider domain in certain respects though it can be lesser in certain others. Francis Bacon spoke truly when he said that all human power depends on understanding what causes yield what effects.[145]

152.

You must never say that a given thing can or cannot exist without having studied the proofs. Among these, the experimental proofs are preferred to testimony, because the former can contradict the latter and not the other way round.

153.

Mankind is now and then subject to periods of fierce aberrations. If you find yourself caught in one of these and can keep your head, try to avoid it as you would the plague, unless your importance and authority constrain you to the sacred duty to devote your life to trying to cure people of their insanity.

154.

A rich person without work tends to travel to convince himself that he is accomplishing something.

---

[145] ['Knowledge and human power are synonymous since ignorance of the cause frustrates the effect.," Bacon, *Novum Organum*.]

155.

The saddest days of your life are those in which you have regrets.

156.

It is much more difficult to write one good word than to erase a thousand and destroying the lives of a thousand Herostratuses[146] would not have been equivalent to the effort to build the temple that a single one destroyed. But finding and removing weeds is like fighting and removing errors and is not destructive.

157.

The highest difficulty is to recognize a true error and know how to correct it effectively. But you can certainly find erroneous opinions that contradict natural and eternal laws, and over time they inexorably fade away.

158.

People consider having wealth or not to be the inverse of having or not having great problems. All other issues are for the most part mere pocket change. This is why we find that the pursuit of gold is mankind's primary and continuing objective.

159.

I have to admit that gold helps intelligence in two ways. It enables people to take the time to exercise their minds, and, at the same time it increases the value of those who truly succeed in increasing their intelligence.

---

146 [Herostratus sought fame in the fourth century BCE by burning down the temple of Artemis in the Greek city of Ephesus. He was executed and a law was passed prohibiting anyone from mentioning his name orally or in writing.]

160.

Money makes one rich, but character makes one a gentleman; therefore, you will find poor gentlemen and rich misers.

161.

When others are praised, we may be indifferent or annoyed, while people enjoy reviews and criticism of others' defects. If you look you will find the first phenomenon in those you admire when they approach you, and thus you have the illusion of great people appearing smaller in your eyes.

162.

Poets and novelists describe women in love as chatterboxes, which in nature they are not. Among birds, it is the male who sings; among people women tend not to bother with words to express their feelings. Rather they speak of their great love with the untranslatable language of their eyes.

163.

It is easier for a bad cause to find an excellent orator than for it to find an honest one.

164.

Even the greatest minds are not exempt from the illusion that they can replace the creations and images of others' imaginations with the severe and exacting conclusions of proper reasoning. Thus, the precepts taught by imposters, men of bad faith and the ignorant appear authoritative to many people.

165.

One can make an analogy between the sum total of human intelligence and a sphere whose shape furthers progress. The most elevated individuals and the lowest are at the antipodes, but all are pushing in the same direction, some with their heads and the others with their arms.

166.

Some leading people make a routine practice of pretending to stand aloof from daily human affairs either to generate publicity about themselves or to position themselves above others.

167.

Becoming illustrious is the most powerful revenge that one can have against others' insults.

168.

Their pride causes many brave men to isolate themselves, which neutralizes and sometimes destroys their power. This tendency runs counter to the normal human desire for sociability and action and is not the correct approach to acquire or maintain the esteem of others. The man who indifferently closets himself will fall unless he is proclaimed great for his past deeds, in which case he will be as one who has died famous. A similar fate befalls institutions which isolate themselves, because this activity runs counter to their intended purpose and is incompatible with doing good works.

169.

When a democratic government is not based on an educated populace, it can easily degenerate into a collection of petty tyrannies. What then happens is that its decrees run counter to the laws, and in place of its suppressed king[147] it produces many minor tyrants.

170.

On the contrary, when a society has a reasonably high level of education, any principle of authority that is not based on free elections might be tolerated for some time, but it does not have sound roots. Therefore, it follows that the primary and most important foundation of any despotic government is the ignorance of its populace.

171.

It has always been the case that the devout sanctify the use of force, violence, and fierce zealotry for their cause. These sanctifications are the parchment scrolls in which justice is quashed. On that account, be careful not to be among those of whom a holy prophet can have you fed to the wolves because someone yelled, "Turn him over to the bald man!"[148]

172.

If you have a vivid imagination and you enjoy mystical concepts, do not detach yourself too much from the world around you. Seek above all, to take pleasure in doing good and take into account the needs of those around you; aspire to reach Paradise by so doing even if you believe that only mystics will go there after death.

---

147 [At the time when Levi was writing, Italy's government was a constitutional monarchy. After the Fascist coup in 1922, Parliament was effectively overthrown and the king became Mussolini's puppet.]

148 [During the Middle Ages and Renaissance, friars and monks, and most notably, the rabble rousers among them who incited anti-Semitic pogroms, generally shaved their heads as a sign of sanctity.]

173.

The simplest ideas are often the most difficult ones to discover because of what surrounds them or the fuss that they cause among the people of the time.

174.

True eloquence is only acquired through accurate and impartial study of the work of those who disagree with our opinions. Unfortunately, we find it repugnant to dig through such writings and we fear finding our ideas undermined in the process. Thus, such eloquence is seen only rarely.

175.

A famous man wrote in his celebrated book that in the future, the moats of the mind will be filled. One could say the same about wisdom.

176.

In the mind of a donor, a gift is intended either to repay a debt or to establish a credit.

177.

Each debt that one takes on weakens his liberty, and this in turn entails a partial loss of his rights.

178.

People's laziness causes them to find it easier and more comfortable to be told what to do than to be self-directed. This causes them to readily adapt to tyranny both at home and in their government.

179.

One of the fatal consequences of despotic government is that the most influential people, the ones who come to mind for their fame, their lineage, or their leadership, are forced to set aside their own judgment and instead court the tyrant's approval to protect their own fortunes. Without exception this happens to all of them, as happened to Seneca before the parricide of Nero.[149]

180.

The liberty that people love most is that which allows them to follow their passions. To unfetter themselves from scruples, many ignorant people become followers of the deniers of God and his justice beyond the grave. But not even an avowed atheist finds value in the applause that comes from his vulgar followers.

181.

Do not dwell on your troubles. They are like a rope around your neck which you should not grab onto lest you strangle yourself.

182.

If you like to use your brain to shape ideas, do not let this desire detract from the time required to do your duties and supply the necessities of life. In Italy, certain clouds and fogs tend to spoil the kernels of grain, and you must never forget this.

---

149 [Seneca was a Roman playwright and moral philosopher. Agrippina, mother of the emperor Nero had installed Seneca as one of Nero's tutors, and he went on to serve as one of Nero's closest political advisors when Nero assumed the imperial throne at age 16. Nero has been accused of the later murder of Agrippina, who initially sought to rule through Nero and Seneca.]

183.

In speaking with someone, it is neither permitted nor useful to condemn people he holds or should hold dear. Doing so would be to assume that this person favors you over them, and therefore instead of interesting him, it causes him to hate you if you are wrong and embarrasses him if you are right. In either case it will cause him to consider you obnoxious.

184.

If you wish to be a real man, take everything seriously and avoid superficial foolishness in passing judgment.

185.

The thoughts produced in us in reaction to their opposites are always stronger than those that arise spontaneously. Thus, our feelings of friendship and love for someone we initially disliked are much deeper and last longer than those which spring up quickly. And the opposite case is also true.

186.

Each head has its world and each heart its theater, but they are like portraits. Even though they differ one from another, they all have one mouth and nose, two eyes and two ears. For this reason, whenever you express an idea, each person understands it in about the same way even though those understandings are never precisely the same.

187.

The only reliable indicator of true affection is self-denial.

188.

Action and inaction lie behind every good or bad deed. Between the wise and fair person who rues having done or not done something, and the fortunate one who laughs and boasts of his success, the remorse is the more legitimate emotion. My reasoning is certain on this.

189.

When rendering judgment on others whose activities are similar to yours, you risk drawing erroneous conclusions. Speaking from your brain, you could encourage your son to become a pastry chef, when he might want to be an architect or vice versa. Speaking from your heart, you could create or envy an unhappy person or deride someone who is content. Finally, if you are speaking of actions, you may criticize a wise person and denigrate an honest person or applaud their opposites.

Overall, an orderly brain will be open to the right path and a sensitive heart will respond to situations as it feels them.[150] Distrust your knowledge and tolerate things of which you disapprove. Openly and wisely condemn only those things that clearly threaten human life or knowledge. In these cases, you can be certain that your judgment is sound, that you are doing your duty. and you are not simply acting in response to your imagination.

190.

Poverty results in urgent demands and injustice. Wealth creates egotism and cruelty. When these two extremes meet each other, they do battle.

---

150 In this maxim as in others, I distinguish between the brain and the heart following the common view that the brain is the center of reason and the heart of emotion, even if this is not quite scientifically sound.

191.

Boredom does not cure sloth. In adults, this passion, vice, or defect is cured only by necessity.

192.

Gluttony, luxury, and amusements are made for those who can enjoy them. Thus, poverty can stimulate the development of knowledge because it cannot survive actions that work against it.

193.

The only situation in which people increase equally in dignity and honor is when they work together.

194.

Only for those who are entitled to public honor on their own merits is it permitted to publicly claim friendship with famous people. Nonetheless such claims are frequently made by ordinary folks. You should avoid doing so in order not to insult the relevant famous people and appear ridiculous.

195.

A person cannot be held to account for his lack of intelligence, or for his status due to birth or any number of social mishaps outside of his control that may have befallen him. He cannot be denied the dignity due to any worker, regardless of the nature of his work, unless he has willfully chosen infamous, ignoble, or servile work.

196.

We view our own value through the end of the telescope that enlarges, while others see it from the other end. Grow rich and powerful and the telescope turns in the opposite direction, both for us and for the others. Only the worthiness of the dead can be judged with the naked eye, and even then, not always.

197.

Wherefore doth the way of the wicked prosper? Wherefore are all they secure that deal very treacherously?[151]

Wherefore do the wicked live and grow old, and wax mighty in their power...they sing to the timbrel and harp and rejoice at the sound of the pipe.[152]

I was meditating one day on these passages from Jeremiah and Job ... why? ... why? and I said to myself, when people have neither scruples nor remorse, they happily cheat, swindle, deceive and steal to the sound of the organ, and then repeat until they wallow in wealth.

198.

It was the prophet Habakkuk, a holy prophet, who drew forth the argument about the seeming prosperity of sinners, when he said that God does not have eyes for evil. I who am neither a prophet nor a saint, say that each person says he is unhappy many days of his life, and in too many days he is in fact unhappy because he does not know whether or not God is truly blind to evil. I understand full well why it is wrong to thunder against such people in the Sabbath sermons.

---

151 [Jeremiah 12, which Levi quoted in Latin, given that all educated Italians in the 1800s would have been conversant in that language.]

152 [Job 21, 7-12, again quoted in Latin]

199.

One day a friend of mine asked, "Why is it that the Supreme Legislator, he who claimed to be the source of divine justice, proclaimed that children should be punished for the sins of their fathers?"

I responded, "In those days, children produced by those sins were the products of ignorant slaves and the impoverished masses, and today they are created by those who ride in carriages.[153] In the end, he who eats should pay, and doesn't that seem to be just."[154]

200.

Given a wide avenue and a narrow shortcut, both of which lead to fortune, the poor honest man will not get there, or will arrive too late to get his share, because he always chooses the first way.

201.

No one in the world is always virtuous, and no one is always wicked. The overall judgment of someone's life is the result of collecting and comparing his deeds and inclinations. If you then find that his bad outweighs his good, you can lay the bulk of the blame on the officials of the public education system.

202.

More often than you might expect, the public good is a gentleman who, when encountered on the street, is most often met by people who are not looking for him or is taken care of as dogs tend to do to

---

[153] [In ancient times, illegitimate children were born to the poor or enslaved and thus were themselves condemned to poverty. In modern times, they tended to be born of the rich, and thus were less likely to be condemned to poverty.]

[154] See maxim 207.

metal signposts. Among these people are too many who like to make a show of their own prosperity instead of helping the public at large. Nonetheless, this gentleman gains even from their insults.

203.
The modesty of famous people and other worthies can be compared to the indifference that beautiful women show toward their clothes. In the one case as in the other, people understand that there is no need for artifice to enhance the genuine.

204.
In every epoch there exist people who are above the law, which is an absolute black mark against progress and explains their social mobility.

205.
Music does not prove anything, but it excites and moves the emotions. Therefore, it is considered the most powerful, efficacious, and impressive element of public worship.

206.
People willingly imitate and learn reluctantly. They are drawn to imitation by jealousy and are kept from learning by their teachers' affronts to their self-esteem.

207.
There are cases in which the mandated legal sanctions should not be carried out because the punishments create greater wrongs than the original crime. Therefore, the balance of justice cannot always undo an accumulation of minor crimes. However, while death brightens the good, it cannot cancel out people's misdeeds.

208.

Men's preoccupations that gnaw the longest and most vividly are most often those inspired by envy, and those of women generally involve jealousy.[155]

209.

We should always protect our judgment from the impressions that it receives from our emotions because they are easily shaped by everything that surrounds us. They cause us to believe, doubt, deny, re-believe, re-deny, absolve, or condemn by unconsciously sculpting words and deeds, angels, and demons. But our reason can perceive the sculptor's chisel and either avoid or confirm its products. Therein lies the freedom to judge, and our ability to reason is reinforced by knowledge, and a body that is vigorous for its age and health.

210.

Many times, I succeed in overcoming an ugly mood by exercising my intelligence. And if I am unable to do so today or tomorrow, I will succeed in the following day. In these cases, neither my understanding nor my effort changed; instead, what changed was my strength. And when I succeeded, I would clap my hands and exclaim, "This much farther I can go."

211.

A man is always impatient for his pleasures; we all know that obstacles to them stimulate his appetite. Ambitious women know this also and use it to rule over men.

---

[155] See Maxim 111 in the Volume A.

212.

A person may believe that he can further his own interests by exaggerating another's capabilities, but never in discovering them.

213.

Do not isolate yourself if you do not wish to be lonely. And, if you wish others to come to your business, in search of useful or pleasing things, decorate the showcases as best you can. But you should remember that not everything which is pleasant is useful. Buffoonery and affectations are suitable for clowns, just like obscenities are to perverse fantasies, and you should never confuse a smile that brightens the face with the sneers that contort it.

214.

> "She had a pleasant face, sober clothing,
> A humble look in her eye, serious demeanor,
> A kind speaking voice, and so modest,
> She seemed to be Gabriel saying 'Hello.'
> But the rest of her was ugly.
> But she hid this wicked fact.
> In a long wide dress, and under that
> Always carried a vicious knife."

It was Lodovico Ariosto[156] that thus described Fraud and Deception in the sixteenth century.

Today she is much richer, and in addition to the long wide dress, often changes her clothes and in truth I can no longer distinguish her from others. But many times, when I thought of her as a queen, I discover from her acts that I have been fooled.

---

156 [Lodovico Arioso (1474-1533) Italian poet and diplomat from Modena]

215.

Concern yourself only with the material needs of your peers and permit them to take care of their own spiritual needs. But you should remember that teaching can do no harm on the latter front and will reflect well upon you.

216.

If you arrive at the point of well-earned public esteem, the first indication that you have gotten there will be when others affect disdain and direct unfair criticism and other poisonous arrows toward you. When you see such rage due to frivolous envy, which is as impotent as it is nasty, you should be happy and remember Maxim 167, which I repeat here: "Becoming illustrious is the most powerful revenge that one can have against others' insults."

217.

A person of genius is one who can see, express, or act better or earlier than everyone else.

218.

The duration of pleasures or physical pain gives us a sense of the duration of moral joys and pains. Being with your beloved and all manner of successes are joys that last an hour or maybe a day. Gout, cancer, other chronic diseases, falls, losses and the like are pains that last for months, years, or forever and are perhaps life threatening,

Is this the justice of God? This is the wisdom which is embedded in the law that governs the life in us for its current mode of being. Because if pleasure lasted as long as pain, we would commit suicide, or kill each other or we would rest upon our laurels, or we would be reduced to idiocy by dwelling on our pleasures.

And why doesn't our existence lend itself better to prolonged pleasure than to perpetual pain? I know how I am, or I endeavor to learn it. I do not know how I will be, or if there might be another mode of being different from what I am now. We should never discuss the properties of non-existent beings or of people we do not know.

219.

It is unwise to forget that in everything you say and do, people always suspect good or bad motivations, Sometimes, success perverts judgment. A person may keep quiet, or mask his thoughts, or exaggerate to appear at the peak of his reputation or power. Thus, the written story may not be the true one. Oh, how many statues would be reduced to mere cement or small coins if the light of truth and justice were shone upon them; and how many graves that yesterday were neglected would today be bedecked with flowers!

220.

You should erect a monument to your mind if you can. It alone can be believed without any legitimate doubt if it withstands the judgment of time.

221.

In political struggles, there is a great difference between those who battle in good faith to produce that which is for the public good, and those who battle simply for the triumph of their own ideas and to achieve personal supremacy. In truth these two types of political battles cannot be easily distinguished. But between these types, you will recognize the better one by how the patriot behaves. He is firm in his convictions, speaks little but does much, does not seek power, does not require us to chain ourselves to him, focuses on principles and the interests of society as a whole, and only rarely on the interests of the people and things that are close to him. And when he does act in his own interests, it is only when they are consistent with the principles and interests of society. The nation is what matters to him, and he walks with his head held high without paying attention to the gold that is being spread at his feet, preferring to live modestly than to stoop to collect that money. His objectives are the current common good and a laudatory page in the history of the times as it will be written in the future.

The ambitious person instead will help himself to that gold and public adulation, using terror, slander, and all manner of seductions to gain them. He afflicts, pressures, corrupts, and is always ready to put on a mask, riding roughshod over every principle, stepping on and defiling every noble idea simply to acquire more power, honors, distinctions, medals, and titles. He is indifferent as to whether he does good or evil, and is an archangel today and a devil tomorrow, because he is high, powerful, dominant, and a prince.[157] Such a person follows the formula of "After me, the Deluge.[158]"

And thus are the two extreme types of politicians; between these two extremes there are many gradations.

222.

Even knowledge can result in ridicule or intolerance of the poor.

---

157 ["Prince" in the Machiavellian sense.]
158 [This quote is generally attributed to King Louis XV of France; Indeed, his successor, Louis XVI lost his head to the guillotine during the French Revolution.]

223.

The road up from zero runs along the edge of cliffs and is as narrow as the blade of a knife. Furthermore, there are breaks in it that require you to jump, from zero to five lire, then back to three. It is a great miracle that most itinerant peddlers do not slide down at break-neck speed.

Also, next to this path there are certain holes that lead directly to Heaven, but their entry ways are closed to those with large tender hearts. To enter, you must have a heart that is so small and hard to serve as a knife. Mix together the verbs *play* and *win*. Know how to show that to *absorb* is not a synonym of *to rob, and* you will be able to pass through those holes in a gilded carriage without falling and smashing onto the rocks at the bottom.

Nonetheless, you will reach a quiet town at the top of that narrow road, generally after a long and arduous journey. Courage, poor brother, and endure the pains to your hands and feet on that harsh journey along that straight and narrow road and you will reach that town by the sweat of your brow. Above all, avoid the holes that lead the devious to the temple of fortune, and avoid that fancy carriage. Remember that those others are skirting the laws and will or should end up before a judge, where their bad reputations will destroy their public image.

224.

Knowing how to proceed in every situation can render us proud and disdainful of our peers, which all too frequently results in people rightfully saying, "That one thinks he is God in the flesh."

225.

Honeyed words offer sterile promises. The benefactor frequently uses the word *give* and rarely the word *say*.

226.

When people who have risen to the speaker's rostrum or achieved an office of high honor look out at everyone else from on high and imagine themselves superior to those down below, they must remember that down below is the person who will judge them. Easily achieved honors can be the Capua[159] of merit.

227.

In love, women tend to show off their beauty and men their good minds. In this way the stronger sex strongly shows its nobler and less egotistical spirit.

228.

Great political revolutions do not occur without stimulation from the people's unmet fundamental needs or the hunger that threatens or afflicts the masses. The real motives of such revolts are always "bread and life." In such revolutions, however, those needs are often masked by ambitious hypocrites.

229.

Our intelligence is measured by the range of our observations and experience. Any other metric is merely conjectural or imaginary. It is pointless to complain that two plus two equals four if what you wanted was three.

---

159 [Capua was city north of Naples that was repeatedly destroyed by invaders, first the Vandals and later the Arabs.]

230.

Every new discovery is based on new reasoning, and to overturn the prior understanding, you must show it to be false.

231.

Above all else, we prefer our own judgments, and therefore it is exceedingly difficult or impossible to root them out. Our laziness causes us to gladly adopt the testimony of others with whom we agree, even if their assertions are illogical.

232.

Move closer to the distant image that appears through the shadows to be a man lying on the ground with a rifle aimed at the street and you will find a tree.

233.

However great a man may be, his reason frees itself only occasionally from the middling culture in which he was brought up and in which he continues to live. Accordingly, rejection of that culture is essential for all who aspire to fame for great deeds.

234.

Time is a sponge which often can erase all in one formidable sweep. It is beneficial and provident when it glides over everything and makes it disappear, as it generally tends to do.

235.

Civilized people never lose their original propensity to organize themselves into distinct families, tribes, communities, and nations. Among primitive peoples, physical valor served to designate their leaders and grant them royal esteem. Today, when various social circles represent the tribe, community, nation, or complexes of related nations, leaders are selected on the basis of their daring, shrewdness, subterfuges, and their art of exploiting the inertia and indifference of the many. In some cases, cliques or riches, however they were acquired, determine leaders, and in others, abstention, partisan spirit, and the strength of the many meritorious people outweigh personal valor as criteria for selecting political and administrative leaders. And, as you may know or sense, the leaders' authority is weakened because various public offices are no longer recognized as unquestioned sources of public esteem.

236.

It is truly the case that many people's views of themselves are fictional characters drawn to enhance their self-worth. He who believes such images of false praise and false defects is a fool.

237.

Those involved in the hard sciences tend in general to dismiss too easily all other areas of study, a tendency that exaggerates their own self-respect. Those who observe the truth through experiment or calculation tend to have that approach as a personal value in their daily lives; this is a most exaggerated metaphysics, one that thinks everyone else is a torch that is going out. The science types think themselves superior. While maintaining maximum respect for those among them who are great scholars, and even more so for their important discoveries, when I see such behavior, I privately laugh to myself.

238.

Every object of human thought can be subjected to analysis and synthesis. But the extreme ends of such analysis fades into the unknown. Everything is a long chain of which only some of the links can be seen. This truth is known to the wisest people, whether or not they see it willingly, and this makes them humble.

239.

One of Envy's methods is to make itself an enthusiastic advisor.

240.

It is an essential part of any vocation not to be discouraged by adversities, obstacles, or falls.

241.

Never trust promises made contrary to your passions.

242.

Love, no matter how elevated, and luxury both have the common objective of possession; honest commerce and gambling both have the aim of profit. By their different means and not by their objectives do we distinguish between virtue and vice.

243.

I note that human society is divided into different classes; people of the lower levels look upwards and envy, hate, criticize, abuse, slander, condemn, and curse those above them or, speak well and love them. Those of the higher strata appear to not concern themselves with their inferiors, hardly glancing at them, and use their inferiors as mere stepstools to enable them climb to higher levels.

I wish that a powerful and broadly distributed element of teaching would cause each person to see that society is organized in its natural and ordinary way. Then each person could look at himself in the mirror and discover that the happiest people on earth are those with the healthiest bodies and the most cultivated minds.

244

Constancy is a virtue that takes work. However, it is the prime driver of achieving results, be they derived from good or bad motivations.

245.

People are drawn to the news of the direst catastrophes because of their desire to hear about new things, and not because they feel a perverse joy in others' misfortunes. We enjoy hearing about new things, then we shed a tear over the disaster, cordially commiserate with the victims, and deplore the consequences. The unfortunate part of this behavior is that somehow the "I" of personal action does not enter into the situation, and bad news merely tickles the heart a bit.

246.

The imagination is excited by a natural desire to see magical wonders and to encounter the unknown. The mind often conjures up false images in place of what would come from judgments produced by careful and deep study of a given situation. These images are based on desires and are usually devoid of reason which would cause them to dissipate and result in disappointment.

It is precisely to avoid this disappointment that many people's lives and deeds are driven by these fantasies, and they silence their inner voice that would tell them to think, study and then judge.

247.

Above all else, people need to love and believe, and frauds are built upon this need.

248.

Brilliant minds are characterized by the ability to assemble diverse ideas into coherent arguments that the public accepts or that result in works that are broadly pleasing or useful. Sooner or later people who can do this will receive public acclaim.

249.

People sometimes become widely recognized because of their condition, good luck, physical endowments, or some other special quality, but when this condition passes, their lofty renown often lands them in a ditch.

250.

The essence of human reason is founded on the principle of contradiction. We cannot reliably make judgments without facing their opposites.

251.

A person's crazy desire to control others turns into bullying, which results in his having to fight continuously to maintain his position.

252.

Always seek to say the most you can with the fewest words.

253.

No matter how good or helpful a complainer is or how much he is loved, people do not listen to him.

254.

I have always sought to overcome my defects, and admitting to them is the first step. Sometimes this remedy is also sufficient, but it always makes me feel better.

255.

People have an intense desire to make others have sympathy for them. You will find few people who won't tell you tales about the fortune they narrowly missed earning, the great job they did not get, or how they were only one digit shy of winning the lottery.

256.

Block a plant from growing in its normal shape and you will produce a monstrosity. Such is also the case with people.

257.

People do not always admit to themselves the reasons for which they move their hands and feet.

258.

Widely distributed bread renders people less fierce and evil. Therefore, the Minister of Finance is the high priest of public morality.

259.

When money is the only measure of value of ideas, beware of the benefits that are said to be created. The more that people dress up savings in these terms, the sooner the storm will break.

260.

The profit column on the income statement of stock market speculators has to balance out with what others have lost or paid.

261.

Ten clever billionaires say, "Give us a desert and we will plant vegetables and form a company to float a stock offering under our leadership that will rise to a premium in the public. When the company is wound up, the shareholders will share in the profits from the harvested beans," And then they will succeed. Good for them.

262

The current mania of getting rich quickly and without effort by any possible wicked means has diverted many bright minds from vigorous study and beneficial undertakings. Industrial development and the increase in its associated commerce, and the increased honors and pay associated with them can go at least part of the way to remedying this unfortunate situation.

263.

To free himself from serious concerns, the vulgar and unprincipled person speaks easily except when fear forces him to tell the truth.

264.

When we exaggerate about the value of a given thing, our mind diminishes the value of other things, and thereby we use doubly false judgment.

265.

Keeping silent about your innermost thoughts is said to be concealment. To espouse ideas contrary to own thoughts is said to be hypocrisy. Concealing your thoughts because of shyness is often called prudence, just as prudence in some cases is another name for fear. In any case, willing or not, keeping some of your thoughts to yourself is indispensable for social peace and tranquility. On the other hand, hypocrisy is a form of worship of another person and always is motivated by a desire to mislead others.

266.

Given two people, one of whom always looks at everything only from the bad side, and the other only from the good, the latter will be cheated more easily, but will have a happier life and be considered the better man.

267.

In the course of one's life, there are significant occasions when luck shines. It is important to recognize and take advantage of them because, once they are past, they will never return on account of the continuing change that is an inherent part of our lives.

268.

Progress increases the sum total and our understanding of virtuous acts, and therefore we cannot have a fixed, rigid understanding of morality.

269.

Hope is a counterfeit currency that we all take to be minted gold coins.

270.

In the moment that a person claims to be totally disillusioned with the world, he shows himself under the power of an illusion.

271.

The fastest way to become obnoxious and hated is to claim to always be right in judging everyone else's thoughts and deeds.

272.

The public tends to make way for bold and ambitious people, and to applaud when they fall.

273.

The pleasure of having others obey your commands is greater than that of familial love. One's self-esteem appears to be tickled more by others' fear of you than by their love.

274.

Envy alone is insufficient to push someone to denigrate and minimize the distinctive accomplishments of others. Generally speaking, it also takes a generous dose of ignorance to convince him that he can succeed in so doing.

275.

People do not love those they fear or love them only slightly. Some men have the perverse idea that there are some women who become attached to men who beat them.

276.

In making judgments, people tend to progress from the specific to the general. Thus, many people attribute the bad action of an individual to his race, his caste, his family, or his ancestry. But this type of group responsibility for the action of an individual is inherently unjust, and furthermore also suffers from the effect that people tend to remember the bad more willingly than the good. In this way the obligation to stay on the straight and narrow path is imposed not only by duty, but also the requirement for justice for others.

277.

Who knows, for example, who Pietro Mattei was?[160] When I think that even though Giulio Strozzi's[161] work was noted in the historical annals of the King of France written by the great Tacitus[162] of France, and whose works were translated in London by the secretary of the Venetian ambassador, that those works along with their author are completely unknown today, I am struck by the impermanence of fame. When I see you, dear brother, strutting, boasting, and carrying in your arms a sheaf of printed pages spread out like a peacock's tail, I can

---

160 [Pietro Mattei was a Pre-Dantean Italian poet of the 1200s, whose work has been largely forgotten.]
161 [Giulio Strozzi, a Venetian poet of the 1600s and the librettist for several of Monteverdi's lost operas]
162 [Levi is making an ironic reference to an official French historian comparing him to Tacitus who was born in Gaul and was perhaps the greatest historian in ancient Rome.]

imagine your thoughts that you are making an impression of "I am the Lord" based on the way you are presenting yourself, and I shudder.

278.

Study and write if doing so gives you pleasure; Endeavor to do your duty to be useful and seek to keep healthy. Your fantasies of being an eternal flame or of becoming one are a hope which, so long as it remains sealed within you, cannot become the source of ridicule.

279.

The smile of a woman you desire spurs you on and that of a woman you have won is often a fire extinguisher; the whip, a goal, a prize, a chain, or another clipping of the wings, these things are the soft wax of which the male sex is made.

280.

When a strong passion wells up within you, your poor reason shrinks, and should it timidly speak up, you shrug your shoulders and set it aside for a better time. In very many cases you hear its voice too late; my poor reason, how right you were!

281.

You will find the perfect gentleman among the most independent people, and the perfectly gentle man among the neediest.

282.

Never push your presumptions to the point of having no doubt about your strength nor your modesty to the point of self-loathing. The former causes you to jump over graves[163] and the latter renders you impotent.

283.

Our passions are not all at the same level. Reasoning ought to lord it over all the others but that is not always the case. That is why there is so much discord and misery in the world.

284.

Why do reasonable people constantly ask us to teach and educate the people to make it possible for the community's higher values to dominate over base ones? They do so because people's personal interests motivate their activities, but their accomplishments are driven by their passions, if those passions are noble or elevated, so will be their accomplishments.

285.

Our need for the admiration of others is the real representation of God among the people on earth.

286.

There are people who attribute value to various individuals, and this value is always measured relative to their power to produce. A rich man can borrow, a wise man is admired, and monuments are put up to commemorate exemplary people, all in proportion to what their power and subsequent production were beforehand. Later on, people correct the errors in their views of those who merit revised reputations in proportion to what followed, so that others will not be misled by false witness.

---

163 [i.e., take undue risks.]

287.

In general people like to hear stories. It is important to examine the facts underlying those tales before believing them.

288.

We can define *justice* as a series of ideas that are consistent with the law and guide our judgment as to how to protect and extend human life and intelligence. We can define *morality* as the practical application of justice. But we must not confuse the concept *application* with that of *guide*. The laws which guide our ideas of justice exist outside of our personal will and knowledge while morality is exercised only to govern our personal actions or inactions. Each judicial ruling is necessarily related to the laws and therefore extends the series of ideas that comprise justice and its applications. Thus, it is said that morality effectively evolves over time.[164]

289.

Some people who were unrecognized in their lifetime are later seen as more important, either because of merits that were unknown in their lifetime or because of unrecorded or forgotten misdeeds. In the first case it is a question of justice being served and, in the latter, they have become eminent merely on account of good luck.

290.

A sign of true modesty is having a character that is always affable and merry and being someone that gives little importance to his own "I." Truly modest people never appear as benefactors because of their desire not to seem powerful, which renders their virtue worthy

---

[164] See Maxim 268.

of gratitude rather than praise. In fact, the truly modest rarely go unthanked.

291.

The practice of dueling constrains men to undertake manly training; it brings them to the same level in important situations, reinforces the respect that men owe each other, supports the principle of equality, and serves as a safety valve which helps to avoid fierce and predatory vendettas in response to low and prolonged disputes.

Even if we permitted duels on the theory that the sacrifice of a few people's lives would protect the many, we logically should consider this practice to be inherently immoral. It is immoral simply because it is unjust; the plaintiff must allow the responding party the free choice of rules and weapons. Instead, we should leave the cases that used to result in duels to be decided by fair and impartial third parties who would decide how to resolve issues of honor and fair recompense in the cases where there is no voluntary resolution between the parties.

292.

Paying compliments, forcing the face to deliver a faint smile and exercising the voice to issue honeyed words is hard work for a gentleman. Therefore, face to face encounters are unpleasant, as these require bowing and scraping and people avoid doing this willingly, just like they try to avoid running into a creditor to whom they owe money when settling up would be difficult.

293.

Holding fast to your principles in the face of facts that seem to point in the contrary direction is truly a sign persistence in great men. This difficult capability is admirable because it reveals an unusual force of will and, above all, shows courage.

294.

I always feel well disposed toward those who tip their hat toward me, notwithstanding my long experience of the emptiness of this gesture.

295.

The offenses that unprincipled people make are the mental seeds of their hatred toward their victims.

296.

Houses built close together with multiple stories for better illumination, and current fashions in clothing, household furnishings, and modern cookery all have a strong influence on customs, practices, religion, and legislation.

297.

When things happen that you could not have caused or prevented, and these result in a good or bad outcome of an undertaking of yours, it is said that you have had either good or bad luck. In such cases, praise or disapproval are equally inappropriate, even if they are customary,

298.

In practical life physical attractiveness and sweet manners often erase the provisions of the penal code.

299.

Some are born rich and at the entryway to the temple of glory; others who are poor are disdained or ignored.

Princes, dukes, other nobles, billionaires, and the "vile multitudes" are all equal in the grave, but we vainly speak of equality during their lives. If Vauvenargue[165] had not been a marquis, and Leopardi[166] a count, they would not have been lauded, respectively by Voltaire and by Giordani,[167] whose praise made them seem great.

300.

One could believe that the mysterious force called attraction is the fundamental cause of all the phenomena of the universe and its ultimate end will be a big crunch. It is generally observed as attraction and repulsion, aspiration and respiration, aggregation and disaggregation, or life, death, and life renewed. But one of the effects of this attraction or what it causes must in some way be consciously and willfully compatible with intelligent life. If its end is to be an infinite crunch, its ways of proceeding are manifestly infinite, and in the choice of these methods there must be one or more intelligent arbiters.

If all is constrained to operate in an unchangeable cycle to contribute to new aggregations, those who have a certain amount of judgment can accelerate or retard a given moment in this process, either supporting or impeding one of those processes within the limits of their own strength. Understanding the ongoing operations and the natural end of this overwhelming force is knowledge. Arguing in favor of these processes to the degree of one's knowledge is just and good, while

---

165 [Luc de Clapiers, Marquis de Vauvenargue (1715-1747) wrote a volume of moral essays and aphorisms that was praised by Voltaire.]
166 [Count Giacomo Leopardi (1798-1837), an Italian philosopher, essayist, and poet]
167 [Pietro Giordani (1774-1848) an Italian writer and literary critic, who defended the classical Italian literary tradition from the criticism of Mme. De Stael, who thought Italian writers should adopt the then fashionable French romantic style.]

arguing against them is unjust and bad. The former is to be praised and the latter punished.

And the underlying cause of this force, mediated or not, is it something supreme? Absolute cause?! People cannot reason about things of which they cannot conceive.

CHARGE

Descendants who might be alive a century from now, assuming that you have read this writing and carefully meditated upon it, if you agree with it, please erect a stone tablet over the bones of he who wrote it. On it incise one or another of these maxims assuming people's inattention has not dispersed them and that they have become elements of the collective unknown.

End of the Maxims

ILLUSTRATIONS

ILLUSTRATION I

2. Today's civil marriage laws contradict true morality in that they do not recognize the role of physical beauty and are contrary to the breadth of people's ideas.

No other of my maxims has rendered me as hesitant as this one before I decided to leave it as written, even though I had long ago become persuaded of its truth. This truth is based on careful and accurate observations and deep meditation. These laws clash so violently with deeply rooted and most precious communal ideas. It includes an accusation that it is closely tied to the influence of Jewish thought on the western world. And, in the end, they strike violently against many dictates of the religious, civil, and penal systems. Even a mighty tome would be insufficient to give an adequate and well-illustrated magistrate's analysis of this issue. This slim volume, which by its nature is only a synthesis of ideas, is not the proper place for such an analytical exposition. The reflective mind which is composing it does not want, and not wanting, is unable to publish preliminary studies on this subject.

I choose to discuss in brief one of these maxims on such a weighty subject to please those who enjoy reflecting on varied subjects. I do not mean to write an essay expounding the development of my ideas with detailed and weighty arguments. And, besides, where would I find the time and money to do so? Would I write a daily journal whose success would earn me great riches and flattery in exchange for my good or perverse thoughts or for such information that the world would deem valuable? Absolutely not! Would I write comedies, dramas, tragedies, or fragments of such as I have seen done? Would I paint images of human nature such as Phryne, Medusa, Minerva, or Atropos,[168] great figures with feet of clay, or dwarves who become giants by standing on the backs of the blind? Should I depict crocodiles weeping for the victims they have devoured or laughing at those they have killed, monsters who kiss people sweetly, or angels who allow themselves to be martyred? And how many things would need to be included in the picture? What different colors must I use and mix together so that impossible images would emerge from the haze, which no one would believe other than those who can see the sadness of spilled blood or the sin in the foam on the lips, all the while giving intoxicating joy to those who imagine it pure. Most people would dismiss these as insane works, or the work of Harlequin[169] who howls and laughs scornfully at his victims. And a few people would engage in careful study, lengthy meditation, febrile hesitation, and settle their mind on a profound conviction that all this stormy turbulence is based on a deep understanding of the human spirit. They would obscure and obfuscate the true vision of the work for long periods of time.

---

168 [Phryne was a Greek courtesan of such extraordinary beauty, that the judges were dazzled and let her off when she was on trial for impiety; in Greco-Roman mythology, Medusa was a woman so hideous that men turned to stone upon seeing her and Minerva (or Athena in Greek) was the goddess of wisdom and Atropos was one of the three Fates.]
169 [Harlequin was the jester in *La Commedia del Arte*.]

Oh, my will and firm judgment, what perchance would be your prize? Harlequin's motley clown suit? Should I remain eternally closed up like a plant in a cave, which grows and grows to show its pale though perhaps enduring flower through the narrow opening?

This project arose partly of necessity, and partly because, wrapped up in my cloak, I find it a sweeter pleasure to work than you might expect. And as you can easily see, I have digressed from the maxim that I had undertaken to explain to follow the whimsy of my sometimes-angry pen. Therefore, please excuse me and listen carefully.

It is a natural truth that the sexes attract each other (and do not laugh too soon, remembering M. La Palisse[170]) but this attraction acts differently according to whether you consider it in general or as it applies to specific individuals.

In general, whatever its cause, that attraction is stronger in males than females, probably because of their exuberant strength that drives their powerful need to reproduce. In the case of individuals, love, desire, respect, compassion, sympathy, and the like are not necessarily found to the same degree in two people of opposite sexes who are joined together. That results in the attractive force working to differing degrees between them. Also, it can be changed in one or the other spouse by hundreds of different circumstances in their private and social lives that work to undermine it day by day and hour by hour. In the majority of cases, it is finally destroyed in both spouses, or at least in the unhappier one of the pair.

---

170 [I.e., as plain to see as the nose on your face, taken from the satirical song, *La Chanson de La Palisse* which mocks chivalric virtues. The song takes its name from Jacques II de Chabannes, Seigneur de La Palisse, an officer in the French army who was killed in battle at Pavia in 1525, of whose glorious death it was said, "Poor La Palisse, if he were not dead, he would be yet alive." There is now a candy in France, Vérités de la Palisse, which comes wrapped in papers imprinted with the verses of the song.]

But such circumstances are not entirely natural because there are two types of jealousy with fundamentally different roots. One is a natural result of the human condition and the other is purely artificial. The natural one is that motivated by the desire for exclusive love from the beloved. The artificial one is that which arises from that presumed right, and from the fear that children born outside of the marriage will intrude and lay claims upon the wealth and affections within the family.

From this factual distinction emerges a corollary that, while natural jealousy is an inherently and unavoidable human sentiment, the artificial one could be removed if we modify or remove the underlying rules from which it originates. The Oriental ideas that were introduced into Latin culture have come to tie a woman to only one man for the entirety of her adult life, and to make him a thing that she possesses for life.[171] Once this idea was introduced into the western world, it expanded, as such things tend to do, to the point that it triumphed over all the ideas of common sense.

This triumph was both a benefit, in that it resulted in the abolition of polygamy, and a detriment in that it excluded divorce, a practice that we think of as barbaric practice, but one that could help restore happiness to the human race.

The invention of mechanized warfare and industry and many other factors have favored the spread of sybaritic luxury, enervating habits, and cheap pleasures. Also, the creation of mass movements, a direction in which all of mankind is turning, is reducing the drive of individuals. These forces and many others are producing a veritable decline in the energy and strength of the people. It may be the case that the need to oppose this weakening will force civic political measures to permit divorce as a public health measure. What I mean is that this

---

171 [In Italy, divorce was illegal until 1970.]

logic will inspire the practice of free choice in marriage among the strongest and most attractive.

When we read that in antiquity some great men would lend out their beautiful wives to friends who wished to have attractive children, this fact justifiably arouses in us a sense of horror and disgust. That was a direct consequence of the detestable idea that women were mere playthings without hopes or power of their own.

But then today we see cruel parents who frequently condemn their children to a living martyrdom, tying the young to the old, the beautiful to the ugly, the healthy to the sickly, all for financial gain or vanity. Consequently, we see beautiful people remaining barren, facing the choice between remaining painfully unsatisfied for life or being subject to sneering ridicule whenever they appear in public. From this arises misery, discord, vice, abuse, and self-denial. The victim and her executioner are mated together, violently constrained to be paired off for all time. We should feel horror and disgust at such a situation. Thus, I have found over my many years ample reason why our children should seek to remedy these problems with our current marital laws.

ILLUSTRATION II

3. Do not worry about having excessive progeny. Remember that there have been few only children who have become great men.

Benjamin Franklin was the fifteenth of Josiah Franklin's seventeen children. It is our good fortune that his father was not as scared by the arrival of the fourteenth, as you and I might have been.[172] He knew his wife yet again, to use the chaste Biblical expression, and from that union sprang the great man.

However, I would not advise any friend or you, dear reader, to express yourself in such a great number of children in the hope of producing after the fourteenth, a Benjamin Franklin; but, by the faith in God, I would like to give you some brotherly advice., If you are greatly afraid of being surrounded by a great number of children, do not marry. There are certain things you must master in any calling, at the risk of things going seriously awry.

If you marry, God willing, a chaste woman, with whom you undertake to exercise certain desires of brotherliness, friendship, and obeisance, either you will create a story in which your desires will be satisfied by the time that the curtain falls and you will fall asleep, or better yet, you will both fall asleep, concerned only that you might produce the twelve tribes of the Bible. Conversely, if your marriage is not consummated, your wife will become an embittered complainer, an angry, hysterical, mortified, anxious, and dejected woman. And that is what you will have in place of being surrounded by children you did not want. You will need to hire a doctor and adopt the pharmaceutical handbook as your prayer book. It would be horribly shameful to marry a young woman to give her over to leeches, to be cauterized, or to be burnt with silver nitrate.[173] For shame!

If you marry, God forbid, a woman of fiery spirit and then, my son, you treat her as if she were your sister, she will behave like a wife with other men. In such a situation, a great man like Benjamin Franklin

---

172 [Recall that Levi and his wife, Benedetta Debenedetti, had twelve children; after his death she married Levi's younger brother Samuele and upped the total to fourteen.]

173 [Silver Nitrate was a common 19th century antiseptic. The reference here is to potentially induce sterility.]

might be born in your household, and you would be at fault for not having caused this. The result would be that you would undergo the punishment of those poor little birds that wear themselves out raising a cuckoo.[174]

Marriage is a serious business that has to be undertaken seriously. This is a perfect example of the saying from the satirist, Marchese Colombi, "Things are done or not done."

ILLUSTRATION III

14. A focus on making money is an undertaking that can lead to a quiet ferocity in which throats are cut politely or even while laughing. How many nooses have been hoisted with gloved hands? What does it matter if the acquired money is minted from mud? It is picked up anyway. You do not even see their money lust which masquerades as Thalia.[175] In fact, the respectable public drunkenly cries "BRAVO" to the teacher as his money banishes their perception of his evil deeds.

It is said that this situation is fair because lending money to the person who owns a building entails less risk than loans to poorer people. There is no doubt that there is higher risk in loans to the latter and good heaven, one needs to pay for this risk. I claim that while you can borrow at five percent, an honest poor person either has to pay through the nose or duck his obligations with myriad strategies.

---

174 [The cuckoo is a parasitic bird, which lays its eggs in the nests of smaller birds and burdens them with the work of raising a nestling that is not their own and that kills their legitimate offspring.]
175 [In Greek mythology, Thalia was the Muse of comedy and bucolic poetry.]

Consequently, a person might agree to a loan at the usurious rate of 1000%.[176]

Now I will argue the other side. I have observed that the risk is the pretext which makes it possible to charge more for a loan than it is worth. Suppose you lend money to a worker at a rate of thirty percent or more if you can, with an agreement that repayments will be made with monthly installments taken from his salary. There is still a risk, but it is a risk that can be mitigated with life insurance whose premiums are understood to be tied to the loan. Thus, if the borrower dies, the loan would be repaid.

Alas, the workers to whom one makes loans are for the most part young and relatively few of them are worth bleeding.[177] The government believes that its staff should be protected from this feast of the vampires.[178] That is a serious error. For the few among them that need substantial loans, the risk is thus raised, and the banks are pulling out of the business. It used to be possible to repay the excessive amount charged by appealing to the sympathy of the lender. Today when there is an elevated risk of getting no repayment from government employees, banks are limiting their loans to them to small amounts at high interest rates. As for loans in excess of one thousand lire[179] it would not a take a Mr. Minghetti[180] to see that banks would not offer unsecured loans without the payroll guarantee.

---

176 [It is worth noting that Levi's paternal ancestors were Renaissance money lenders, somewhere on the spectrum between bankers and pawn brokers. Also, his wife's paternal ancestors were Renaissance bankers of the more conventional sort, mostly engaging municipal and sovereign lending.]

177 [That is, for only a few of these people is the return worth the risk.]

178 [i.e., from payroll deductions to repay their loans]

179 [1000 Lire in those days would translate to about $14,000 in modern money.]

180 [Marco Minghetti (1818-1886) was an Italian politician who led several different cabinet departments over the years, including the Finance Ministry from 1860-1876.]

And here I would like to publicly expose many examples, but that is not permitted. However, having removed the public employees from the talons of money lords (I assume that you will not object to this non-standard term), these employees would be exposed to the same risks as railroad workers[181] and would pose the following as yet unsolved problem, that of knowing whether their net pay (after debt service) had been reduced by half from three thousand lire per annum[182] to less than the pay of a railroader.

Pawn broking and other loan guarantees have their own risks, but certainly not so much as to justify the high interest rates charged. Those rates also serve as a fee for the quick and easy service provided over and above the interest for the loan. The borrower's short-term need for money renders him improvident, trusting without measure that nebulous future events will enable him to repay the loan. Oh, illusions and hopes! How many times have you faded away in the face of the combination of time and arithmetic![183]

I see things clearly from on high. I know about the abundance of Dutch and English gold. I also know more than anyone that money is offered at a cheap rate only to those who do not need it. But I also know that in every country there are those who speculate on the tears of simple people who show their hunger or overdue debts to their friends and families when they ask for help.

Oh, social economics is such a lovely *science*. On this point we should explain who turned this into a noble occupation. It once was the case that Jewish and Lombard[184] bankers charged people 18 percent

---

181 [I.e., the working class, of whom railroad workers would have been a prime example in the 1870s.]

182 [Translator's note, about $42,000 in today's money]

183 ['combination of time and arithmetic." i.e., compound interest.]

184 [The Lombard tradition in banking survives in the term, *Lombard rate*, the rate at which European central banks make short term loans to commercial banks against sound collateral.]

interest, and these lenders were in a separate part of town, like lepers. Today what happens? Don't they produce financial reports, issue discounted notes, and issue shares for others to buy, and then trade in and out in those shares? And for this some of those bankers are awarded knighthoods, perhaps because they ride other people's horses so well.[185]

And don't we find such people everywhere, indeed, insolently riding in fancy coaches earned by speculating in telegraph company bonds, or profits squeezed out from the distress of the needy?

I know well that our society operates in this way, though I feel that it should not be so. And when a society can no longer continue on its course, by God, sooner or later it rights itself. It may sweat blood by the bucketful, but it does sort itself out. This prophecy is much easier to make than you who laugh at it might think.

Shifting to another argument in support of the fourteenth maxim, I will talk about Sir John Herschel[186]. In all of his life he probably earned less from his knowledge and wisdom than did Richard Adam Loke with his little book in 1835, claiming that Herschel had seen lunar people and animals with wings and horns. I am not complaining about this state of affairs. People are like children who like marvelous things and believe in them past the point of absurdity.

Drawn to that which their imaginations conjure up, they desire to create and believe in real-life things based on images that appeared in their dreams. They are entranced and delude themselves. They will sacrifice money, life, and reason in pursuit of these images from their own minds. In this way, they learn, live, and die, by turns terrified,

---

185 [In Italian, a knight bears the title *Cavaliere,* which literally means *horse rider.*]
186 [Sir John Herschel, Baronet (1792- 1871) was a noted English mathematician, astronomer, chemist, and botanist. Among other things, he promoted Leibniz's notation for the calculus, in place of Newton's, discovered double stars and many nebulae, named the moons of Saturn and Uranus was the first to apply photography to astronomy, and developed blueprints and the use silver nitrate emulsions for photography.]

encouraged, resigned, and becoming fierce or calm. One day, they will pay those who will show them such marvels, albeit in obscured images, such as bodies that rise and float in the air, or the dead who come back to life. The other day people were kowtowing to someone who was reported in the newspaper as having predicted that the universe was about to be overturned, causing rivers to run back toward their sources and the oceans drying up. In other cases, they may believe a report that he had passed through a spider's web without damaging it in order to hide from an enemy. And people tremble with fear when there is an eclipse, a mirror shatters, or olive oil or salt are spilled. Others will seek to predict their futures and those of their dear ones using the hallucinations of a delirious person or in the dreams of their brains resulting from indigestion caused by overeating prior to going to bed.

You laugh, dear reader, you believe that you and I are above all this nonsense. And I also know that there are madmen who all in good conscience proclaim their sanity.

I can also excuse those who ask others to pay to see the wonders that they have on display. It is possible that those showmen themselves were the first to have been fooled.

But what I cannot excuse are those who sell scandals or who show scenes of filthy or perverse practices. Those are the people who bend art toward the obscene, showing the shocking filth of the basest passions with the paintbrush, pen, or engraving tool. It is never permissible to use the mind to paint bawdy images of other people, to make the reader witness adulterous kisses sealed with tears to shock the public, to expose the prostitute who has to sell her teeth one by one in order to pay for food for her child, or to depict someone who, after a corrupt life of orgies, is now dying of love, having been seemingly rehabilitated by a false piety while trying to convince you that it is easy to conquer vice and be pardoned, when in reality vice is very hard to overcome, and true pardon is never possible.[187]

Oh, unhappy ones, it is time to balance the books and write stories about these diabolical authors. May your pen be used to increase the numbers of them who cannot earn a living in this way, or at least to decrease what they earn in order to degrade them. You should introduce slimy slander into their private lives, no matter how clean they are. Rage at them in your writing with the sublime and eternal feeling of a superior intelligence because you are not in a position to pay them back face to face. Always adopt a tone of protest against their pleasures and whims; may our country, families, laws, customs, and authorities pay you well for your outrage.

Are there writers such as I have just described, or are they merely the dreams of a perhaps ailing mind? Perhaps I am deluding myself instead of helping you with your work, oh unhappy ones. Perhaps I am deluding myself when I believe that I can understand how difficult your path will be in the weakness of your adolescence, in your emasculated youth when money becomes your god, when you have been abandoned by your woman, with morality having become the slave of fashion, or when a satanic grin too often pressures you to block those honest and

---

[187] I digress here to note that I have been publicly and privately criticized for my maxim 151 in the first volume which expresses the idea that, with due respect for my critics, true pardon is impossible. I wish I were wrong, but I am profoundly convinced that it is true. I have known women who strayed into adultery who were *pardoned* by their husbands, evil children who have been *pardoned* by their parents, noted people whose ill-deeds have been *pardoned* by their peers, but after many years when I draft people's wills, they tell me what sort of pardon was given to those wives or children, and history tells me what happens to those notable people. To give a single example, Armand of Saint-Arnaud was named a Marshal of France, but his marshal's staff could not keep Victor Hugo's pen from remembering that as a young man he scraped off the gold from the royal throne. Not even the Pope knows how to forgive those who have offended him.

tender feelings that are imposed by a violated and disobeyed nature. O Pen of a deluded one, please be quiet.

ILLUSTRATION IV

16. It takes many years to have solid proof that you no longer stumble with the usual foot.

While a man of sound mind learns as he grows older, it is important that he be well taught for him to truly mend his ways. It is easy to express regrets for a misdeed and beat one's chest; the difficult part is to avoid such misdeeds in the future when similar situations arise.

Disrespect for the rights of others is a major source of breaches of trust, which frequently arise from those who ignore such rights and do not recognize the importance of protecting them in the interest of the overall community. Education can sometimes succeed in curbing bad tendencies.

I do not see any other remedy. Maybe religion could help, but only rarely does fear of future peril prevail over near-term interests. And then, some lack religious feelings, and for the others, the problem is the promise of God's forgiveness to those who repent; only rarely do those who sin fail to promise to repent at some indefinite future time.

ILLUSTRATION V

28. In general, people are judged more or less in proportion to the values of their leaders. But leaders whose minds are capable of offering wise leadership and guidance grow ever scarcer, as the number of followers and the scale of their society grow ever larger.

Society is a great chain of subordination. If you try to catalog the acts that are truly of free will, you will have to admit that they are marvelously rare. Reader, as you stand there with your book of John Stuart Mill in hand, I see you smiling as you say, "Acts of Free will? None." This is an absolute statement. Allow me to question your "none." A few examples, yes, and legislators should study those examples deeply and assiduously, which I do not believe they have done to date. In particular, I do not think these examples have informed our laws. So many crimes have been provoked by their victims! And yet, this provocation serves as a very thin excuse when in fact it should always be ascribed directly to the guilty party and not just implicitly.

Husbands, those of you who head your households, who drag your wives through the mud, and indeed into the courthouse, because she is fascinated by guilty desires. You claim that she has cursed you while you never did anything to remove your image from her heart. Her heart, hearing another man's true or pretended affection saw a contrast between it and your neglect, indifference, arrogance, and non-stop contrariness, solely to show your autocratic and egotistical power. These behaviors have reduced your woman to merely witnessing your outrageous whims and blunders.

Fathers who are lamenting their sons' appearances before the courthouse judge, that you have to witness their guilty verdicts, what did you do to teach them about affection and doing good? Are you truly innocent of their misdeeds?

Your daughter whom you honored and whose only sin was to suddenly abandon you and run off for the kisses of a snake. Your daughter, that half-crazed person, had forgotten that she could become a mother. She reminded you of the blot she brought to your honor and the shame in which your fault became evident to your parents, your family, and to all your friends. Her abandonment especially upsets you because of your fear of the scorn, the scoffing, and the false comforting from others whose embarrassments have not yet been exposed to a corrupt society that heaps scorn on those whose faults have been exposed. Even if you were convicted of being a perverse mother, a baby killer, and were in the hands of the executioner or the chains of servitude, you would be seeking to purify your delicate polluted flesh of such an embarrassment.

I have seen many fathers seeking to cleanse themselves of the sins of their children, children who are stingy in help for their ailing mothers, wives marrying their husbands for financial gain, husbands reducing their wives to choosing between basic financial needs for bread and clothing, for the rich brother who forces his poor relation into liveried service in his household; the well-off sister who repays her poorer brother's offer of a helping hand with slanders and reproofs for his having produced too many children. Oh. Horrors! And I have seen a son, rich from inheriting a fortune from his father, skimp on the funeral niceties as too fine for a cadaver.

I do not condemn these children or those others whose excesses I have kept to myself as the only guilty parties. I also condemn from the bottom of my heart those who are even guiltier for having provoked or misdirected them toward the wrong path in life. Instead, I think of the flip side of the coin. There I encounter the true sources of honesty, action, charity, justice, patriotism and all the other virtues. Blessed is the breast that gave you life and the father who created you, for the parents play a great role in developing the virtues in their children, and their work can be a boon or a curse to the community.

This maxim Number 28 is not only suggested to me by the direction of individuals' actions in the course of their personal and family lives. I see that true social merit becomes ever more difficult to inculcate as the degree that human progress takes on a greater and greater scale. It is hard enough to govern one's own behavior, more difficult to govern the behavior of one's family, and yet more difficult to govern the behavior of a large population.

Today, it is becoming more and more difficult to impose despotism, not because of society's paucity of base people to impose it, but because of the rapidly growing number and complexity of international and domestic relationships.[188]. Under the current state of affairs, it would be impossible for one man to take on the sole direction of a nation; for that reason, if a single person tried to rule, he would have to behave like a blind person who is so concerned that he might be surrounded by the edges of cliffs, and thus walks about the town always afraid that he might of fall to his death.

The reality is that social relationships have become so numerous and complex because of the multiplicity of capabilities that need to be developed in a modern society. These require considerable learning and wisdom. It used to be that almost anyone had enough knowledge to marry wisely and carry on his business in most situations. But now, with civilization's progress it is difficult to achieve the level of knowledge and reason needed to carry out today's higher level of civic responsibilities. The coarse man is satisfied in his basic necessities: sufficient shelter, food, and clothing. But the exchange of goods and services has become much more complex as people become more civilized. Perfecting the mind requires perfection in one's work; thus, the need to acquire broad knowledge is a necessity in all the

---

188 [Just four years before Levi wrote these words, King Vittorio Emanuele II completed the process begun in 1848 of unifying under one constitutional monarchy the plethora of despotic petty principalities that had ruled most of the various parts of the Italian peninsula since the early Middle Ages. Levi saw this as part of the positive sweep of historical progress. Of course, he did not foresee the appearance of Italian Fascism that was to come power in 1922 during his children's lifetimes, let alone the rise of Communist Russia and China and of Nazi Germany.]

exchanges of services in order to meet the buyer's expectations. This requirement has a great influence on popular and political movements. In the major cities of today, people can earn a living using whatever skills they have, which is why there is such a strong migration to the most populous cities.

The political approach needed to successfully lead the large populations gathered in the greatest cities necessitates that there be sufficient transport and communications for the continual distribution of newspapers and periodicals. These journals are needed to develop sufficient breadth and depth of knowledge among the people to deal with the growing complexity of the urban society. This is why as time goes by it becomes ever more difficult to become such a famous leader as to be one who will be memorialized for the ages.

ILLUSTRATION VI

30. A powerful mind is so attractive and strong that when it speaks, it blocks the ideas of all weaker thinkers. That is why one should judge people not only by their words, but also by their deeds.

There are educated and eloquent people who know how to win praise from small groups but who remain incapable of speaking before public gatherings. They feel that their physical or intellectual strength diminishes as the group in which they find themselves grows larger. The odd part is that they are not intimidated by the number of people around them but by their presence. When I see someone like that, who would not dare to give a public speech as long as those of Friar Onion,[189] I suggest

---

189 [In Bocaccio's *Decameron*, the subject of the tenth story on the sixth day is Frate Cipolla, Friar Onion, a man so gifted in oratory that he could extract major donations from

that he publish his ideas in the newspapers aimed at the terrifyingly omniscient public. In those cases, I think of myself as listening to a bully celebrating his own heroism by delivering a monologue.

When faced with a crowd, he hears a high-pitched buzzing in his ears, his voice trembles, his heart pounds, and his arteries visibly swell his wrists. He is terrified before a profoundly silent audience with hundreds of eyes trained on him and hundreds of ears ready to listen to him. But if he does not see these people who would judge his ideas, there he is ready to propose new laws to the government while smoking a cigar and lolling with his feet on the table.

Could that be why we have hordes of politicians, reformers, and statesmen and a scarcity of, for example, good teachers in our elementary schools? What a joke! Anyone can claim to be a lawmaker with his pen, inkwell, and a printer who is seeking his fortune, while to become a first-grade teacher requires passing an examination. But in truth, the story would change if the laws covering certain subjects were truly liberal and were not merely licenses to publish drivel.[190]

ILLUSTRATION VII

48. If curing oneself of his depravities were as independent of his free will as engaging in them, virtue would not have a name.

---

poor peasants for his order's treasury. He did this by charging them to see his phony holy relics, including a parrot feather that he passes off as a feather from the wings of the Angel Gabriel, and lump of charcoal which he claims was part of fire in which Saint Lawrence was roasted alive.]

190 [In Levi's book, *Piemonte e Italia* (p.117), he proposed that (1) managers of newspapers should be at least 35 years old to have a certain level of maturity, and (2) that they be required to have a university degree in journalism which required profound study and rigorous examinations.]

One can say that gambling, luxury, and all manner of vices have become an epidemic disease that subtly becomes your master. The primary cure, the most radical one, and perhaps the most heroic approach, is to flee from the environment in which the germ that causes this plague enters your body.

However, it is not sufficient to merely abandon such places; one should also have the wisdom to select new, healthier environments, given that gambling dens and upraised skirts abound in every inhabited part of the world. Fortunately, this germ mainly attacks the rich, who, if they wish to be cured before they are bled dry, can move frequently to new places and not settle in any one place until their bad habits have been broken, and their spirit has lost its bad turn.

Those without virtue can only hope in vain to be cured. The gambler who has lost his money and his credit and can no longer play still feels the violent desire to do so. He squeezes money from his family whenever he can to satisfy his hunger to throw it on the green felt table.

Luxury does not create a thirst by natural means. Instead, it shifts and rules every fiber of your being, tempting you with bursts of ugly mockery in ways which only the human animal is capable of. My only remedy for the greedy person would be to send him to live for a few years among the Bedouins.

Enough of simple-minded solutions, and for this, I apologize. Live within your means and do not mistake everything you could possibly acquire for what pleases you. In this way we have the one possible remedy to this disease, one that drives the wolf from your door.

Occasionally I have seen people cured of the foregoing disease by an unexpected and important life event or misadventure, which caused a change of status. However, I repeat, the normal cure is that of changing your environment, and to remove yourself from the fatal attractions of your normal activities and beginning that cure entails traveling.

This remedy is so difficult and painful that it causes even the strongest to cry when they are forced to abstain from their bad habits. However, those who know how to cry and thereby cure themselves, cry alone and only a little bit.

I know well that it is easy to preach and, in the end, those who adopt this prescription are those that do not really need it. Meanwhile the truly ill reject it and simply toss it into the trash basket. But that fact that in certain cases people do not take the straight and narrow path does not exempt one from the duty to show them the right approach.

Oh God! And to think that in many circumstances, to subdue such a habit requires the totality of human virtue to know how and be able to escape from it. And no sir, the subduer does not know how to execute that escape. Truly I am ashamed of my own weakness on this point.

ILLUSTRATION VIII

49. To state known facts and deduce from them the likelihood of a future event is said to be foresight and wisdom. On the contrary, predicting future events from present circumstances without any natural cause and effect linkage is said to be prophesying and is idiocy. Indeed, it is idiocy and malevolence when you predict another's misdeeds because you must know that predicting bad events in this way is a form of wishing for them to happen.

Only rarely is an oldster happy about the passage of time; he is, as they say, a white elephant. If you then add to the sadness of old age, taking offense at and passionately disapproving of the newer generation in the rare opportunities that an old man has to speak from the heights, you produce a new prophet Jeremiah. A time for licentiousness, perversity, lying, iniquitous justice, bodily corruption, and lost souls will lead to tempests, fire, pestilence, and war, the punishments of God. Those who survive will see cataclysms and the end of the world. To these old men I would add a few worthy men with perverse ideas; I would say that these men suffer from the disease of *spermatitis*, that is, reentrant sperm.[191]

Oh, for the sake of peace! Come out of the fog, good people, and do not curse a world that you cannot or will not enjoy, while preaching that it is on the edge of a precipice! I don't know if I am speaking suitably but a bit of defogging would better position the eggs in the basket.

Always God the terrible, always God the punisher, always God who brings forth bad events and that makes judgments over this and that in order that his banner will emerge triumphant over the piles of corpses and mountains of ruins at the end of the slaughter,

Good people! Take a bit of Catherine, some skirt[192] and, here before you, the terrible God has become maximally good. When you have children, I will tell you that you will find the Eternal Father is too good to make them cry, or at least you will hope so, and you will leave the dreaded prophesies to fortune tellers.

What good does it do to draw one's hands across his chest after having cursed the reprobates, the heathen, and the heretics? Instead, pray for them, that God will pardon and redeem them, that He will open their eyes to the light so that they will not trip in the darkness in

---

191 [Levi is suggesting that such men suffer from both figurative and physical impotence.]
192 ["Take a bit of Catherine, some skirt" are figurative allusions suggesting that men should marry and have children.]

which they grope their way. After all, He knows that the reprobates, the heretics, and the heathen, are the ones who use a microscope to observe the grandeur of God, and thus, if you please, the protozoa that live, swim, eat and, heaven help us, reproduce (profaning God!) are doing the worst even in the font of holy water!

According to the old, the enraptured and fanatical, the heretics, the heathen and the blind have always been and continue to be the young, the ones who do not eat or dream in the same way as their forbears, and for the ill-tempered, everyone else falls into this category.

There is still the category of worriers, people who like to predict public disasters, thinking that by so doing they can gain consolation for their own problems, knowing that many others will also have problems. One should have more sympathy for this type of unhappy prophet who draws horoscopes from his book of unfortunate events. At least he does it for himself, rather than for others because at least he does not deny himself the help that perhaps he could receive from God.

Well! Who can give me a happy, tolerant oldster who knows how to take the world as it comes and does not want to reshape it? Such a person is religious and recognizes the Divine hand in the story of mankind. Philosophically, he views scientific discoveries as steps toward a better understanding of the Eternal One and a benefit to the brotherhood of mankind. He welcomes and preaches the good in man and can only imagine doings of evil people. He can see death as a necessary part of life and not as punishment, and on the final day ends his existence serene in his righteousness and leaves to his friends the sadness and regret of his absence.

Oh, such a person might not find himself in the calendar of the saints, but he would be remembered by people as worthy of being there. Who can name such an old person who can be an example to everyone else? Once upon a time, when I was young, I thought that I had found such a person, but it turned out to be only a dream; come springtime the dream vanished.

ILLUSTRATION IX

52. Poverty is not a sin, but it is a plague that causes revulsion in those who see it.

When I encounter a certain crowd that is so hell-bent on making money that it does not matter to them if it damages this or that, I say to myself, "Is it possible that those people do not know that in thirty or forty years their strongbox will be made of four wooden boards held together with nails and the treasure that it contains will be their bones?"

In fact, they know it very well, but they do not remember it. And then ... and then it is not all to have food, drink, and enjoyment that such people engage is such knavery, but it is to avoid the frightful poverty, or even the appearance of being poor.

Unfortunately, poverty can be found everywhere, and in every corner, there are unhappy people. Rascality does not always inhibit admiration, and in some cases, knavery actually promotes it.

See the little ones eager to be seen with a gold watch and chain, the ladies who seek out used velvet gowns, and the workers dressed in used secondhand suits because these mask their powerlessness, and everyone desires to have power.

The lecturer laughs, "Oh, you knaves, cheats, and swindlers, be careful not to be caught in the talons of poverty." He says to a beggar who lacks the money for so much as a clove of garlic or a loaf of bread, "Tell me why you behave this way."

Now, among most poor people it is understood that each person must cover his shirtless body with a patched multi-colored military cloak in order not to appear simply to be a scarecrow. There are certain people who know how to adapt their bodies to very few needs, and to measure these needs to their resources. However, their fasting puts them at the risk of contracting serious illnesses such as consumption.

There are those who know how to maintain an outfit that twelve years previous still had some style. There are also those whose talents enable them to achieve high office even if their pockets are empty.

If the sick do not complain and the needy do not beg when they are unhappy or unfortunate, no one would hear them cry.

But are the people who were born naked and who have addressed their own needs and also helped to raise up others with their own efforts, labor, and virtue truly poor? The ones who could not produce, who had to do without, those are truly poor. We can assume that their poverty is the result of some unknown misfortune. They alone know the secret of how to hide their misfortune with their virtue. While such people are rare, they are to be highly admired.

ILLUSTRATION X

54. The difference between an opinion and an understanding consists in the latter being based on proven truths, and the former only on beliefs. People will fight to maintain their opinions, but for solid truths there can be no discussion by virtue of the evidence supporting them.

55. It is permissible for people to confuse their own opinions with true understanding, but it is not permissible to impose that confusion on others.

Believing that the earth rests on the back of a turtle, or that Mithra, a member of the Persian trinity, offered a sacrifice to Ahura Mazda as a redeemer and savior, to atone for the sin of the first man[193] are opinions, whereas believing two plus two equals four is a fact.

It is worth noting that learning facts calms the spirit. When a person communicates them to another, whether coldly or joyfully, there is peace and the pleasure of learning. But when one is dealing with opinions, the situation changes because contradictions can emerge from the lack of certainty with the latter. This lack of certainty inherently irritates the mind, especially when the believed truths are based on opinions that strain credulity.

However, these contradictions that support or refute what we believe offend our self-esteem, and that offense is the root of intolerance. Today one must admit that the world is undergoing a great revolution. The weight given to facts which make up mankind's scientific inheritance far outranks the power of opinions, even those of highly recognized subject matter experts.

We have begun to feel that good taste requires us to express opinions only sparingly and not to be offended by the opinions of others in order not to cause angry reactions. It is no longer fashionable to promote the idea of consorting only with people who agree with our opinions.

When we cannot support our ideas with facts or derive them logically from the same, we have only poetic opinions. Such opinions

---

193 From the letter of Felice Layard to Augusto Nicolas: *Études Philosophiques sur le Christianisme*, tom.2 pp504, 506

can sometimes help us to intuit the truth or dress it up in ways that are admirable and sublime. On the other hand, a hypocritical opinion can be a sort of banker, encouraging the passions of weaker minds. To the former go the rewards of the world to come, and to the latter payments in the here and now.

Becoming a saint in Heaven is much sweeter to contemplate than the prospect of Hell, especially when one can ride there in a carriage[194] during this life.

ILLUSTRATION XI

59. Few people can make the painful calculation of the future gains that will compensate for today's loss or deferred gratification. Most find it easier and prefer to waste their money in exchange for immediate gratification.

63. One day I was reading a column about the annual toll of suicides in a major city. I thought about it and then said, "Who can count how many of these were truly suicides? Could we all be wise and strong enough to sensibly control our impulses throughout our lives?

No one knows how to precisely measure his own strength. The smartest people are those who discount their own strength and always stay on the right side of presumption. They always moderate their eating, sleeping, drinking, walking, working, studying, speaking, and so on.

But I hasten to add that I do not know anyone who is like this, and I imagine such wise people only as an ideal. Many control their

---

194 ["one can ride there in a carriage," i.e., one is well-to-do.]

stomachs but not their brains and vice versa. I know others who avoid alcohol, but whose intemperate conversations attack the marrow of my bones. For such modes, wisdom is measured in sips: for you one gram, for me only a half. I must confess that viewing matters in this way ruins any sermon. Given that good health is the basis of well-being, and people are only marginally capable of intending, aspiring, and committing to curing themselves no matter what they think and believe they can do, I find it rather ridiculous to preach on this topic except in the terms that were incised in the walls of the temple of Delphi, "NOTHING IN EXCESS."

These three words contain within them a code of wisdom which far outdistances the wisdom of King Solomon, who in turn had dictated proverbs that I believe were not his as he sat with sixty queens, eighty concubines, and innumerable young ladies in his lap.[195]

Therefore, if I were to enter a church or synagogue and hear the preacher say, "My weak brethren: I tell you that eating, drinking, sleeping, procreation, studying, working, speaking, moving, lying down, or equivalently, sitting, spending, saving, arguing, believing, disbelieving, crying, laughing, valuing life, fearing death can be things of wisdom or insanity. Everything should be done in moderation." I would rise, thank the speaker, and kiss him fraternally on the cheek and I would say, "I believe in your religion."

One should further reflect that this principal obstacle to acting upon this wisdom is that there are many competing ideas within it. Do you have a young and eager wife? Chances are you are no Solomon let alone a Great Turk, but in the end, you are a man. If your wisdom whispers in your ear, "My friend, I see medical issues in your future, indigestion, dizziness, and gout are knocking at your door; be careful not to open it;" And in the other ear your love and the pleasure of

---

195 Song *of Songs*, VI: 8

kisses on your mouth are yelling "Enjoy! Get on with it, come what may!" And you choose to obey the latter.

Do you have children? Suppose that just when you are having a migraine one of them brings home an excellent report card from school and he says to you,

> "Papà, won't you take me to the theater tonight, like you promised?

And you say to him,

> "That is true, but right now I have such a hammering headache that I can't see straight. Wait until tomorrow night."

And the boy bursts into tears saying,

> "No, no, no! You promised!"

And you respond,

> "I will give you the money; go with Peter, our butler."
> "No, I want to go with you!"
> "But I can't. Believe me. I am in agony."
> "Phooey! I knew your promises were useless!"

And now your wife intervenes,

> "What is the big deal about meeting your promise to the boy? I am sure that if you go to the theater, your headache will pass; Get some fresh air. You will enjoy it. Go ahead, do me a favor.

Finally, you say in a resigned tone of voice,

> "Okay, I will do this for our son."

And so, dear father, you go to the theater, and, arriving late, you have to hold your son in your arms so that he can see over the heads of all the people in front of you. And thus, your headache redoubles in pain, and after two days leaves you so exhausted, tired, and depressed that you can hardly write two lines without your just calmed temples feeling the hammer coming back.

Do you have a friend? He is throwing a big party in honor of his daughter's recent marriage, and he wants you to come. You don't really feel like it and search for a suitable excuse, but to no avail. Your friend, his wife, and the young couple all want you there.

> "Okay, I will come." you say, while thinking that you will find a way out of it.

> "Please remember that we sit down for dinner precisely at six o'clock, and we look forward to seeing you."

> "Okay" you reply and then go on your way, thinking, "Come six o'clock, I will find an excuse and not go.'

Arriving home, you say to your wife,

> "Today I just don't feel like a spending three or four hours eating a monstrous meal."

To which she responds,

> "You are doing the right thing. Better that we have a simple dish of pasta at home that to overtax your stomach with all that."

But just as you are about to sit down to your quiet supper, you hear the doorbell ring.

> "Who's there?"

> "You rascal. Aren't you coming? I have my carriage right outside your door. Everyone is waiting."

And your friend does not let you respond. He finds your hat and your cane, and helps you put on your coat. In vain you try to speak, to excuse yourself, but he drags you out the door. And in vain, your wife has tried to come to your help.

> "No excuses! And you, Lady Eugenia, Dorothy, or Sophia. We missed you at the wedding. It would have been such a pleasure to see you."

> "I'm sorry. I just couldn't come."

"And dear lady, I understand. But for this event I will not accept any excuses. Let's go! Let's go!"

And you, dear father, you went.

And then when you were at the table, (In reality in the major cities this extravagant practice has gone out of fashion among the better sort of people, but in the smaller cities it is still in full flower.) you hear yourself constantly being called,

"Will you have some of this? Won't you taste that? See how delicious this sauce is."

And the host and hostess keep refilling your plate with each serving.

"This wine is a '37, that other a '58, and the third is a '60. Will you have a sip of this one? Won't you drink that one? How about trying the third one?"

And you, dear sir, furtively loosen your belt to try to make room for it all as you eat some of this and drink some of that, down, down it goes to avoid the embarrassment of leaving a drop behind, let alone being unable to button your pants for several days thereafter, as you pay for this sauce and that wine with bicarbonate of soda and tamarind, and maybe worse remedies.

Oh, you wise old Greeks! I proclaim you to be the unsurpassed benefactors of mankind for your maxim NOTHING IN EXCESS.

ILLUSTRATION XII

79. Hearts of stone tend to be long-lived.

The story is told of a saddler who lived to be 113 years old. He was presented to King Louis XIV who had wanted to meet him.

After asking a few polite questions, the king asked him what the secret was of his having lived long. To which the man responded, "Sire, When I was fifty years old, I decided to regulate my life according to two rules: close my heart and open my wine cellar."[196]

With this remark, I do not mean to indict gray hair as though all who had it had hearts of stone. I just insist that a sensitive man has a much lower likelihood of seeing old age than one who is excited by few if any events, and who in any case does not deprive himself of lunch or supper. Those who are never caused to weep die happy. I know that is commonly said that those who never experience pain do not enjoy pleasure, and to some degree I believe it. However, in the end, one who does not feel the sting of misfortune, or the death of his loved ones, who suppresses within himself any feelings other than self-esteem, and any care other than the will to live, has avoided many troubles and denied himself many joys. What remains for such a person is to devote his time on earth to pursuing blessed life. Nothing short of the end of the world would disturb his sleep.

The story is told of Fontenelle[197] who shared an inordinate love of asparagus with his close friend, the abbot Terrason. The one point of disagreement about this vegetable was that Fontenelle preferred them prepared in olive oil whereas Terrason thought they should be dressed with butter. One day the philosopher invited his friend to a dinner in which ample quantities of asparagus would be served and gave his cook orders to dress the asparagus for each person according

---

196 *Sire, depuis l'âge de cinquante ans, j'ai réglé mon existence sur deux principes : j'ai fermé mon cœur et ouvert ma cave.*
(Revue Britannique, août 1861, p 408)

197 [Bernard Bovier de Fontenelle (1657-1757) was a failed lawyer, poet, and dramatist who in later life found success as a writer of popular accounts of major scientific discoveries, a biographer of famous scientists and a philosopher of mathematics.]

to his preference. Terrason arrived at dinner time, but no sooner than he was seated, he had a massive stoke and died.

You dear reader, probably think that Fontenelle would be beside himself with distress and fright upon seeing his friend collapse, calling for help, doctors, servants, and medicines.... In fact, it was just the opposite. He immediately ran into the kitchen yelling, "Dress them all with olive oil, thinking that nothing was more important at that moment than to make sure that no asparagus were dressed with butter.

Fontenelle lived to be one hundred years old.

ILLUSTRATION XIII

89. Promising payment for good deeds and punishments for evil ones turns every action into one tied to personal interests. This approach has resulted in many dark pages of history because it induces actions for the wrong reasons. Philosophy teaches us that one should do good for the simple love of it.

The human spirit is carried in a chain of contradictions that stem from one fixed idea, which is inadequately expressed as *self-esteem* or *egotism*. This is the love that we each have for our thoughts, our ideas, of a scribbled line we have written which causes us to take offense if someone touches it and to defend its presumed value, sometimes even at the cost of our lives. It is this effect that, to coin a new term, I will call *authorism*.

For example, you might believe in an entity called God, who is omnipotent, the creator and manager of the myriad worlds distributed through the infinitely large universe, just, benevolent, merciful, who punishes the doers of bad deeds and rewards those who do good. If you do not see contradictions in this opinion of yours, I do not wish to oppose your view. I will simply tell you that your concept of reward and punishment make that great God of yours a very small God, and thus you have contradicted yourself. I am not speaking about your definitions of good and bad deeds. History will tell you that your criteria on this subject up until now have been the source of much disagreement.

I must confess, covering my face, that there was a time when I would have thought that I would have been dammed to the Devil if I had a bit of pork or a slice of ham; you might then have confessed that you would be punished if you had undertaken a great voyage without certain precautions, or if you ate meat ravioli on Friday.[198] And a Turk would confess that for a glass of wine he had eternally lost the kiss of Houri.[199] Poor Turk!

Be good and answer truly: Have you ever asked the Creator of the Universe to play the lottery or the stock market on your behalf? Have you ever asked Him to help you in your business, that he gives fine weather or rain, that he shows you favor in managing your theatrical productions or tours, or ... or ... or something else that I have not mentioned? Have you never followed the example of the good prophet and king in asking that your enemies be annihilated, to leave their women as widows, and their children as orphans and for you to emerge triumphant in their ruin? Have you never invoked His thunderbolts in support of the free play of your thoughts, opinions, and hatreds? And confidentially so that no one can overhear us, the day when you loved a young lady but your hopes were unrequited, did you ever raise your

---

198 [Translators' note: Prior to Vatican II in the 1960s, Catholics were not supposed to eat meat on Fridays.]

199 [Houri was one of the beautiful virgins that accompany those who are in the Muslim paradise.]

eyes to the Supreme Ruler of innumerable worlds and ask for ... oh great God for ... her to be your prisoner?

Have you never done anything of this sort? Go forth, for you must be a great man. However, Old Man, heavenly man, who, according to the Kabbalists is the image of the ideal man.[200] I recognize you and do not believe you.

On the day in which you said Merciful God, you conceived of pardon and you destroyed eternal justice. If he pardons you and not me, where is there justice? If he pardons both of us, again where is there justice? And if He pardons neither of us, where is his mercy?

Old Man, the day in which you made your God a punisher and rewarder, you subjugated him to your ideas of good and evil, and in this you are deceived and mistaken. The inconceivably divine Majesty knows it and you would too if you thought about it.

Now therefore, what is the point of surprising you as I have just done, if your reason is unwilling to recognize that your God, the rewarder and punisher, the origin of morality that should guide you to in all you do, is so firmly set as that contradictory Being?

Laugh and cry with me, Old Man, and not only for the enormity of having created in your imagination a Creator of the universe, a servant of your shabby interests and your deplorable errors, but to have dared to invoke the true Entity, the great Entity, the Entity felt in your thoughts, and then having injured, plagued, and bled you for your love of the same, having indiscriminately trampled and derided them both.

---

200 *Adam Ileà, Adam Kadmon.* The most elevated, the most complete of all the divine manifestations of God, source of all forms and ideas, is the supreme thought that is said to be the Word. It is important to distinguish between the absolute form, the universal form of mankind, and individual people who are the more or less weakened copies of the former. The former is called heavenly man.

Jacob Frank, *The Kabbalah*, pp180, 257-258

It is a noble and modest thought for which you do not assume that your intelligence and strength, such as they appear in this little world, are the best in the universe. But when you think about your deeds, rejoice in modelling them according to those laws which enable you to use reason to illuminate your mind and to avoid or minimize your suffering.

It is ignorance and pride to pretend that those laws are modified in your favor without any explanation. Always, a part of you can suffer from indigestion and for that reason die; Old Man, you know that you can always cut off a life or limb, with a steel blade, a lump of lead, or a poisoned drink, or shorten it with slander, betrayal, adulterous intervention and a hundred other approaches that you might dream up. You also know that the eternal law has been inexorably applied in similar cases. Therefore, if the laws were not constant, inviolable, and inexorable, wouldn't God be able to allow sin?

How many times did you choose not to look, and the blade, lead, poison, slander, or betrayal sent people to the grave? Old Man, does it matter if you then seek revenge? A vendetta repeats an evil deed and does not prevent it.

Just this once, allow me to digress to explain what I mean. What is the point of seeking an explanation of the value of good deeds in books of which your right hand might approve and your left might not? You will not find the answer to this mystery there. Can you find it in what is useful to you, perhaps at the cost of ruining the love that each part of you has or must have for the rest? You would have harmed your nature in that way and disguised what you had done, and thus you would not find the reason for doing good works. Can you find it among the things you approve of? Your opinions about things change from day to day as you accumulate experiences while the Good is immutable.

Try to formulate your idea of the Good based on immutable principles, study those principals, and with that study you will be able to discover true basis of good works, good habits, and morality. Oh, Old Man, the biblical legend of the serpent was right; understanding the good and bad can bring you to the level of divine wisdom and therein lies happiness.

In that understanding alone are the foregoing principles. It is a prize in itself; come what may, knowing and following the good is its own reward, the sole reward of a high-minded person who is capable of sensing that Majesty that is incapable of contravening his eternal laws without contradicting himself and dissolving into nothingness.

Study, Old Man. The apple of the tree of science was only nibbled by our ancestors; much of it remains. Old Man, since your component parts will die when you do and only God knows when that will be, study! Who knows if one day, having become wiser in your understanding of the infinite wanderings that lead to the Good, that in your lifetime you may be able to drive away the angel with the flaming sword who blocks you from the earthly paradise!

And you, my brother, an individual person, endeavor to live a healthy life and take care of your brethren. Seek to recognize and know for your benefit and that of others. Listen and preach that you do all this without being paid because *a healthy life and a wise mind are in themselves the Good in the world.*[201]

Do you love to believe in God and in his support of virtue in this world? Do you believe in the eternity of the life principle that is manifest in you and subject to eternal justice?

If this feels like it sustains and comforts you, gives you courage, consoles you, gives you hope, and directs you toward the Good, do not seek to comprehend the incomprehensible. Listen and enjoy

---
201 See Maxim No. 20 above.

because this is the path toward the Good and leads to happiness in your life without hurting others. But please remember that becoming a missionary or a martyr for these ideas is no longer considered to be in good taste.

ILLUSTRATION XIV

125. In modern society, there are many orators and few doers who espouse the principles of liberty, equality, and fraternity.

The problem arises because these three words, liberty, equality, and fraternity mean different things depending on the biases of the person interpreting them. If each person were to add three adjectives to these three nouns, *political* liberty, *legal* equality and *social* fraternity, the areas of disagreement would become more limited and with that, the potential for abuse would too.

If there no longer were kings, barons, and abbots, the word *liberty* without this modifier would begin to take on a vague and indistinct meaning. The wishes of each person with respect to public governance could become the banner of the most uncontrolled passions among all sorts of malcontents. The definition of liberty would be to demand change, which is natural among those who feel aggrieved. There are more fiery demagogues than you may believe, who desire to have a revolution and complain of governmental tyranny only because they are short of money.

Without this modifier, there would be confusion in that shout of liberty. It could amalgamate many different ideas: a philosophical concept, freedom of speech, which touches upon morality and civil rights. It could have as its objective the exercise of legal rights and protection against abuses of power. It might also include the freedom to heedlessly proclaim subversive doctrines, slander other people, trample on the laws, or to declare that we want to change our form of government for our benefit exclusively, even at the cost of public disorder and civil wars, and to hell with anyone who disagrees with us.

I openly declare that if we limit the term liberty to political liberty, the natural direction would be toward republican government. However, before we get there, we need to raise the educational level in the country. The majority would need to learn to regard the nation as a whole as an entity with higher prestige than the authority lodged in any one person.[202]

Today there are still too many who need to put on a reverent look for those who are watching as they kneel. Certain indiscretions, uses of violent language, and sharp insults do not cause anything other than reactions which are contrary to true liberty. These end up causing a continuing confusion, which is believed to be the speaker's objective when he is caught in the talons of need.

To profess true liberty and prepare for its eventual triumph, one must speak about the need to educate the masses and deliver such education to the limits of one's ability. Let schools be set up in offices, the countryside, the garrets of the slums, factories, villages, and farmsteads with schoolteachers like the chaplains that are required to be attached to each military regiment. Let this continue until these means banish ignorance, much as public health measures are taken to eliminate lethal diseases. Only when ignorance has been eliminated will the apostles of liberty be able to turn their minds to other issues.

---

202 [Louis XIV of France famously declared, "*L'etat c'est moi,*" *I am the state.* Contrast this view with the oath that American politicians take, in which they swear allegiance to the United States Constitution and not to any one leader.]

And for this purpose, one should note that knowledge brings the maximum possible level of political equality If a person is to enjoy equal rights, and to assume equal obligations, he must understand what his rights and obligations are under the laws of his country. Also, equality indicates that everyone has an equal reasoning ability and participates equally in the gifts of Madam Fortune.

In truth I would like to see a law that would grant me the right to pool my holdings with the many Rothschilds, and then to divide it equally among all the people of the world, provided of course that such a division would not leave me impoverished. But of course, I could not vote for such a law because it would make idiots equal to intelligent people, the active with the passive, the industrious with lazy, the frugal with the prodigal, and so on.

Until that day I will be satisfied with the little that I have and I will hope for the triumph of the possible equality, in which the motto will be: Everyone equal before the law.

Fraternity! A rich young man dressed in the Italian style sang out at the top of his lungs,

"We are children of the same father!"

To which a good time Chalie who was chronically short of money called out,

"Lend me a thousand lire"

In response, the young man asked,

"Who are you?"

"I am a son of the same father as you."

"To the Devil with you!"

And then the rich young man turned his back and continued with his song.

Oh reader, in this anecdote is a look in the mirror of true fraternity as practiced among people. It is not that I am suggesting that you should act differently; I am only arguing that the word fraternity should be excised from the democratic project because it embodies hypocrisy and is useless.

Liberty! Liberty! Who does not want it? Everyone preaches it as once upon a time people preached religious faith or the crusades. However, the reality behind this term is often a government controlled by a narrow clique, and that provides only a very minimal public education,

Equality! Two people are not equal to a third person if the latter lacks the wisdom, strength, and rectitude of the first two combined to balance his inequality with the pair of them.

Oh words! Oh Charm! How many times have you followed the straight and narrow path to ruling the world!

ILLUSTRATION XV

167. Becoming illustrious is the most powerful revenge that one can have against others' insults.

This maxim, which I believe to be among the truest of all, was suggested to me one day when I was afflicted with impotent rage. It is perhaps a sterile wish but one that consoled me and made me feel better.

In any case, to illustrate this maxim I have attached as an appendix an essay written by me on October 27, 1872, in which I narrate what happened to me on that day.

And why do I leave it to an appendix? First of all, it is to show you, dear reader, that if gentle souls must always be courteous to each other, it would be a good policy to adopt in dealing with people we do not yet know and vice versa. Secondly, because on that day I felt my dignity as a man of letters unjustly insulted, and I promised myself to adopt the term *Bodonian Invitation* as an insult. I have kept my word. *Homo sum, humani nihil a me alienum puto*[203]

ILLUSTRATION XVI

178. People's laziness causes them to find it easier and more comfortable to be told what to do than to be self-directed. This causes them to readily adapt to tyranny both at home and in their government.

One day, a well-to-do 28-year-old, who had tired of insincere and purchased kisses, began to notice the children that he saw passing on the sidewalk below his windows. Oh, what a pretty little girl, what beautiful blond hair she has! Oh, what a handsome little boy, with such lively eyes! And he said to himself, "If only I could have a child of my own. What a great pleasure it would be to hear myself called Papà by such an angel. Oh, why not?"

Then he mentally reviewed all the young women that he knew to determine which one would come closest to his ideal choice. The first couple of passes through his list were interrupted by a shrug of his shoulders as he said to himself, "I have time, I will think about it." But that mental list kept on returning to him, almost becoming an obsession. Finally, he went to the church of San Filippo or San Lorenzo[204] to have a another look at a certain attractive, warm-hearted

---

[203] [Translator's note. Man am I, and never do I think anything that would offend others.]

[204] [San Lorenzo and San Filippo are two ornate Baroque churches in Turin Italy than tend to have well-off congregations.]

young woman. After having studied her carefully during the mass he decided, "I like this one; my decision is made."

Having been introduced to the family and to her through mutual acquaintances, he is welcomed. And in the course of the next month or two, he finds himself alone for the first time with this chaste, well-bred woman of about twenty years. She is as shy as a dove and confused by the flood of emotions, of which the foremost is apprehension. However, within a few days she warms up to him and shows interest in his life and his activities, and if you will, the future reign begins. Today she asks him to smoke a fancier sort of cigarette, the next day she criticizes the collars of his shirts and the colors of his neckties. After that it is the shape of his beard and mustache. And our hero, a most gallant man, instead of smiling and responding with an innocent kiss on the forehead, decides to make her happy. Here comes the razor.

Up to this point no harm has been done, but each day the criticism expands, until finally after four or five years, the combination of his interest in an intriguing and lively woman, combined with his inertia, have brought him to understand that the expression, "your lady," a term often used to refer to a man's wife, is neither a simple compliment nor a light jest.

One day he says,

> "Lina, I would like to go to Milan; I will be away for a day or two at the most."

To which she replies,

> "Oh sure! Let's go to Milan in order to waste a bunch of money to see the museum of the Milanese ladies."
>
> "All right, you should come too!"
>
> "You know very well that I am busy with our little boy, managing our household and a thousand other worries about what could go wrong if I were not there."

"We could bring our son with us."

"And the cook and his governess?"

"Lina, why don't we all go?"

"Are you really dying to go to Milan?"

"What do you want? I need to get out for a bit, have a change of scene and to breathe some fresh air."

"But it will cost too much for all of us to go."

"Oh, for goodness' sake. One moderate expense won't bring financial ruin. After all, we only live once."

And there is our hero, a father who in order to get permission to spend a day in Milan has had to emulate Saint Martin.[205] And so, bit by bit, he finally gets to the point where he has to ask permission to gamble a few lire at cards, where he has to endure her complaints after his second losing hand, and her prohibition from further play after the third.

In this little story I described the situation between husband and wife. But I have also seen sons and daughters putting the squeeze on their parents, priests who abuse their families, bullying uncles, and other similar cases. Such situations are so common that you, dear reader, could easily sketch many more of this sort.

But such misuse of authority within the family has no consequences except for those who tolerate it. Further, I have to admit that they do not always lead to bad ends. Sometimes, these are not just the result of personal inertia, but tacitly reflect a truly superior intelligence or other virtue.

The worst harm occurs in the cases where laziness leads to bad governance. Why haven't you registered to vote and joined a political

---

205 [St. Martin was a Roman Catholic pope who disagreed with the Eastern Roman Emperor on matters of church dogma. The latter had him arrested, tortured, and exiled to Crimea, where he died from the injuries sustained during torture.]

party? Having registered, why didn't you vote? Why do you avoid the political meetings that precede the elections at which you could educate yourself about the merits and values of the candidates? You let these go by; you permit the meddlers to shout out their slogans, and then one day you complain about the conduct of public affairs, run with an iron fist that sneaks in laws you disapprove of such as those involving hidden payments, and you see before your eyes a government that that would embarrass even the most shameless bankrupt.

Get up, you lazy-bones. The sun is already high above the horizon, and you, still in bed, are allowing your strength to ebb away. Wake up and arise, for once exercise your hard-won rights. Put on your glasses and unblock your ears. Defend yourself from the loud mouths and their illogical arguments.

Do you want to laugh and cry simultaneously? One day not long ago, the local newspaper published the official text of a new law concerning property taxes that had not been previously communicated to the agents in the city Tax Department in Turin.[206] In France, a country whose legal system was a model for our own, the laws are officially communicated to the subordinates with accompanying instructions based on the parliamentary debates that preceded the enactment of the law. These instructions explain that the law was specified or changed for the following reasons to remedy the following problems.

With us there is complete anarchy, and everything is left open to debate. Can you imagine the impact that this has on the tax agent whose job it is to allocate the annual spending of the local and provincial governments into property tax bills in a process that limits him to a single sentence for each taxpayer? The result is an avalanche of hatred and rage that heaps up on our national government.

Why is this so? What can I make of the underlying politics?

---

206 This a true story related to me by a most reliable person.

Many times, I have gone to the theater and heard a cry of approval or disapproval from someone in the audience, and it often seemed to be speaking common sense. I like to pretend that it is my voice.

ILLUSTRATION XVII

207. There are cases in which the mandated legal sanctions should not be carried out because the punishments create greater wrongs than the original crime. Therefore, the balance of justice cannot always undo an accumulation of minor crimes. However, while death brightens the good, it cannot cancel out people's misdeeds.

It is very well to say that riches should be equally distributed to all at death. It is not the case that all riches are acquired through litigation and combat, deceit, greed, or theft. Neither is it always the case of some popular idol that in no time receives great homage and deserves major honors. It is generally the result of more serious thinking and work, indeed according to many people, exclusively the result of serious thinking and work. To speak of God, the soul, of human destiny, and to pretend to know of virtue, passions, or habits is a pastime of fools. Serious people speak of assets, mansions, land holdings, stocks and bonds, and rents. If one of these were to propose marrying your daughter, your first question would not be whether he is healthy, strong, well-educated; rather, it would be how rich is he? The other questions come later, and unfortunately, if the answer to the first question is satisfactory, you do not put much weight on the answers to the others. This mania about becoming rich in financial assets is without any possible doubt necessary up to a point to increase well-being. After all, the combined efforts up to a certain point produce an increase in the general level of abundance which is needed to support a growing population. However, this mania far exceeds what is necessary to achieve this desired benefit.

Unfortunately, greed and laziness frequently combine to raid the nests of others in order to feed their own progeny. In those cases, intelligence and hard work are unable to join to produce truly increased value, and violence, fraud and other similar sins only move existing value through tortuous routes. A kilogram of iron can be used to produce clock movements or burglars' tools. In the first case, it has produced value, and in the other simply enables existing value to be shifted from one person to another.

However, burglars' tools are not the only way to move value from one person to another. There are many hidden ways of doing this and the laws are so stretched among opposing interests that while they stop the majority of such issues, a minority of them still slip through. There are so many loopholes in the laws that the human spirit can find infinitely many ways to avoid punishment under our system of justice.

And so it happens that not all riches are the product of intelligence and hard work applied in their natural ways. There does exist a means of tempering this mania to acquire things to the degree of becoming possessed by this evil hunger, but they come at the price of damaging property rights and causing other injustices. If we could judge everyone at their deaths as was the nominal custom of the ancient Egyptians and distinguish which assets were acquired legitimately from those that were acquired illicitly, we could confiscate the latter and by this shift of assets achieve a remedy for the misdeeds previously committed.

If we attempted to abolish the right of inheritance, we would destroy a deep and very useful family bond, whatever may be said about it. The result would be to divert human industry from stable, productive investments such as in agricultural land, our common mother, to highly liquid assets which can be used impulsively to satisfy every human whim which would become their primary love, almost like that for their own children. To satisfy those whims, people would certainly be tempted to and generally succeed in evading and violating the law in order to leave their accumulated assets to their children. Also, deprived of the motivation to accumulate assets to leave to their descendants, some people may lose desire to work hard and have children. The result would be more people choosing a dissolute life in place of raising a family, and thus reduced growth of our population and all the benefits that accrue therefrom including the sense of patriotism and civic duty. In its place we would build a system of uncontrolled egoism.

Such would be a few of the primary effects among many others of an effort to attempt to collect and redistribute ill-gotten gains. Little if anything can rebalance justice in these cases, in that the human desire to accumulate wealth is so tightly bound up with its productive efforts that we cannot attack the one without destroying the other, which would harm not only the current generation but also those of the future.

ILLUSTRATION XVIII

235. Civilized people never lose their original propensity to organize themselves into distinct families, tribes, communities, and nations. Among primitive peoples, physical valor served to designate their leaders and grant them royal esteem. Today, when various social circles represent the tribe, community, nation, or complexes of related nations, leaders are selected based on their daring, shrewdness, subterfuges, and their art of exploiting the inertia and indifference of the many. In some cases, cliques or riches, however they were acquired, determine leaders, and in others, abstention, partisan spirit, and the strength of the many meritorious people outweigh personal valor as criteria for selecting political and administrative leaders. And, as you may know or sense, the leaders' authority is weakened because various public offices are no longer recognized as unquestioned sources of public esteem.

I had considered whether I should keep quiet about this maxim or shine a light upon it in the form of an illustration that would give a glimpse into how my mind would work on it. I was inclined toward the first approach, but my conscience bothered me. The argument seemed to be too important not to be recalled in a way that would focus the reader's attention on this maxim. Also, my mind would not be satisfied by a simple nod to a maxim such as this one, buttressed by a couple of examples, because it contains a very deep observation. Here I would add that I was concerned that people might accuse me of making an impertinent statement in the form of a maxim. Thus, the need to express my full thoughts on this very serious theme, further supported by the need to protect myself from such an accusation, has led me to speak about it at length.

I will not speak of the intrinsic truth of this precept in current times. That, dear reader, I will leave to your judgment. Instead, I will speak of the causes that underlie this social phenomenon, for the reason that any simple peasant can pretend to be like Marcello[207] and run the risk of incredible violence such as people can inflict on each other in innumerable ways.

---

207 [Benedetto (1686-1739) and Alessandro (1673-1747) Marcello were Venetian noblemen and musical composers whose work was admired by Bach.]

Now, please lend me an ear and I will begin my discussion with an analogy. A person who is in the eye of a hurricane does not sleep during the few hours of treacherous calm therein, but instead anxiously looks at his barometer to alert him to the return of the danger, and studies the rotation of the wind and repairs and fortifies the ship against the overwhelming force of the wind that will attack it within a few minutes or hours.

Then, having experienced the blasts of this terrible wind, he would study the relevant physical laws and record its appearance as to place and duration. He would notice that the rotational direction of the wind is in the opposite direction in the southern hemisphere as compared to what it is in the northern hemisphere, and that the most violent wind is adjacent to the calm in the eye of the storm. Finally, having withstood the storm, he would then know how to avoid it in the future or enter into it knowing the best means of surviving.

This is how a person learns from each crisis, and when someone shouts to him, "Brother, our guiding principles are being miserably undermined day by day, base and guilty passions are taking over. An insatiable mania about getting and having things is causing our past and the present achievements to fade," he should watch out. Today many would work themselves to death thinking that they would be better off tomorrow and run about shouting, 'Long live the future! Long live the unknown!'"

A person so forewarned either by others or himself would seek to study the society in which he lives, to learn the causes and draw conclusions about the causes of the danger in which he finds himself. If he has the strength, he will seek to rise above it to see it and avoid it.

I do not regret the past. Indeed, considering the entirety of the human race, my personal dogma sees the future as better than today, just as today is better than what has come before. However, progress does not exclude the possible arrival of many evils that might beset us. Because man is imperfect, every moment in history has had its share of troubles. And studying the past will help us avoid or at least mitigate some of those bad effects.

Because inductive analyses entail approximations, forecasts of the nature and scale of these future bad effects based on present experience is an undertaking that cannot be just the opinions of a single mind. Rather they require each of us, meditating on various subjects as it is our nature to do, to investigate root causes and make educated guesses as to their consequences to the best of our ability and thereby we can collectively predict what will happen.

Above all we need to observe and remember that in the grand scheme of things, some people have a narrow view of the world around them while others see things more broadly. And besides, people tend to consider it an essential duty to take a broader or narrower breadth of view that is proportional to their station in life, so that it is similar to that of others who were born to or have risen to a similar level in society. That is, the head of the family, the president of an organization, the leader of a bank, a mayor, the head of a national government department, a member of parliament, and so on are all required by their duties to take a wider or narrower view of the elements of modern life according to the scope of their responsibilities. In fact, the minds of these leaders drive the bulk of the prosperity and failure, growth and retrenchment, and strength and weakness of their families, organizations, and the government.

Considering the great longevity of the influence that certain of these actions have or could have on future generations, it is not difficult to be convinced that, above all else, the choice of leaders is a serious matter. Once leadership has been conferred, it has to be religiously respected, so that the leaders can have the strength, power, and freedom to act appropriately. Neither the freedom to act or direct is possible unless it is with universal reciprocal consent.

There was a time when despotism was violently imposed, claiming to derive its power from will of God, and making league with the Church. The despot alone would choose the government officials and was responsible for coordinating their activities. The legislative and executive functions were founded on the principle: *As I want, so I do*. And in this way, he disposed of people and benefits. This involved privileged castes, feudalism, bloody wars, vulgar displays of wealth to the point of immorality, waste of the public's money, and following exclusively the passions of a single individual and his family, often in ways contrary to public opinion and the national interest.

Such government lasted and continues to operate where it is possible to violate human nature, but in such places the winning hand is shaking and breaking the despotic yoke. The people are discovering that it is not always a given that a single mind alone, to whom all others must bow, can have the breadth of outlook to properly see to universal justice in every circumstance and for every person's needs.[208] It came to be that the principal of authority, in which all power was concentrated in the monarch, perhaps guided by religious principles, was respected and venerated for centuries, finally collapsed among civilized peoples because of its intrinsic flaws.

And it is important to recognize that while religious support helped to extend the duration of such despotic rule, it could not prevent its eventual collapse. It is certainly true in all times that if a

---

208 [Levi was born shortly after the ghettoes were reestablished under the despotic kings that returned to their thrones after the defeat of Napoleon. He lived to see that form of government overthrown and replaced by a constitutional a monarchy in 1848, the year when the ghettoes were reopened. The last such despotic government in Italy, that of the Papal State, was overthrown in 1870, shortly before Levi wrote his two volumes of maxims.]

government does not have intrinsic merit that renders it respectable, no power on earth is strong enough to sustain it. And this consideration shows how vain an effort it is for those who try to confuse the respect due to the government with that due to religious figures, and from that to conclude the decay of one of these with that of the other. Every governing principle must find within itself the strength to sustain it, and if it decays, it means that it lacks that strength and cannot regain it.

Certain of those universal governing principles are necessary during a given historical period and are accepted and approved of by the majority of the people. But when those principles begin to decay, they cannot be revived in the same form. That decay is their way of dying, and, once dead, no power on earth can resurrect them. A corpse cannot be brought back to life! It can be subjected to an electric shock and briefly recover a crude transitory semblance of life, but the corpse is irrevocably dead.

Thus, once a despotic government decays, it cannot return. And those who attempt to bring it back are doomed to failure. Sometimes people try to revive such a government by more or less masking its nature, but the momentum that it used to have would no longer have its vital driving energy; that vitality, once gone, will be gone forever.

This rule, however, does not prohibit that a given government title can be revived, even if the underlying form is no longer the same. For example, Louis XIV of France was not king in the same way as Louis Phillippe, even if they both bore the same title. The Roman republic was not a republic in the same sense as are Switzerland or the United States of America in our times. The governing principal is not determined by the title of the head of government. That principal will have died along with the generations of people who made it possible.

Scientific progress, and the broad range of different doctrines, opinions, customs, objectives, and levels of prosperity change the character of the populace and, with that, the character of the legislative system that governs them. But precisely because an existing legal canon has been unable to achieve the broad public acceptance necessary to sustain it in a given time period, it begins to decay. Then, when the existing canon is in decline, the spirit that sustained it lives on, albeit in another form. People always find a new governing model necessary for their life as a society if neither the old model nor its removal matches up to their needs or gives them satisfaction. But this new governance is subject to variations, and thus of being reformed. Initially the reform operates according to public opinion until it is irrevocably codified in statute and the revolution is complete.

However, the laws that coordinated and moved the majority's aspirations in a positive direction, whose power drove and continues to drive the revolution, are and must be the product of a long period of time. This time was one of trials and experimentation, as it were, a period of groping, during which people know more about what they don't want than what they do want. That is why, in almost all cases, during such periods people resort to imitating different governance models with greater or lesser success.

However, in each of the cities and provinces that together constitute a great nation, there are local practices, opinions, and biases that retain within them elements of the governing model which is collapsing or has fallen among the majority and so in some of them the former governing principles are still accepted by many people, for it is impossible for everyone to change or disappear in a single day.

Therefore, this undeniable fact is the real root cause of the existence of minority political parties that endure for long periods of time, holding on to the past. They cause the transitional period of experiments and trials to be very difficult.

It is best if a governance model is broadly accepted for it to function at full strength. To be accepted it has to truly address the public's opinion on what are the new requirements of a broad cross section of the public. It is useless, or at least not at all supportive, to attempt to draw from one population a new government model that works for another. For example, the British constitutional system has not worked well in France, even though it seemed to have been suitably adjusted.[209] While the British system has resulted in Britain seeding the world with its colonies, France has merely let its own colonies vegetate.

This is not due to differences in the level of education between Britain and France, nor to differences in the abilities of their leaders or to other similar reasons. Rather it is due to essential differences between the two populations. The British are tenacious observers of their laws, while Frenchmen make laws and then destroy them and reduce them to caricatures. The latter idolize their own soil and do not pay attention to anything that happens outside their national boundaries, while the British idolize their flag and for them home is anywhere that their flag waves.

Therefore, the governing model has to be based on needs, desires, tendencies, and passions of each nation, or of the majority of the different peoples who make up a nation.[210] That model needs to carefully address the public's views on moral values as well as the most important national customs, and the need for broad prosperity. Unless a government can find a single approach that addresses all

---

209 [During Levi's lifetime there had been several attempts to establish a constitutional monarchy in France. These were repeatedly overthrown, the last being in 1871 when Napoleon III was driven from power.]

210 [Levi thought of Britain and France as monocultural nations but was well aware of other models such as Switzerland, Belgium, and Austria-Hungary whose national boundaries include peoples who viewed themselves as being of different cultures.]

of these factors, it sets itself on a path to failure, driven by its own ineptitude.

But to substitute one governance model with another one, whether it be for a state led by a king or a president at one extreme, or replacing a head of a family at the opposite extreme, it cannot be a work of just one or a few years, if it is to be accomplished harmoniously and push the society toward the well-being for the majority of those under its administration. It is precisely for this reason that each time an institution undergoes a radical transformation, the new leadership must review every law, regulation, custom, and usage in order to firm up its leadership before it can claim victory,

Thus, the result can be external wars and broken commercial relationships, and internal persecutions, fights, violence, coercion, and interim legislation covering a wide range of subjects in order to protect the main elements of the new order. In similar cases in the past, it has included making common cause with Cicero and Cato who both died or with one who courted Seneca.[211]

Today, politicians often vacillate, with little confidence in themselves; they might wait a bit to change their position or excite themselves and those around them by changing position, seeking an adjustment that satisfies the inexhaustible and often changing desires of the multitudes in order to further their own unbridled and overwhelming ambitions. But in either case, when this happens the unfortunate result is to disgust supporters who need to live normal

---

211 [Cato (95 BCE-46 BCE) was a Roman senator who opposed Julius Caesar's attempts to overthrow the Roman republic. He died during the civil war between the followers of Caesar and Pompey. Cicero (106 BCE - 43 BCE), another Senator who opposed Caesar, was killed by Caesar's political heirs in the aftermath of Caesar's assassination. Seneca (4 BCE-65 CE), a noted playwright and stoic philosopher, was Nero's tutor and personal advisor, though he too fell from power during Nero's reign.]

lives. In many cases they run the risk of falling into vulgar and inept hands.

People cannot achieve their desired ends in this manner, which is to say, the optimal well-being and its consequent improvement in the lives of the long-suffering social classes remains out of reach. In this way, the latter approach promotes terrible actions which it then lacks the power to stop, while the other, former approach opens leadership roles to mediocre people, who once in power, masquerade as great men and maybe appear to be so until the point where their miserable actions reveal their petty minds.

The result is that many people mourn the loss of the dead regime and about these people I have already spoken; and yet they attempt to revive it.[212] But that revival turns out to be impossible. After a reactionary period of reversion, the masses throw themselves into desiring to accomplish extravagant changes., Then this becomes the objective of one and all, replacing that of leading a life of perennial quiet with distrust of every power that governs them. Judging by their resulting poverty, we see that they had little sense of what was difficult or possible. They all hurtle toward the unknown shouting "bread and circuses."[213] Deplorably, they thought that these could be easily obtained by shouting in the city square or massacring their neighbors. Faced with this perverse aspiration, there was no remedy except to enforce respect for authority as represented by the laws and officials.

And, unfortunately, at this point the people fall into a vicious circle since they are not well schooled in how to choose leaders.

---

212 [During Levi's lifetime he saw the post-Napoleonic reaction in which The Congress of Vienna (1814-15) sought to reimpose the old despotic regimes of continental Europe from the 1700s, most of which were subsequently overthrown in revolutions in the following several decades, most notably in 1830 and 1848.]

213 [It is said that the in ancient times, the Roman government kept control of the masses of poor citizens in the City of Rome by promising them free bread and circuses.]

They no sooner make their choices, than they hold these leaders in contempt and trample them under foot, and this is a vicious circle. The second problem is a direct consequence of the first one. It is incorrect to say that that this state of affairs is simply a consequence of the revolutionary new facts and ideas. A person cannot be criticized for reaching new conclusions based on his understanding of new facts. Likewise, he cannot be held to account when trying to fulfill obligations dictated by a strong conscience. Under such conditions, the revolution arises from the logical necessity imposed by the facts and thus operates on its own.

How, for example, can someone be accused if a physical truth demolishes a prejudice? And yet this is a revolution, a perfect image of larger ones. Now therefore I argue that the complaints of prejudiced minds are just as unjust as the accusations against revolutionaries. No, the error is not in making a revolution, but in the neglect of education, the lack of wisdom, or its failure to follow the law, and in any case from the mob of incompetents seeking offices. This is the true problem, and in my opinion, the great danger from revolutions.

But I hear myself asking: "Do you want a government by the betters, the aristocracy? Is that you speaking?" In common parlance, the word *aristocracy* has lost its etymological meaning, and today has come to include no one who favors human liberty, and its use is indefensible in this discourse. Today no one could possibly desire a government by caste, or the creation of privileges for the few to the detriment of the many, ideas that correspond to the concept that the word *aristocracy* has taken on. But that word must be used when we observe that the democratically elected leaders of the great nations can have no explanation other than the selection of the best citizens to govern the republic and the cities, and these people constitute an aristocracy in its original sense. Now, should we seek the good in the value of the word as it has been currently perverted or in its true meaning?

Nations can have glorious periods and relative prosperity under the leadership of a sovereign surrounded by a court of privileged men; but when these countries rise to a higher, continuous, and long-lived level of power, it is under a government of the most elevated citizens. At the same time the men who were preselected to rule constituted an oligarchy; however, I think that it is the duty of a good citizen to proclaim that *an oligarchy composed of eminent men that accumulates meritorious people without regard to privilege, title, or caste is the single possible ideal among the various possible means of governance.*[214]

That is the only means in which one can achieve a true democracy; after all, after the passing of the small ancient city-states in which the people would take a direct role in public governance, today the only way is for the people to select their delegates, thereby creating an aristocracy based on popular vote. It is certainly not credible that the head of every level in the immense governing ladder that rules the society of a great nation is filled with an active, wise, and honest man. This is an idealized image which should and must serve as a means for comparison with various historical governance ideas for the purpose of perfecting them. In the domain of actual human experience there is no people who meet this ideal, especially not the Italians, the great majority of whom are only in the beginning stages of developing a national government.[215]

---

214 [This sounds suspiciously like Plato's notion of philosopher kings as expounded in his *Republic*.]

215 [Italy's wars of unification (1860-1870) brought together under the rule of the royal House of Savoy the prior series of mostly despotic and often corruptly governed independent principalities and foreign-controlled territories on the Italian peninsula. The Savoyard kings reigned under a democratic constitution granted in 1848, that replaced

Even if we have no hope of fully achieving this supreme ideal, aiming for it is better than doing nothing or the contemptible and exaggerated opposition of meritorious and honorable men that can be fatal to public life, as was noted above. The lack of ambition for honors for those who merit them reduces their prestige and adds the most serious evil of always devaluing their legitimate influence over the government.

Aristocracy and also oligarchy based on popular elections may not be perfect but they are better means of governing a population with diverse aspirations than all the others, even if they are not universally supported. This is self-evident.

Thus, from this point of view, we can conclude that for a capable person to refuse to take on a public role is perhaps as culpable an act against the public good as soliciting or working to obtain a public office. The only justifiable exception to this rule would be in cases of pressing other duties that cannot be set aside.

However, I have to add other considerations on this very serious theme. Due to the geography of their local territories and its influence on them and their history, the distinct Italian peoples have diverse personal characters, temperaments, customs, opinions, biases, fundamental beliefs and by extension the means of expressing them. For example, the miracle of San Gennaro[216] which so emotional for the Neapolitan masses would not have the same influence among the populations of any of the major cities of northern or central Italy.

The national union, having created new interests and relationships which in turn sustain and strengthen it, is a great leveler; but at the

---

their former despotic rule over Piedmont, the Aosta Valley, Liguria, Sardinia, and the counties of Savoy and Nice in what is now southeastern France]

216 [In Naples it is said that if the dried blood in the reliquary of St Januarius fails to liquefy on one of his feast days, then a great disaster will befall the city.]

same time its process proceeds very slowly, like any process that operates broadly on great multitudes of people.

In truth, the idea of a unified nation is a concept that warms the heart of every Italian who can articulate even a faint reason for well-intended national pride, even if for no other reason than the existence of a mysterious law that in these times pushes people into great agglomerations under a single flag, Italy has become a nation.

But the aforementioned dissonances are influencing the transition period with contending approaches to fix the problems of the different approaches to government, as represented by the laws and the officials. We see in our country divisions and political factions that I will not call parties, but which point toward much discord in the conduct of ordinary politics, in administration, and in many social issues.

The clerical faction and the aspirations usually attributed to it truly exists, though I believe that it includes many fewer people than is commonly believed. There are partisans favoring various political forms of government, and disparate factions concerned with the administrative structure, military affairs, taxation, education, on the rights and duties of workers, on the emancipation and role of women, and on social and family law.

And, because each thought has its voice, every act of the authorities that is not consonant with the feelings and opinions of the speaker is criticized, therefore leaders are driven to the difficulty of understanding all the discordant voices:

"The king should be a president."
"No, the king should be a king."
"The pope should be the king."
"No, he should not."
"We want regional governments."

"The regions will disunite us; we do not want them."

"We want education to be optional and to include religious teaching."

"No, we want it required and secular."

"No, we only want it required."

"No, we want it required and free of charge."

And thus with all the other issues until finally there emerges on the horizon an angry group of poor people, and God knows how many, who say: "We want to be rich, and to enrich ourselves, we are told that the goodness of God does not require the sweat of our brows for that end, but we can take money wherever we find it.... And what keeps us from it? The Force! What Force? The Force is our poverty; we do not know any force other than that which is imposed by the demands of our needs." Perhaps this is not spoken aloud, but people think that way, and the majority of them believe in and act upon it, or worse.

In the midst of these disputes, accompanied by this threat and our search for a better system, replacing yesterday's laws with those of today has resulted in the populace losing its respect for the laws. Taking direction first from one version and then from another, the people become anxious and become confused as to their interests. They lose confidence in and can easily rebel against an unstable legislative process and no longer believe they can trust it as a foundation for their present and future needs. To these divisions, worries, and concerns about greed and changeable laws, we can also add the problems caused the multiplicity of government officials involved in each change of government, starting with combining pairs of government departments covering related but different functions.[217]

---

217 [During Italian unification in the decade from 1860 to 1870, just prior to the writing of this book) seven independent governmental regimes, each with its own laws and governmental bureaucracy, were rolled up into a single government. One can imagine the

And precisely because it is not a given that we will achieve the ideal state described above, we must do all that is possible to fill the government posts with knowledgeable, active, and honest people. Thus, the more that we can decrease the number of officials, the easier it will be to make good staffing choices and the more difficult it will be for the reckless, crafty, arrogant, grasping, well-connected, merely lucky, two-faced, and loud-mouthed to solicit and often receive government jobs.

In order for the government to understand the needs, desires, and aspirations of the various factions, they should each get at least one representative in the new parliament. But above all, in order to conform to the liberal ideal that the public be governed by a great council of popularly elected representatives, it is highly desirable that the public be educated on how to choose those representatives.

People possess brilliant attributes, which despite their inherent lack of public utility, succeed in empowering the masses and the seducers because these abilities make it possible to easily ascribe value to often non-existent facts. Such abilities include handsomeness and eloquence.[218] Write a wise book, create a masterful painting, or sculpt the head of a satyr as well as Michelangelo; if with that you become famous, you may receive a call of "Bravo!' from one or two of your contemporaries, and from you will come many future followers. Give a harangue in the city square, shout about some tragedy, and there will be much applause and your name will instantly become

---

confusion that resulted while rolling seven parallel government bureaucracies and legal systems, into one.]

218 "And it happened to them (the drinkers), as in the famous fable, that the beverage was very good and useful to mankind, but when it was taken by a madman, it is very bad, and in those cases, it has become the greatest pestilence." And it was a judge who spoke, Mr. Bono Giamboloni in his *Tractate on Virtues and Vices.*" [Giamboloni (c.1240–c.1292) was an illustrious and scholarly judge in medieval Florence.]

famous. Above all, people want to be seduced by what speaks to their immediate feelings, and that is accomplished most easily among the ignorant. However, according to an ancient proverb, among practical people who wish to protect their fortunes, it is much more effective to judge people by their deeds than by their brilliant oratory.

There once was a time when the most powerful groups in Italy chose industrialists, pioneers, or businessmen as leaders of their states, and those states prospered. Today the great entrepreneurs and men of action are becoming eminent among the Nordic peoples. Lord Waterlow, a printer, was elected Lord Mayor of London. The American, Horace Greely, who was a candidate for president of that great republic, rose to great honor from low beginnings. And we could add hundreds of other examples since the beginning of modern times, starting with the printer's apprentice, Benjamin Franklin, to our day.

But among today's Latin peoples the time of the comedians has not yet passed, and candidly I say that it is deplorable that there are still few politicians of whom it can be said, I prefer this person who knows how to make me a fine tunic than that fellow who talks a good story.[219]

You may accuse me of being against the so-called positivism, and ostracizing eloquence and its sisters, poetry, music, and the fine arts. That would be a mistake! Would it be possible to banish the desire for the beautiful from the human heart and mind? And do you not see that those who seek their well-being as the fruit of their labor and wish to win the esteem of others, those who know how to improve their situation with their deeds, they all give proof to this idea by promoting every sentiment of aesthetics because aesthetics refines behavior?

---

219 [I.e., a person who knows how to accomplish something rather than one who can just talk about it.]

We only ask that those people operate according to this principle: and this, like it or not, consists in having money and living well. Are the people who have fallen or are so prostrate in their misery that they wish only for a crust of bread, also the ones who sing hymns and become ecstatic over an image painted on canvas or sculpted in marble? Would they consider erecting everlasting monuments if they were beaten down almost to death under the rule of a despot? On the other hand, if they were well off, they could become poets or enthusiastic for poetry in all of its manifestations.

But for this to happen, we must first develop general prosperity, based on which private fortunes can be built. This, in turn, requires that the public select as its leaders those whose good works have created value and demonstrated their wisdom and then accord respect to these leaders for their persons and for their actions.

It is necessary that everyone be persuaded that the actions of those in power can be improved through constructive criticism and degraded, suffocated, and destroyed by destructive attacks. And we must never replace the one approach with the other because constructive and destructive criticisms are in themselves contradictory.

Everyone must believe that hard work, savings, and patience are the three cardinal rules for building one's fortune, perhaps slow but very effective., Grant these their due respect and you will succeed by means of this path.

And when hard work and patience are applied with real science but do not succeed in building a fortune, you will discover that unfortunate but most noble truth of the benefit of effort.

In the end, everyone must recognize the equality of all citizens in their relations with one another and before the law, and that freedom to express criticisms against others is not true freedom but license, disorder leading to actions that degrade and violate others.

When there has been ample and broad education of the common people in these thoughts, then the principle of proper authority will emerge, unlike the corrupt version of today, and in the future, we will be able to avoid many dangers.

ILLUSTRATION XIX

238. Every object of human thought can be subjected to analysis and synthesis. But the extreme ends of such analysis fades into the unknown. Everything is a long chain of which only some of the links can be seen. This truth is known to the wisest people, whether or not they see it willingly, and this makes them humble.

Somewhere in his writings, that great man, Sir Isaac Newton, said that he had succeeded in merely collecting a few seashells on the beach of the that great unknown ocean of the Truth. And this blessed ocean has certain areas from which discovering the center of Africa would be like finding the Via Po for an inhabitant of Piazza Castello.[220]

Go search for this desired truth! Once, when there were prophets and apostles, people accepted the world as it was, and celebrated the otherworldly. Today, instead, we have people who see every natural phenomenon as translating itself into a special type of motion, for which it would be possible to say, *everything is nothing but a form of motion;* but the blessed cause of this universal motion, its particularities, its infinite number of different modalities, and is innumerable effects, who understands any of that?

---

220 [Via Po is an avenue from Pizza Castello, a major square facing the former royal palace in the center of Turin, Levi's home city, to Piazza Vittorio Veneto, a large square opening onto the Po River.]

This idea brings me to

ILLUSTRATION XX[221]

300. One could believe that the mysterious force called attraction is the fundamental cause of all the phenomena of the universe and its ultimate end will be a big crunch. It is generally observed as attraction and repulsion, aspiration and respiration, aggregation and disaggregation, or life, death, and life renewed. But one of the effects of this attraction or what it causes must in some way be consciously and willfully compatible with intelligent life. If its end is to be an infinite crunch, its ways of proceeding are manifestly infinite, and in the choice of these methods there must be one or more intelligent arbiters.

If all is constrained to operate in an unchangeable cycle to contribute to new aggregations, those who have a certain amount of judgment can accelerate or retard a given moment in this process, either supporting or impeding one of those processes within the limits of their own strength. Understanding the ongoing operations and the natural end

---

[221] [When Levi was writing no one understood the "cause" of the force of gravity, nor did anyone have an explanation for the mechanism by which Darwinian evolution operated. These would have to wait until Einstein proposed his General Theory of Relativity in 1915, and the development of modern genetics beginning with Crick and Watson's discovery of how DNA worked. In Illustration XX, Levi used these two scientific mysteries and a series of very convoluted arguments replete with a misunderstanding of Newton's laws of mechanics to try to deduce the existence of a Prime Mover, i.e., God. I have translated his argument as best I could but must confess, I could not follow it completely. The best I can say for this effort is that Newton also engaged in extensive speculations about the theological implications of his discoveries in celestial mechanics.]

of this overwhelming force is knowledge. Arguing in favor of these processes to the degree of one's knowledge is just and good, while arguing against them is unjust and bad. The former is to be praised and the latter punished.

And the underlying cause of this force, mediated or not, is it something supreme? Absolute cause?! People cannot reason about things of which they cannot conceive.

It was between midnight and 2:00 AM that I, eager to learn, was reading through the lectures of two of my professors. The first was a typical materialist,[222] while the other, notwithstanding that he was a Jesuit, might have agreed with the first in certain conclusions had he thought about them. The lamp of my reasoning was wide awake, paying great attention, awake like a mind being kept from sleeping at that hour when faced with similar lessons. I was awake trying to understand their logic, and dare I confess it, in the eager hope of finding a mistake in their lectures, in that I believe in God and I love my idea.

It seemed to me that the materialist was dabbling in metaphysics; I found that the Jesuit, evidently to satisfy the mystics, threw in a Prime Mover, an eternal Author, whose will determined the *first* limitation of the intensity and direction of actions, and then removed Himself from intervening in his creations. Once He had given the command, the initial impulse (my deduction), everything remained eternally. Alas, his God is none other than the modern version.[223]

---

222 [Materialism is a philosophical position that nothing exists except matter, its motion, and its changes of state. In particular, it holds that consciousness is due wholly due to material agency.]

223 [I.e., the Jesuit was effectively taking the Deist position, that God was a "clockmaker" who retired after setting up the heavenly clockwork of the universe. This theological model was proposed much earlier by Sir Isaac Newton in his extensive writings on theology.]

The Jesuit thought he had found a weak point in the position of his adversary, or to say it better, of his adversaries. Even as he recognized that the law governing forces could be reduced to motion and was constant, he also opined that it was not absolutely necessary that it be so. He called it a free law, which is an invariant law that could also be cancelled.

I began to perspire as a read this defense, and I found a tear in the corner of my eye. I reread the lines of Maxim 218 in this second series and did not erase them. But I repeat, I thought that I had found that the materialist was metaphysical, and I consoled myself thinking that I had caught him in a circular argument.

My thinking, my faith, to use the word, which exists in me today was not inspired by anything outside of the spectacle of the world, which appeared to me as a faint ray of light, perhaps driven by my needs and feelings. My faith exists, unless there is evidence to destroy it, and the evidence needs to be tested. "He who sees in the movements of natural bodies only the means to achieve a certain purpose, falls under the concept of a certain personality that, by necessity, is due to matter and its properties.[224]"

In other words, motions are *properties* of matter.

"Matter is always measurable (The most esteemed Father Secchi[225] believes that it is inertia and not gravity that is the essential property of matter. See *L'Unità delle forze fisiche* [The Unity of the Physical

---

224 Moleschott, *La circolazione della vita*, pag. 258, Milano, 1870. [Jacob Moleschott (1822-1893) was a Dutch-Italian professor physiological chemistry in Turin and later in Rome. He pioneered the theory that thoughts and emotions had a physiological basis, and was noted for the statement "No phosphorus, no thought."]

225 [Father Angelo Secchi (1818-1879) was a Jesuit priest and director of the astronomical observatory at the Pontifical Gregorian University. He pioneered astronomical spectroscopy and was the first person to establish that the sun is a star.]

Forces), Vol. I, p. 277.]) It occupies space and is unchangeable. Without matter it is impossible to begin to discuss these properties.[226]

Here we no longer have the action of moving; instead, movement is a *property*, the possibility of motion, that is, of being mobile, which is not the same thing. "Thus, if something moves, the cause of that motion returns always to a property of matter."[227]

But the three inherent *properties*, mass, occupying space, and the capacity for motion imply in and of themselves that a property is the cause of a property, that is motion is caused by itself. Here we no longer have a physical law, but a purely metaphysical affirmation in response to a radical question. We simply have an incomprehensible *eternal requirement* in every order of the human mind which tries to understand its own basis.

In fact, when you see a moving object, you seek to find the force that caused its motion and you then ask yourself, what was the cause of the first motion, the one with no precedent. The words *always* and *eternally* cannot make sense without pointing to a notion outside of our sense of time, and consequently outside of our comprehension. Thus, a materialist who tells me that a given phenomenon necessarily has always existed, he has no more authority than a theologian when he uses the same affirmations using the same words.

We have seen the circularity of an argument based on the word cause of motion. We have also seen how the word always when applied to a property of matter takes us back to cause, and to avoid quibbling, we admit that the word property applies to things besides motion. That said, the human mind is not satisfied. It seeks the cause of this property. When confronted with that which makes no sense, the mind recognizes that it is not and cannot be a final cause because

---

226 Moleschott, op. cit. p. 259
227 Moleschott, op. cit., page 261

such a cause would have to come from itself without help from some intermediary. At that point, the mind glimpses the magnificent order, the stupendous, and the universal harmony of creation and kneels and begins to pray.

It seems to my great common sense that in any list of the essential properties of matter at least one is omitted, and this property takes us into the unknown. This essential property is the *ability to react against gravity*, which carries with it no less than that the movement of matter is non-destructive. With that I see an *equilibrium* and I conjecture an *intelligent power*. I will explain by returning to my favorite example, the example that causes me to believe in God.

I am about to fall, and *something* reacts against the motion that would result in my falling, using the laws of statics. This reaction manifests itself as a sort of wisdom because it is perfectly aware of equilibrium even if my mind is unaware of it. This awareness exists and opposes the laws of physics because of my wish not to fall, that is, it blocks natural movements.

Therefore, you have, even for those who consider that each phenomenon is to be understood of and by motion whose cause always arises from a property of matter, certain of these properties, which strike each other with opposite effect.[228] Therefore, they are necessarily different. While on the one hand they cannot be analyzed, on the other hand they persuade us without doubt that that motion must be conserved because it is blind and depends only on a single constant and invariant physical law.

Now I say to myself: You are confused; you have mixed up the property with the various ways in which it manifests itself: every force is driven by another force, just as motion is produced by other motion,

---

228 [In this passage, Levi appears to be very confused about the basics of Newtonian mechanics.]

agree or you contradict the law of gravity, a property that is always conserved. You yourself, in the precept on which you are commenting, have you not posited that gravity is the root cause of all phenomena? Therefore, what does it matter what type of force is involved, since force is conserved and is necessarily material? What does it matter, what type? But perhaps it is the type of force that determines the different properties of an object.

If I admitted to a universal cause or intentional and willful director, I would admit to a property of action or of reaction. Therefore, I repeat, if a unique[229] active agent existed, no *stable* movement or phenomenon could exist contrary to his direction. Absent the agent's intent or will, the properties would also have the potential for reaction. It would be possible for matter to move instantaneously in reaction, say to the eruption of a volcano, resulting in the explosion of a planet, thereby contradicting the law of gravity, while immediately after fully obeying it again.

It is the characteristic of *stability* that is imposed by a few actions that exist more or less continuously that contravene the law of a reactive force. This stability, which is visible to us as an ability, is given uniquely by will and knowledge. Certainly, it is limited, like the property that produces it when it is the work of an animal, such as the pyramidal nests of small swallows, and can be effectively measured.

Can this be refuted using reason? We use the words *motion* and *matter* and discuss the few properties of this and processes of that to deduce absolute negations that depend on much we do not know or do not want to know.

But this seems to me to be weak logic. If you give me a material being whose lifetime surpasses any notion that we have about time and suppose that it is able to think and act willfully and has the double

---

229 [e.g., God]

property of action and reaction, a property that we do not possess as we have shown, this Being must be God.

I do not ask whether this conclusion can be drawn with a positive argument, but I do ask whether, based on our knowledge, we can declare it impossible or useless that there exists such an entity. Perhaps we know enough about the make-up of this substance that we call matter, its limits and laws, to be able to judge what is possible and useful relative to it.

According to the Roman professor[230], the difficulty arises because we are used to denying the existence of everything that we do not sense directly (p. 276, Vol. I) from which it follows that we block our thinking from the remarkable power of reasoning by induction, even though that type of reasoning constitutes the greatest part of our ability to think and is the basis of every scientific discovery.

Nor is this property of being able to react knowledgeably in certain cases the only mystery. I cannot preoccupy myself with creation. Creation, taken in the sense that it is ordinarily taken is simply inconceivable; but even on this subject, my overall common sense and *impartial* observation, convinces me that these properties of matter cannot be the same for all time. In the present we can only vaguely judge what they were like in the past or might be like in the future.

And, for example, I am firmly convinced that the life force or the phenomenon by which it is manifested in composite materials, loses energy over time.[231] Up to this point we are dealing with a common

---

230 [I.e., Moleschott]

231 [This is scientific nonsense, but in his day, it would have been serious science. There was a theory (vitalism) that dates back to the 1500s and survived into the first half of the 20th century that all living organisms had a mysterious property called the life force which gave them life independent of chemical processes. This life force enabled these organisms to synthesize organic molecules, which was thought impossible to do outside of a living

truth. But applying this truth to all living things we find the reason why life is possible without having changed into different types of beings, that is of being able to create them. Life is only able to sustain itself by reproduction.

Darwin's theory asserts that the wolf and the goat are simply variations of a single type of animal without giving so much as a vaguely conceivable argument as to why this is so. But we can conceive and explain the origin of the various types of life forms that populate the Earth and many other worlds based on the different types of energy and certain properties of matter.

Observe that living things, those we think exist or at least that are most likely to exist, acquire and retain, up to a given point, the energy with which these pallid figures of ancient creation are able to reproduce. Then little by little, while remaining alive, this energy disappears as the animal ages.[232]

The earth too is aging. Therefore, it is difficult to judge what the properties of matter were or should have been in the past. Today we are unable to understand, even approximately, what properties and forces there must *necessarily* have been in order to populate the world with so many different varieties of living organisms. Nor can we judge up to what point an active and reactive will could have contributed to the creation of the species, neither affirming nor denying its intervention.

---

being. Levi then adds the observation that as organisms age, they are less energetic, and concludes that this mysterious life force must be leaking energy and will continue to do so until the organism dies.

232 I assume that in the area of the Nile Valley, there is a point in which Europeans lose the ability to reproduce. And it is certain that that force is being extinguished among the red people of America [e.g., the Native Americans.] but who would dare to assert that the vital energy has declined in that race? Oh, if only I could, I would like to study that most ancient lineage. Certainly, its antiquity would not be a counterexample, but it would be a major element of it.]

As I have observed above, we can only state that the human mind can conceive of this possibility when it recognizes that certain motions have the property of willfully reacting contrary to natural explanations.

Wanting, thinking without organs? If there are organs, could they have fixed attributes that cause them to be eternal and keep them from changing as we have seen in matter? Oh, if I only knew, if I could respond! But because I do not know, I can say this: In order to refute the above argument, you must bring me back in certain respects from the present to the past and from the known to the unknown. Doing so assumes that there was only one mode of thought and volition, and that it would be impossible to be mistaken. Could it be possible that the organs of the plants endow them with thinking and volition?

Already, Father Secchi warns us that one can assume that the universal cause of gravity is that *imponderable material* entity that is commonly called ether.[233] Does this ether exist? Where does it come from? What are its properties that have not yet been discovered?

Man can imagine a material entity with no known origin, active or passive at various times, and essentially invariant, the vehicle through which light propagates to us, including the warmth of the sun and planets and which extends to them. Can't we also conceive of a similar entity, whose necessity was already known to and predicted by Isaac Newton, and then claim the great first cause is blind?

Oh, in the realm of the word there can also be my comforting feelings that imagine a sapient and supreme will which directs the movements of matter in motion and orders them as part of the larger universe.

---

233 [In the 1800s, physicists posited the existence of a medium called *ether* through which light waves were propagated. The Michaelson-Morley experiment in the early 1900s definitively proved the non-existence of ether, and therefore the ability of light waves to travel through the vacuum of space without any tangible medium.]

I wanted to expound these brief ideas on the greatest subjects in order to show to wise men, my sole audience, that my approach to religion as encompassed by the several lines of my 300th maxim is based neither on blind and arrogant ignorance, nor on prejudice, but instead on observation, the only weapon left to me by my brotherly fellow men.

THE END

APPENDIX[234]
TO THE 15TH ILLUSTRATION

THE BODONIAN INVITATION

or

A Day's Visit to Saluzzo

* * * * *

Homo sum, humani nihil a me alienum puto.
Liberal Translation: Man am I, and courtesy,
courtesy and a half.[235]

Traitorous Hebrew, barbarian Hebrew, go away you overthrown language that has played a mean trick on me! See if ever I write a single additional letter of you, I would want as punishment to be invited once again to go at my own expense to a festival and dinner in

---

234 Concerning a Latin epigram coined by Professor Sir Andrea Gualdi, a classicist, which was translated into ten other languages on the dedication of a statue of G. Bodoni in Saluzzo. The author of this book produced the translation into Hebrew.
235 [Literal translation: Man am I, and never do I think anything that would offend others.]

Saluzzo with my host, the noble publisher and printer, Sir Francesco Lobetti-Bodoni.

Oh, precious reader, do you not know what happened to your most devoted servant? But I have already told you!

The above-named person invited me on his account and that of the city of Saluzzo to go to that town on the occasion of the dedication of a monument to Bodoni.[236] But my gracious host forgot to mention in the note he sent me that the invitation was at my expense for transport, hotel, and other costs, and that I could as well have spent the money to go to the theater. Further, the invitation did not indicate that it did not include the post-event ball at the club. I, ingenuous man that I am, left home with only ten lire and thirty cents in my pocket.[237]

I won't tell you that I dressed in my best suit with a black velvet vest, and I pleaded with God to give me the patience to be able to button its accursed cuffs. And, if I must confess it, I also barbarously plucked the few innocent white hairs that had snuck into my mustache in the secret hope of appearing a bit younger at the aforementioned ball.

Human vanity! And all for the sake of writing four lines in Hebrew in honor of Giambattista Bodoni. Strutting and looking everyone up and down with my invitation in my pocket, I departed for Saluzzo at 8:15 in the morning on October 27, 1872. When I arrived, I saw that the city hall, or rather the Commission's office, was where the guests were being received.

I bowed to this person and shook the hand of that one as I stood waiting to be officially received. But the others continued to file out.

---

236 [Giambattista Bodoni (1740-1813) was a celebrated Italian printer and type designer. He was born in Saluzzo in the Piedmont Region of Italy. At one point he was the official printer to the Catholic Church's Congregation for the Evangelization of Peoples, and, among other things, produced a number of elegantly printed volumes in Hebrew and nine other languages. This book is set in a Bodoni typeface]

237 [ten lire and thirty cents in the 1870s would be worth about $150 in today's money]

My heart kept saying, "Esteemed people, recognize me. Don't you see that soon I will be the only one here?" Alas, no one heard my cordial greetings, so I said to myself, "Perhaps they missed me. I am rather small of stature, maybe they did not see me." My mind of course was telling me that in fact I am big. No matter, I continued to delude myself and proceeded to tell myself, "They have not formally received me; I will receive myself."

That said, I followed the others, listening to the music, when after a few steps, I felt someone tapping me on the shoulder. I turned, and who did I see? It was another of the invited guests, Professor Sir Augusto Heer,[238] whose German language had played the same trick on him as my Hebrew had done to me. Heer said to me,

"Were you invited?"

"Yes, I was." I replied, "Were you?"

"I was too; I wrote the polyglot epigram that was inscribed in German."

"But surely you were received by those gentlemen."

"I, no."

"And so?"

"Let's just keep following the others."

I then looked Heer up and down and noticed that he was tall. Then I began to suspect the truth; I thought to myself, "Perhaps the invitation did not include the dinner."

Then I said to Heer, "Why don't you go to the city hall? This is my first time in Saluzzo and I will wander a bit to see the town. We can meet again between eleven and eleven-fifteen by the statue for the dedication."

---

238 [Prof. Sir Augusto Heer founded La Scuola Tecnica del Commercio, an institution devoted to preparing students for careers in business administration.]

I then heard from someone who whispered to me quietly so that Heer could not hear, "Down there, or more correctly up there, since the city hall was up the hill, you will only see them serving hot chocolate, and others drinking it."

So, there I was at 11:15, standing in the municipal pavilion facing the veiled statue of Bodoni. There I stood for a good half an hour, crushed by the crowd, waiting or hoping to be seen, and saying to myself, "I am a little thing, but in the end, the I had written the Hebrew words in the Album,[239] and under them was my good name, and I have the invitation in my pocket, so therefore I won't be abandoned."

I heard the church bells peal at noon and I stood trapped between two lines of people moving in opposite directions, almost fainting. I barely had the strength to hold on with both hands to the wooden partition that formed the edge of the pavilion's dais, near the steps. By God! They will have to pass by here and surely they will see me. And here I remembered that Prof. Sir Andrea Gualdi[240], the man who had had written the kind letter inviting me to this event, had to be in the middle of that crowd. I hoped that he would rescue me from that suffocating mob.

I stood on my toes as they passed and saw everyone, including Gualdi. I tipped my crushed hat to him and shook it so that I would be noticed, but my only consolation was to note that one of those gentlemen smiled back, thinking that I was simply greeting the assembled notables.

When nearly all of them had passed, I wondered what to do. I followed the procession of those climbing the stairs. I pushed and shoved my way through the crowd, yelling that I was among the invited guests, that people should let me pass and I climbed up to the pavilion.

---

239 [The album is reproduced in the attached Translator's Appendix.]
240 [Sir Andrea Gualdi was one of Levi's colleagues at the *Società Filotecnica di Torino*]

If they send me away, I will show them my letter, and if they push me I am a man capable of addressing the crowd, using as a script the *Bodoninaria,* the text of the invitation letter, and to show in that way that I know how to laugh heartily at an awkward situation.

As soon as I arrived at the pavilion, I saw Sir Augusto up there, and I went to him.

> "I should have gone to the city hall with you," I said to him. You figured it out, and you did not have your hat crushed and ruined, as happened to me."
>
> "I figured it out. Oh yes, we had received some sort of invitation. They have already shown me how they serve hot chocolate in Saluzzo, and how the people sip it."
>
> "But how could it be? You weren't properly received at the city hall? And how did you get to be up here?"
>
> "And you, how did you get here?"

We then exchanged tender glances so tender that we almost hugged.

> "Enough said, so be it. With good luck here we are on the dais, and here we will stay. "

The drums rolled, the statue was unveiled, and everyone applauded.

It was now about one o'clock. I had gotten up at six and my fasting stomach wanted something other than long speeches whether or not I listened to them. I ultimately resigned myself to watching a hurried oration by Prof. Maineri from afar.

When I am hungry, I tend to become ill-tempered and see everything only in black.

One person near me said,

> "That statue has such a thoughtful attitude and a long chin."
>
> "It is thinking about the invitations that his nephew sent out, and as for the long chin, that is the effect of the finger on

which he is leaning, which being made of marble, does not appear detached from the line of sight from where we are seated. Maybe the artist did not remember that a work of art is perfect only if it is aesthetic from all points of view."

Then another person added;

"And the belly; it appears almost obese. The belly seems swollen."

"It is not hard to see why, with this blessed speech that seems to go on forever."

In the meanwhile, my ill humor caused my judgment of the sculptor's work to decline. I found the statue's legs to be too slender relative to the body even after making allowance for the clothes. The statue's posture seemed affected, and none of the muscles had the natural pose that would distinguish it as the work of an inspired sculptor. At that moment, only one thing about the statue struck me as praiseworthy, the way in which the physiognomy expressed a thinking mind. That was the real value of a true artist or one who had the potential to become one.[241]

I was contemplating the statue when I saw Gualdi right near me. I won't say that he seemed to me to be the star that appears after the hurricane, because that image would be too lyrical. I will simply say that he appeared to me like a fine meal set before a fasting stomach.

I said to Heer.

"Finally, here's Gualdi"

"Oh, Let's go to him."

And so, we went up to him.

---

241 [This particular sculpture made the career of the then 27-year-old sculptor, Gabriele Ambrosio (1845-1918). On the strength of public admiration for this particular statue, Ambrosio subsequently received many commissions to create commemorative statues of other important historical figures.]

"Well sir, we were invited and here we are. Shall we go right in to dinner?"

Without saying either yes or no, he turned to me, signaling with his hand to wait a moment. He went to speak to another man and returned downcast,

> "Sir Francesco Lobetti-Bodoni says that he is very sorry ... but that there are a limited number of seats at the officials' table ... would they be willing to dine with him?"
>
> "With him?" I said, "We were invited to the festivities, and not to the home of Sir Francesco, a man we do not know! I am amazed Sir, by your most unusual invitations!"
>
> "And yes, as you well know there are things that you say for the sake of saying them." Stammered a mortified Gualdi.

Heer and I descended from the pavilion without saying a word. Once we were out of the crowd Heer then exclaimed in the deep voice of a tyrant in a tragic drama, "Guards, take him away." And then he turned to me and said, "Let's go to somewhere to eat." I replied to him in the voice of a heroine, "Sire, have pity on him, and please calm yourself." And then I continued; "Let's go eat lunch, let's go to The Cock; Just yesterday, Carlo Avalle, a travelling companion of mine had told me that the food is good there."

At The Cock Inn there were two large rooms on the ground floor, a large hall and a smaller one. In the larger one, the Apollo room, the truly invited guests were expected to dine. We were shown into the smaller room. After a long wait as they dealt with a large influx of guests, we were taken to a small well-set table that was near the entryway.

Heer then said;

> "Let's eat the prix fixe meal. Waiter, how much does it cost?"

"Four lire[242]."

As I mentally calculated the contents of my wallet, I replied.

"Four lire! No, let's dine a la carte."

"Gentlemen, please listen to me. It is cheaper to buy the set meal." responded the waiter.

"Tell me truly. Four Lire! And Professor Avalle recommended your hotel to us."

"Really, and how is Professor Avalle? So, for you it will be only three and a half lire."

During this exchange, I quietly thought to myself, "My round-trip train fare had cost me six lire and sixty cents; three lire and fifty for the meal, I can cover this," And I replied, "Fine then, we will do the prix fixe." Idiot! I forgot to figure in the tip.

Because I was seated facing the door, I saw the real invitees pass by as we ate. Among them was Gandolfi, the principal of the Liceo Cavour.[243] "Oh hi, Gandolfi, and Sir This, and Professor That. Please tell Sir Francesco that he played a mean trick on me and that I swear that I will not publish another line without remembering the fable of the fox and the stork, maybe even in a book of philosophy." If I live long enough, I certainly want to memorialize the Bodonian invitation as a proverb!"

As I was speaking, I was eating a mouthful of a most savory meatball. Then Gandolfi said, "Calm down, my friend. I don't understand a bit of what you are saying. I think I understand that you are angry because you are not in the other room dining with us. Do you want me to make a scene among so many distinguished people?" He spoke in that knavish way. because he had his eye on who was

---

242 [approximately $56 in today's money"]
243 [The Liceo Cavour was the oldest classical high school in Turin and one of the most prominent in all of Italy.]

coming, and as he saw the line building up behind him, he quickly slipped away.

Oh, what a consolation! How well you can eat and drink at The Cock. Dear Reader, Carlo Avalle was a true gentleman,[244] not that I ever doubted it, but here we have the proof. If ever you go to Saluzzo, O Reader, I recommend The Cock Inn.

As we finished earing and after we had put our seven lire on the plate. Heer said to me, "Let's leave a tip of fifty cents apiece."

I was eating the last bite of a citron-flavored cookie which I had dunked into the zabaglione. With that suggestion, I choked on the cookie. As I coughed, I thought, "Oh, the Devil! And I no longer have fifty cents." I felt in my pocket the two remaining 10-cent coins, and then said,

> "No, fifty cents is too much. Let's give him just twenty cents apiece. That should do it."
>
> "That's not much."
>
> "That's enough"

Finally, I had to admit, that I did not have any more money, and Heer agreed that we should each leave twenty cents.

We went out and walked around the Piazza d'Armi, and I confessed that The Cock and its fine meal had calmed me down somewhat. We then went to Piazza Castello to take in its beautiful views, here and there, up and down, but what was the point? The rust remained in my brain.

"They sure played a bad one on you, Mr. Leone Levi!"

---

244 Unfortunately, he is no longer alive, and the author of *Storia d'Alessandria*, that energetic and sharp-eyed poet and wise professor, was accompanied to the cemetery by three or four of his students in the same month as two thousand people were queuing up at the funeral of an innkeeper. These are things that cause one's pen to drop from his hand as if by command.

"Well, yes, I am not a Sir; when you are not a Sir, you can understand; BUT you are a Sir."

We went to check on when the next train to Turin was, but there were none before 8:10.

We passed a good hour looking at the manuscripts of Pellico,[245] some of the printed editions produced by Bodoni, and some books produced by American typographers that had been sent for the occasion. We found the American editions most admirable, even when compared to those of the great master printer Bodoni.

Finally, it was getting late. Heer suggested, "Let's go drink a bottle of wine at The Cock." I protested that I only drink wine with meals for good reasons. When we got to The Cock, I asked for a glass of tap water to slake my thirst but drank it with more or less disgust. The water was not nearly so good as that of Turin.

We left the inn to see the city lights, which of course were minimal as compared to Turin: suffice it to say that it would have taken gas lighting to know that the bell tower was white, and the stars shone brightly. Finally, the blessed time came for us to depart, and we left Saluzzo.

As I thought about it during the trip home, all this happened to me by being one of the eleven producers of the so-called polyglot epigram. Barbarian Hebrew! I know that if by some misfortune I was asked to use it once more to honor some famous man, I would say *Timeo Bodonios*[246] with the accent on the first syllable, *Timeo Bodonios dona ferentis.*[247]

---

245 [Silvio Pellico (1789-1854) a playwright, poet, and Italian patriot, was born in Saluzzo. He was also agitated for Italian unification, for which he was arrested by the Austrian government of Lombardy and Veneto and jailed for fifteen years.]
246 [Beware of Bodonians]
247 [Beware of Bodonians bearing gifts.]

But I must say honoring the truth, that Gualdi could only be blamed for believing that he could make us believe the promised *warm welcome*. But it has come to my attention that this courteous and wise man has already rued today's unfortunate events. Truly he could have abstained from that meal. But my God! It was so sumptuous! And then I thought of our ancestor Adam, who had to accept death in order to have a taste of a simple apple!!...

INDEX

A
Aberration, 153
Abhorrent, 271
Ability, 224
Abuse, 144
Act (Virtuous), 20
Action (Human), 89, 188; XIII
Admiration 255, 276, 277
Admission, 257
Affection, 61
Ambition, 128, 166
Ambitious People, 11, 12, 13, 221, 272
Appearance, 95, 150
Appetites, 211
Attention, 166
Attraction, 300; III. XX
Authority, 170, 235; Ill XVIII

B
Bad Judgment, 22
Balance Between Virtue and Wickedness, 201
Beauty, 36, 75, 77, 78, 139
Belief, 121, 287
Benefactor, 225
Benefit (Public), 202, 221
Benefit (From Cheating or Swindling) 197, 198
Birth, 134
Boredom, 106
Bullying, 251
Busyness, 47

C
Calculation, 59; Ill. XI
Chains of Connectivity, 238; Ill. XIX
Cheater, 33, 34, 100, 247
Cheating or swindling, (Benefit From) 197, 198
Children, 3; Ill. II
Cognition, 54, 55, 229; Ill. X
Commitments (Irrevocable), 53
Complainer, 253
Compliments 292, 294
Comportment (Personal), 150
Compulsory Education, 53
Constancy, 145, 244
Contradiction, 85
Convenience, 67
Courage, 293

---

248 [Levi's original index numbers point to the maxims addressing the particular index term or issue. We have followed his model. I have added the corresponding illustration numbers as appropriate]

Cowardice, 51
Credit, 223
Criminal Justice, 17
Criticism, 161, 244
Cruelty, 56
Culture (Middling), 233
Curiosity, 109

D

Daring, 88, 137
Death, 124, 134
Debts, 171
Decadence, 68, 94
Deformity, 36
Delicateness, 133
Democracy, 128
Demagoguery, 128
Descendants, 3; Ill. II
Despotism, 170, 179
Devoutness, 171
Defects, 254
Direction, 28; Ill. V
Discovery, 230
Disdain, 216
Disillusion, 45
Division (of time), 120
Doctor, 142
Duel, 291
Duty, 23, 24, 25, 26

E

Education, 18, 129, 169, 170, 201, 215, 243
Education (Compulsory), 53
Eloquence, 174
Energy, 137
Enrichment, 262
Envy, 41, 73, 132, 208, 239, 274

Equality, 125, 299; Ill. XIV
Error, 156, 157, 231
Experimentalists, 122
Eternal Flame, 278

F

Faith, 121
False Judgment, 183
Fame, 69, 70, 116, 127, 249, 289
Family, 5
Fantasy, 126, 164, 246
Fascination, 62
Fashion, 296
Fear, 1, 18, 275
Feelings, 47, 172
Fiction, 136, 166
Finance Ministry, 258
Flame (Eternal), 278
Foresight, 49, 137; Ill. VIII
Fortune, 200, 267, 297
Fraternity, 125; Ill. XIV
Fraud, 214
Freedom, 180
Freedom of Choice, 104, 105
Freedom of Judgment, 209, 210
Friendship, 69, 185, 194
Functions (Vital) 17

G

Gentleman, 160, 281
Gift, 176
Gold, 158, 159
Good Judgment, 32, 111
Good and Bad Sides, 266
Good-heartedness, 22
Goodness, 20, 89, 92, 113; XIII
Government (Popular), 169

H

Happiness, 57
Hardheartedness, 79; Ill. XII
Head, 186
Heart, 186
Honor, 19
Hope, 296
Hypocrisy, 67, 265
Human Action, 89, 188; Ill. XIII
Human Spirit, 61, 67

I

Idea, 4, 123, 173
Idea Generation 18
Idleness, 97, 154
Ignorance, 51, 147, 274
Illusions, 191, 164, 232, 270
Imagination, 126, 146, 164, 246
Imitation, 72, 111, 206
Inaction, 188
Inertia, 96, 97
Ingratitude, 290
Intelligence, 10, 28, 29, 30, 74, 75, 87, 92, 139, 165, 210, 248, ; Ill. V, VI
Irresponsibility, 104
Irrevocable Commitments, 53
Isolation, 213
Institutions, 168
Instruction, 129, 169, 170, 201, 215, 243
Instruction (Compulsory), 119

J

Jealousy, 208
Judge, 38
Judgment, 82, 189, 209, 219, 231, 232, 250, 264
Judgment, (Bad), 22
Judgment, (Good), 111
Judgment, (False), 183
Judgment (Freedom of), 209, 210
Justice, 65, 104, 199, 207, 288; Ill. XVII
Justice (Criminal), 17

K

Kind (Man), 281

L

Laziness, 97, 178, 231; Ill. XVI
Liberty, 104, 105
Life, 15, 218
Liquors, 86
Longevity, 79, 108; Ill. XII
Love, 21
Love of the Good, 89; XIII
Love of Novelty, 245
Luck, 200, 267, 297
Luxury, 86
Lying, 25

M

Malevolence, 39, 40, 41, 169, 276
Mania (For Enrichment), 262
Mania (To Be Admired), 255
Marriage, 2, 65, 76, 134; Ill. I
Means, 242
Medicine, 114
Merit, 212, 280
Middling Culture, 233
Mind, 82, 139, 217
Mind (Uneducated), 56
Ministry of Finance, 258
Misery, 35
Misfortune, 33
Moderation, 31
Modesty, 203, 282, 290

Money (Earning), 14; Ill. III
Money (Paper) 239
Monstrosity, 256
Monument, 219, 220
Morals, 27, 268, 288
Mother-in-law, 110
Mysticism, 120, 122

N
Nature, 107
Needs (Material and Spiritual), 190, 215, 247
No, 106

O
Offensive, 58, 295
Office, 12
Old Age, 112
Opinion, 54, 55, 93, 111, 157, 174; Ill. X
Orator, 163
Originality, 7
Ostentation, 293

P
Pain, 66, 218
Paper Money, 239
Passion, 99, 117, 185, 219, 283, 284
Patriotism, 221
Pay, 124
Paradise, 172
Personal Care or Appearance, 95, 150
Philosopher (Experimental) 122
Pimp, 44
Pleasure, 23, 25, 66, 218
Pleasant, 213
Politics, 111, 221
Popular Government, 169

Positivism, 237
Poverty, 35, 51, 84, 190, 192
Poor Person, 200, 2202 223
Power, 15, 31, 104, 133
Powerful, 42
Praise, 100, 248
Prayer, 100
Precept, 107
Presumption, 282
Pretense, 60
Price, 264
Principles, 293
Procurer, 44
Promises, 101, 241
Progeny, 3; Ill. II
Progress, 204, 268
Proof, 152
Prophecy, 49; Ill. VIII
Public, 14; Ill. III
Public Benefit 202, 221
Public Company, 261

R
Reality, 123
Reason, 164, 246, 250, 280
Regrets, 50, 155
Religion, 111
Repentance, 16
Relatives (Family), 5
Reprobate, 295
Revenge, 1167
Revolution, 228
Reward, 91
Rich (Person), 160
Riches, 44, 91, 92, 190
Rights (Human), 104
Risk, 88, 137
Roughness (Of Manner), 149

S

Saints, 90
Scam, 33, 34, 100, 247
Scandal, 109
Schemes, 43, 93
Seduction, 37
Self-denial, 98, 187
Self-esteem, 98, 206, 273
Sentiment, 280
Seriousness, 184
Sister-in-law, 110
Skill, 146
Slander, 40
Sloth, 191
Small Head, 105
Small debts, 115
Small thoughts, 105
Social Condition, 83
Society 6, 46, 243
Spirit, 215
Spirit (Human, 61, 67
Statue, 219, 220
Stock Market Speculators, 260
Straight and Narrow (Path), 135
Suicide, 63; Ill. XI
Sympathy, 298

T

Tact, 102
Temperance, 96, 144
Time, 234
Traits (leading to riches), 140
Tranquility, 103
Troubles, 158, 181
Truth, 34, 54; Ill. X
Tyranny, 178; Ill. XVI

U

Unhappiness, 198
Usage, 118
Useful, 8
Utility, 8

V

Valor, 196
Value (Price) 264
Vice, 114, 143, 242
Virtue, 20, 26, 48, 114, 132, 242; Ill. VII
Virtuous Act, 20
Vital Functions, 17
Vocation, 240
Vulgarity, 263

W

Wealth, 44, 91, 92, 190
Weeping, 9
Will, 195
Work, 80, 193, 195
Woman, 37, 75, 76, 78, 131, 138, 162, 211, 227, 279
Wisdom, 130, 148, 175, 218
Wife, 110
Word, 108, 141, 252
Worship, 205

Y

Yes, 106
Youth, 96

TRANSLATOR'S APPENDICES

THE BODONIAN EPIGRAMS

Reproduced with the permission of the
Archives of the Community of Saluzzo
Archivio Storico Antico
Città di Saluzzo
(ASACS) cat.54 fal. 8 fasc.2

NEL GIORNO SOLENNE
in cui
veniva inaugurata
li 27 Ottobre 1872
la statua monumentale

GIOVAMBATTISTA BODONI
Saluzzese

Epigramma poliglotto

यो बोदोनिगमा मुद्राशिल्पसंस्कृतो
नानारूपमुद्रान्तरैर् मुद्रयिवा शुभं।
परदेशेषु यशस्वी विख्यातो ऽभवत्
सो ऽप्येव तनुतानगरे ऽभिप्रशस्यते।

COMM. G. GORRESIO.

איש היה גאה על כל גאים לפתח מלים בספר ויחקו
גאון ותפארת לארץ מולדתו ושמו בודוני
פה תמונת שפתי רבבות בתבונתו ברא
ופה אנחנו ביום זכרון גדלו בשפתי רבבות לכבודו נשיר

LEONE LEVI

ΟΣ ΤΥΠΙΚΗΝ ΤΕΧΝΗΝ ΒΩΔΩΝΙΟΣ. ΟΥΔΕΝΟΣ ΗΕΝ

ΔΕΥΤΕΡΟΣ, ΗΔ' ΑΙΗΣ ΠΑΤΡΙΔΟΣ ΕΥΡΥ ΚΛΕΟΣ,

ΟΤΤΙ ΤΥΠΟΥΣ ΓΛΩΣΣΩΝ ΠΟΙΗΣΕΝ ΠΟΙΚΙΛΟΜΟΡΦΟΥΣ.

ΚΑΙ ΜΕΤΑΦΡΑΖΟΝΤΕΣ ΠΟΙΚΙΛΑ ΤΩ ΔΙΔΟΜΕΝ.

CAV. PROF. S. GROSSO.

QVI FVIT IN TYPICA BODONIVS ARTE SECVNDVS
NVLLI ET NATALIS GLORIA MAGNA SOLI,
AERA IS MVLTIMODIS FINXIT COGNOMINA LINGVIS;
QVARE HVIC MVLTIMODE CARMINA VERSA DAMVS.

CAV. PROF. A. GUALDI

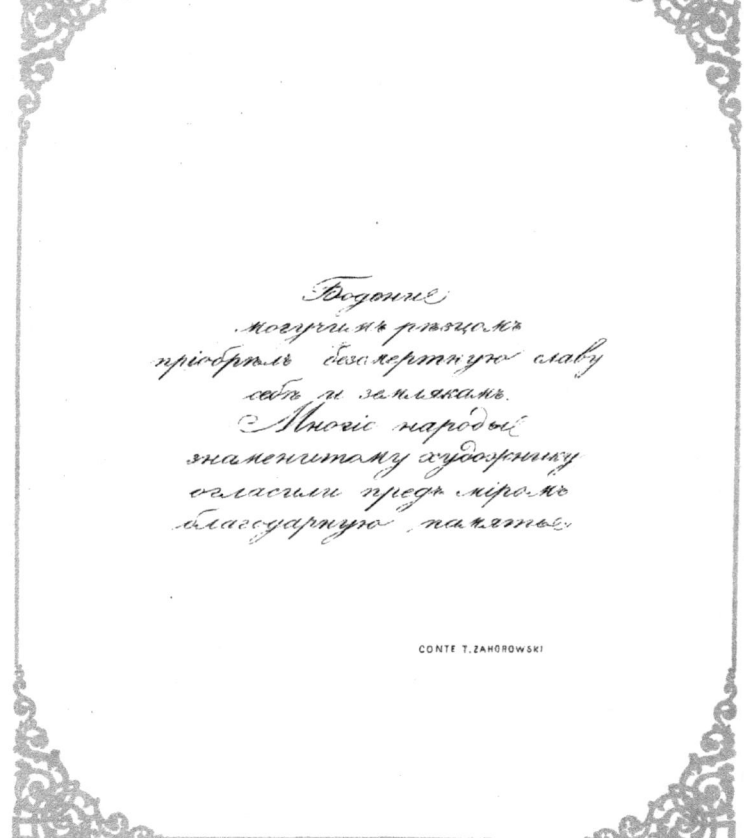

Бодони могучимъ рѣзцомъ прiобрѣлъ безсмертную славу себѣ и землякамъ. Многiе народы знаменитому художнику огласили предъ мiромъ благодарную память.

CONTE T. ZAHOROWSKI

Bodoni, Glanz für Kunst und Vaterland,
  Ein Gruß vom fernen Rhein und Donaustrand!
  In gold'nen Lettern wußtest du zu paaren
  Der Schönheit Ideal dem strengen Wahren.

CAV. PROF! A. HEIR

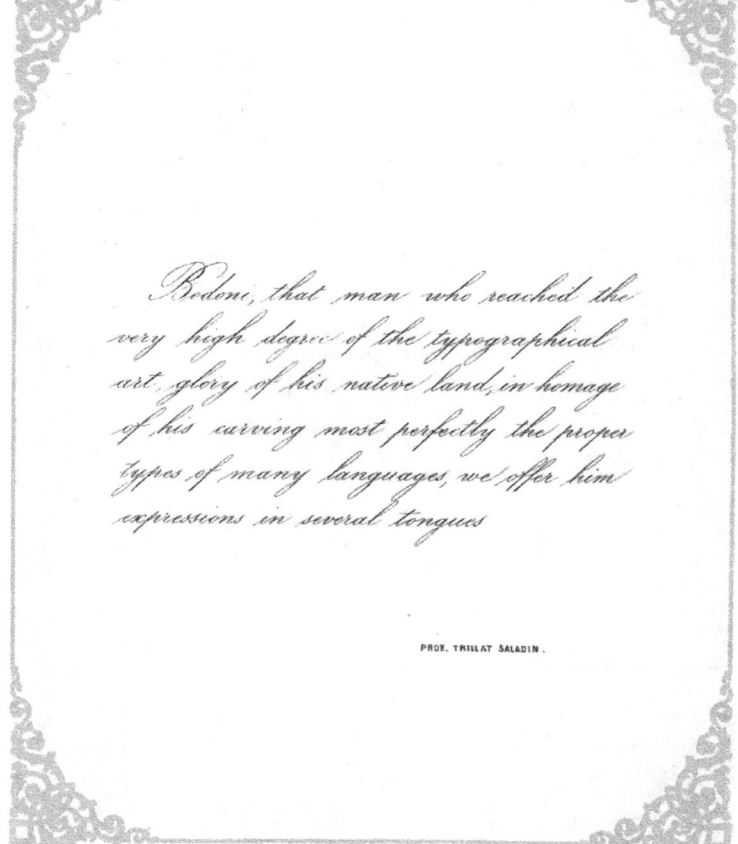

Bodoni, that man who reached the very high degree of the typographical art, glory of his native land, in homage of his carving most perfectly the proper types of many languages, we offer him expressions in several tongues

PROF. TRILLAT SALADIN.

Bodoni, che nell'arte il vanto altrui
Non cede, è di sua patria onore eletto;
Fe' più lingue parlare a' tipi sui,
E or gli tornan più lingue il nostro affetto.

COMM. AB.I. BERNARDI.

Ce nouveau Guttemberg en différents langages
Répandit les trésors de la prose et des vers,
Ne vous étonnez point si nos pieux hommages
Lui sont ici rendus en langages divers.

CAV. PROF. A. SHAS.

A. Bodoni.

Que.Grabando.Caractéres.De.Muchísimas.Lenguas.

Abrió. Nuevos. Tesoros. De. Ciencia.

Aplaude. La. Prensa. Con. Muchisimos. Idiomas.

PROF! ING! E.RUGHI

Bodoni
mistrzowskim rylcem
przysporzył sławy ojczyźnie
a dla siebie
zdobył
różnych narodów
wdzięczne wspomnienie.

CONTE. T. ZAHOROWSKI.

Partial bibliography of Leone Levi's writings

Books

Piemonte ed Italia : saggio di critica storica. (Piedmont and Italy—An essay on Historical Criticism) 135 pp., Tipografica V. Vercellini, Turin, 1866

Lampi sulla Società Contemporanea, (Flashes of light Concerning Contemporary Society) 320 pp., Unione Tipografica, Turin-Naples, 1869

Massime (Maxims), Tipografica A. Oddenino e. Comp., Turin, 1872

Massime, Seconda Seria (Maxims, Second Series), 195 pp., Stamperia G. Borganelli, Turin, 1874

Il Tempio Israelitico di Torino (The Israelite Temple of Turin), Leone Levi, Serialized in *Il Corriere Israelitico*, Vol. XV, p. 54, 1876

Public Lectures (partial list)

Osservazioni su alcune cause del Discredito in cui sono cadute le finanze Italiane (Observations on some of the Reasons why Italian [National] Finances Have Fallen into Disrepute), Lecture before the Società Filotecnica di Torino, March 7, 1867

Il Bastone Magico (The Magic Wand), a novel in sestets, Lecture before the Società Filotecnica di Torino, April 11 and 25, May 2, and June 6 1867

Influenza della Razza Semitica Ebrea sulla Civiltà (The influence of the Hebrew Semitic Race on [Western] Civilization), Lecture before the Società Filotecnica di Torino, June 25 and November 7, 1867

Articles (partial list)

Review of Luigi Cibrarie's book, *Della Schiavitù e del Servaggio (On Slavery and Servitude)*, by Leone Levi, Gazzetta Piemontese[249], p. 1, Sep 15, 1868

Review of Rabbi S. Olper's public lectures on *The History of the Hebrews*, by Leone Levi, *Gazzetta Piemontese*, p.1, July 18, 1869,

Sulla Educazione Religiosa (On Religious Education), Leone Levi, Educatore Israelita, 1871, Vol. 19, p. 13

---

249 [This Turin newspaper was started in 1867, and quickly became a leading paper in Piedmont. In 1894 its name changed to La Stampa, a paper that continues to this day and is noted for, among other things, its publication of many essays by Primo Levi.]

Frammenti Critici Storico-Religiosi (Elements of Historical/Relilgous Criticism), Leone Levi, Serialized in *L'Educatore Israelita*, 1871, Vol.19, p. 3, p. 65, p. 130, p. 193, p. 264, p. 326

Sulle Massime (On Maxims), Leone Levi, Educatore Israelita, 1872, Vol. 20. p. 247

Un Matto (A Madman), a short story by Leone Levi. , L'Educatore Israelita, 1872, Vol. 20, p. 99

Sul Matrimonio Misto (On Mixed Marriages), Leone Levi, L'Educatore Israelita, Vol. 20, p. 259

Una Lettera che non Dovrebbe Morire (A Letter That Should Not Die). Leone Levi, Il Corriere Israelitico, 1874, Vol. XII, p. 11

Polemica (Polemic), Leone Levi, Il Corriere Israelitico, Vol. XII, p. 102, 1874

Legende Ebree: 1. Un Vecchio Rabbino (Hebrew Legends: 1.An Old Rabbi), Leone Levi, Il Corriere Israelitico, 1874, Vol. XII, p. 151, 1874

Legende Ebree: 2. Perché La Propaganda Fosse Impotente Cogli Ebrei (Why Propaganda Has no Effect on the Hebrews), Leone Levi, 1874, Vol. XII, p. 274

Legende Ebree: 3. L'Amore nel Ghetto (Love in the Ghetto), Leone Levi, Serialized in Il Corriere Israelitico, 1874, Vol. *XIII*, p. 35, and continued in Vol. XV, p. 42,

www.ingramcontent.com/pod-product-compliance
Lightning Source LLC
Chambersburg PA
CBHW072147070526
44585CB00015B/1031